THE
ARCHAEOLOGY OF EARLY
ROME AND LATIUM

THE
ARCHAEOLOGY OF
EARLY ROME AND
LATIUM

R. Ross Holloway

London and New York

First published in 1994 by Routledge

First published in paperback in 1996
by Routledge
11 New Fetter Lane, London EC4P 4EE

Simultaneously published in the USA and Canada
by Routledge
29 West 35th Street, New York, NY 10001

Reprinted in 1999

Routledge is an imprint of the Taylor & Francis Group

© 1994, 1996, R. Ross Holloway

Typeset in Garamond by
Florencetype Ltd, Kewstoke, Avon
Printed and bound in Great Britain by
Biddles Ltd, Guildford and King's Lynn

British Library Cataloguing in Publication Data
A catalogue record for this book is available from the British Library

Library of Congress Cataloguing in Publication Data
A catalogue record for this book has been requested

ISBN 0-415-14360-8

T H
AMICITIAE ROMANAE PERENNIS CAUSA

CONTENTS

ILLUSTRATIONS

PREFACE AND
ACKNOWLEDGMENTS

The chapters of this book were originally delivered as lectures at the University of São Paulo in November 1992. It is a pleasure to thank my Brazilian hosts, and in particular Prof. Maria Beatriz Borba Florenzano, for their warm hospitality to me on the Tropic of Capricorn. Two other institutions have aided me substantially, Brown University by granting me a sabbatical leave in the spring of 1992 and the American Academy in Rome by extending to me its hospitality as a resident for four months during the same period. The libraries of both, among the finest in existence for this field of study, supported my work throughout, but the real making of this book has been due to the archaeologists of Rome and Latium, many of whom I have long counted as friends and all of whom responded to my needs with unstinting generosity. It was in 1990 at the exhibition "La Grande Roma dei Tarquini" in company with Dr Anna Sommella Mura, under whose care the archaeological patrimony of the Musei Capitolini and the Antiquarium Comunale resides, that the idea of making a summary of the current state of the archaeology of early Rome and Latium for an English-speaking public was born. Dr Anna Maria Bietti Sestieri opened the pages of her unpublished work on the excavation of Osteria dell'Osa to me and guided me in other ways. To Prof. Maria Fenelli I owe an excellent photographic coverage of the excavations at Lavinium and the results of the work of the late Prof. Ferdinando Castagnoli and of Prof. Paolo Sommella. Prof. Andrea Carandini made me welcome on his excavations on the Sacra Via and discussed his results with me at length. Prof. Lorenzo Quilici and Dr Stefania Quilici-Gigli kindly furnished me with maps, especially of the survey of Crustumerium. Prof. Pär Göran Gierow loaned photographs of grave goods from the Alban Hills. Prof. Adriano La Regina, Soprintendente Archeologico di Roma, assisted me with material from the Forum. Dr Anna Gallina Zevi, Soprintendente Archeologico di Ostia, did the same for the necropolis of Castel di Decima. Prof. Giovanni Scichilone, Soprintendente Archeologico dell'Etruria Meridionale, provided the photographic documentation of the treasures of Praeneste and Satricum in the Museo Nazionale di Villa Giulia. Dr Maria Antonietta Fugazzola Delpino, Soprintendente Speciale al Museo Preistorico ed Etnografico "L. Pigorini," ordered for me the new photograph of the Praenestine fibula reproduced here. Prof. Marianne Maaskant-Kleibrink, formerly my associate in the excavations at Satrianum, has permitted me to make use of her plans of Satricum, a site for which I have also had the help of Dr Riemer R. Knoop. Prof. T. Russell Scott kept me abreast of the latest results of his work in the Forum, as did Dr Alessandro Bedini for Acqua Acetosa, Laurentina and Torrino, Dr Stefano Musco for Gabii and La Rustica, Dr Rasmus Brandt and Prof. Tobias Fischer-Hansen for Ficana. For assistance at the Antiquarium Comunale – Musei Capitolini I am also grateful to Dr Antonella Maganini. Mrs Karen Einaudi, director of the Fototeca di Topografia Antica presso l'Accademia Americana, procured vital photographs for me even when the Fototeca was closed during the renovation of the Academy in 1992–1993.

Once again it is a pleasure to thank Mr Richard Stoneman, Senior Editor of Routledge, for encouraging my efforts and to thank his staff for seeing them into print. Sharing my desk in the stacks of the American Academy Library in the same spot where I first studied in Rome, my wife has been a partner both in thought and expression. The dedication to a friend "di altri tempi romani" is from us both.

RRH
Providence
Exelauno Day, 1993

BASIC BIBLIOGRAPHY

The most recent summary of early Rome in English is *The Cambridge Ancient History* (ed. 2) VII, part 2, *The Rise of Rome to 220*, published in 1989 and edited by F. W. Walbank, A. E. Astin, M. W. Frederiksen, R. M. Ogilvie, and A. Drummond. The development of Rome is set in the context of early Italy by M. Pallottino (1991) *A History of Earliest Italy*, London and Ann Arbor, with useful bibliography.

The annual conferences of the Comitato per l'archeologia laziale are published in the series *Archeologia Laziale* since 1978. These volumes, together with the *Bullettino della Commissione Archeologica Comunale di Roma* and the series *Lavori e Studi di Archeologia Pubblicati dalla Soprintendenza Archeologica di Roma*, are the most valuable sources for reports on current work.

Exhibition catalogues have developed into an important avenue of archaeological publication. Several of these are fundamental for the study of early Rome, in 1976 *Civiltà del Lazio Primitivo*, Palazzo delle Esposizioni, Rome, in 1981 *Enea nel Lazio, Archeologia e Mito*, Bimillenario Virgiliano, Campidoglio, Palazzo dei Conservatori, Rome, in 1989 *Il viver quotidiano in Roma Arcaica, Materiale dagli scavi del Tempio Arcaico nell'area sacra di S. Omobono*, Area Sacra di S. Omobono, Rome and finally in 1990 *La Grande Roma dei Tarquini*, Palazzo delle Esposizioni, Rome. A recent review of archaeological material in relation to Roman private life is given by C. Fayer (1982) *Aspetti di vita quotidiana nella Roma arcaica dalle origini all'età monarchica*, Rome.

All ancient dates in the text are BC unless otherwise indicated.

ABBREVIATIONS

AA	Archäologischer Anzeiger
AC	Archeologia Classica
AION	Istituto Universitario Orientale, *Annali del Dipartimento di Studi del Mondo Classico e del Mediterraneo Antico*
AJA	American Journal of Archaeology
AL	Archeologia Laziale
BA	Bollettino di Archeologia
BABESCH	Bulletin Antieke Beschaving
BC	Bullettino della Commissione Archeologica Comunale di Roma
BPI	Bollettino di Paletnologia Italiano
BSA	Annual of the British School at Athens
BSR	Annual of the British School at Rome
CIL	Corpus Inscriptionum Latinarum
Civiltà del Lazio Primitivo	Civiltà del Lazio Primitivo, Roma, Palazzo delle Esposizioni, 1976, Catalogo della Mostra
DdA	Dialoghi di Archeologia
Enea nel Lazio	Enea nel Lazio, Archeologia e Mito, Roma, Campidoglio – Palazzo dei Conservatori, 1981, Catalogo della Mostra
ER	Einar Gjerstad, *Early Rome*, Skrifter 17, in six parts 1953–1973
Grande Roma	La Grande Roma dei Tarquini, Roma, Palazzo delle Esposizioni, 1990, Catalogo della Mostra
JRS	Journal of Roman Studies
Lazio arcaico e mondo greco	PP vol. 32, 1977
LSA	Lavori e Studi di Archeologia Pubblicati dalla Soprintendenza Archeologica di Roma
MA	Monumenti Antichi
MAAR	Memoirs of the American Academy in Rome

MEFRA	*Mélanges de l'Ecole Française de Rome, Antiquité*
MNIR	*Mededeelingen van het Nederlands Historisch Instituut te Rome*
NAC	*Numismatica e Antichità Classiche, Quaderni Ticinesi*
NSc.	*Notizie degli Scavi*
Platner–Ashby	S. B. Platner and T. Ashby, *A Topographical Dictionary of Ancient Rome*, London, 1929
PP	*La Parola del Passato*
QITA	*Quaderni dell'Istituto di Topografia Antica dell'Università di Roma "La Sapienza"*
QL	*Quaderni della Soprintendenza Archeologica del Lazio*
Richardson	L. Richardson, Jr, *A New Topographical Dictionary of Ancient Rome*, Baltimore and London, 1992
RM	*Römische Mitteilungen*
Roma Arcaica	A. Cassatella and L. Vendittelli, *Roma Arcaica, Documenti e materiali per una pianta di Roma (fine del VII–inizi del V secolo a.C.)*, Rome, 1991
Roma Medio Repubblicana	*Roma Medio Repubblicana, Aspetti Culturali di Roma e del Lazio nei Secoli IV e III A.C.*, Roma, Palazzo Caffarelli, 1973, Catalogo della Mostra
Roma, 1000 Anni di Civiltà	*Roma, 1000 Anni di Civiltà*, Ville de Montréal, Palais de la Civilisation, 1992, Catalogo della Mostra
RP	*Atti della Ponteficia Accademia Romana di Archeologia, Rendiconti*
Skrifter	*Skrifter Utgivna av Svensk Institutet i Rom*, series in 4°

Figure 0.1 Italy. 1, Bologna; 2, Caere; 3, Alban Hills; 4, Capua; 5, Cumae; 6, Ischia; 7, Naples; 8, Pontecagnano; 9, Messina; 10, Tarentum; 11, Himera; 12, Poseidonia; 13, Murlo; 14, Acquarossa.

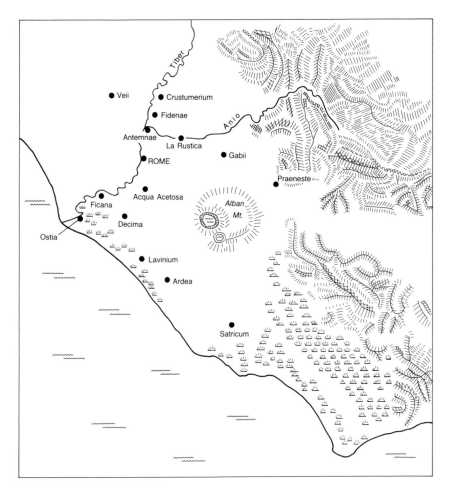

Figure 0.2 Latium.

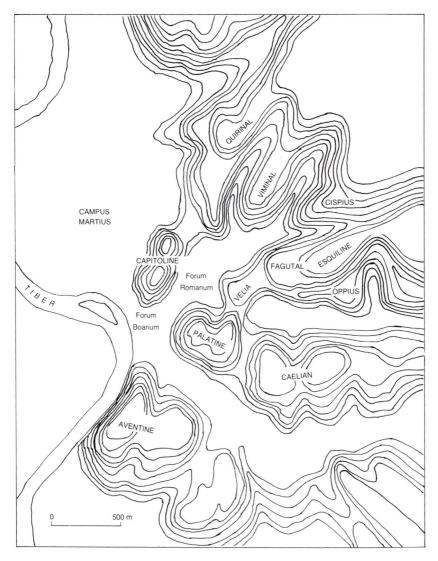

Figure 0.3 Rome.

1

INTRODUCTION

When, during the last two centuries of the Roman Republic, the first writers of Roman history, collectively known as the annalists, set about their task, they looked back into a fog.[1] Here and there a landmark seemed to emerge from the mists of time. The most prominent of these was the Temple of Jupiter Optimus Maximus on the Capitoline Hill (figs 1.1, 1.2). This temple, 62 m (203.3 ft) in width, rivaled, in this dimension at least, the temples of the richest Greek cities of Asia Minor or Sicily. It was reputed to have been raised by the kings of the sixth century BC and dedicated in the first year of the Republic, 509. Inscriptions dating to the centuries before 387, another landmark year in the history of Rome when Gauls from the Po Valley were said to have defeated the Roman army and sacked the open city (while the Capitoline alone held out and was eventually relieved), were few and difficult to understand. A list of magistrates with a sprinkling of events from their years of office was compiled in the late second century by the chief Roman priest, the Pontifex Maximus (the *Annales Maximi*).[2] The reliability of the state records on which it was based can only be conjectured. Livy thought that none survived from before the Gallic disaster.[3] And even following the redaction and reconstruction of the second century, differing traditions remained, as can be seen from the discrepancies among the main continuous sources, Livy (59–AD 17), Dionysius of Halicarnassus (in Rome after 30), Diodorus Siculus (active 60–30) and the *Fasti Capitolini*, the list of consuls (*Fasti Consulares Populi Romani*) and of the victorious generals accorded a triumph (*Fasti Triumphales Populi Romani*), which was set up in the Forum under Augustus.[4] The family traditions of the great houses of Rome, embodied in the funeral orations for their various members, were no better guide to the past. Cicero's opinion (Brutus XVI, 62) was especially unflattering: "These orations have left the history of our state full of lies. There are many things written in them which never happened, bogus triumphs, duplicated consulships, faked genealogies whether by (patrician) assumption of plebeian status or when men of lower condition are mixed up with another family of the same name."[5] An inscription recording the prominent ancestors of an Etruscan family of Tarquinia and their deeds in

1

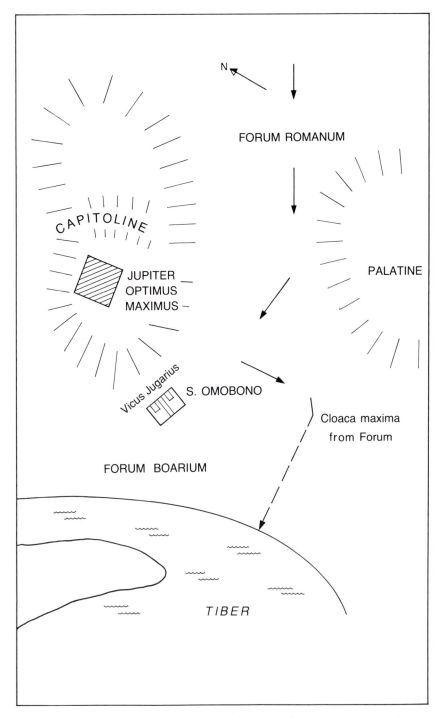

Figure 1.1 Rome, area of the Capitoline, Velabrum Valley, and Forum Boarium.

the fifth to the third century BC has been cited as an example of such *fasti*.[6] But it does not answer Cicero's charge of exaggeration and falsification. Still less reliable as historical sources would have been the Roman banquet songs telling of the feats of olden days. Not one scrap of these has been preserved, but banquet songs appealed strongly to nineteenth-century historians as a possibly genuine source for early Roman history.[7]

The earliest annalists, Fabius Pictor and Cincius Alimentius, both men of importance during the period of the Second Punic War, wrote in Greek for a Greek audience with the intention, it appears, of countering Carthaginian propaganda in the face of Rome's rise to world power. Their works, like those of the other annalists, have perished and are known only from meager quotations and comments of later historians. To judge from the number of chapters ("books") in their works dedicated to early times, they got over early Rome quickly. For the early periods of the city's history they were able to draw on the writings of a large group of Greek historians going back to the Sicilian authors of the fifth century and culminating in Timaeus of Tauromenium (third century) who treated Rome in his account of the history of the west. Much of the embellishment of Roman legend must be

Figure 1.2 Rome, Capitoline, foundations of the Temple of Jupiter Optimus Maximus visible in the Palazzo dei Conservatori, Museo Nuovo.

due to these Greek sources. The second and third waves of the Roman annalists, now using Latin and so writing for an exclusively Roman audience, produced ever more voluminous accounts of early Rome from the same sources, domestic and foreign, that had been used by their predecessors. Artifice and imagination, often stimulated by the urge to glorify one's own clan and vilify others, were hard at work. According to Livy (XXX, 19, 11) one of the later annalists, Valerius Antias, wrote "Shamelessly as to facts, negligently as to omissions."[8]

Such is the background of the connected histories written under the reign of Augustus (27–AD 14) by two rhetoricians, Livy and Dionysius of Halicarnassus. They could not improve on their sources, although Livy, in particular, freely admitted his distrust of them. Livy was writing not as an historian in the modern sense of the word but as a moralist recounting history for the edification of his audience. Dionysius wrote for his Greek readers (which would include all educated Romans of the day) in a similar vein, with less power than Livy and with an unrestrained talent for composing artificial speeches.[9]

In modern times the inconsistencies and improbabilities of the history of the kings and of the early Republic (the archaic period of Rome) were noted not long after readers had printed copies of the classical texts in their hands.[10] After 1800 higher criticism, already at work in the study of the holy scriptures, found another fertile field in early Rome. What Niebuhr began in 1826 Ettore Pais finished a century later.[11] In the view of these scholars, argued with searching detail and no small dose of common sense, early Roman history was largely a fabrication, romanticizing the few traces of real tradition with Greek trimmings. It catered to the vanity of prominent families of the late Republic, inflated the importance of the small city of archaic times and disguised the military weakness of the Romans in confronting their nearby enemies. The Augustan historians, moreover, were unable to conceive of political history without the demands for land distribution that drove the motor of Roman politics at the end of the Republic and the rivalries of the patricians and plebeians as these social orders existed in the same period. The great Mommsen wrestled with the problem of early Roman traditions, but when he came to write his general *Römische Geschichte*[12] he decided that the early centuries of Rome were too uncertain to be presented in narrative form.

Neither Pais nor Mommsen held a high opinion of the usefulness of archaeology as a tool of ancient history. But in recent decades archaeology has played a decisive role in the study of early Roman history because, as the rediscovery of remains of ancient Rome and Latium between the tenth and fifth centuries BC expanded, it encouraged a more sanguine view of the Roman historical tradition. The antiquity of settlement at Rome was first proved in a convincing fashion by Giacomo Boni's discovery of the Iron Age cemetery of the Roman Forum in the years between 1902 and 1911.[13] If the Romans of Romulus' time had their tombs in the Forum valley, the houses of the same period could not be far away, and indeed they were soon to come to light on the Palatine Hill.[14] The historicity of the Etruscan kings also emerged, it seemed, in material form. In 1899 Boni discovered the archaic *cippus* (stone upright) with inscription below the square of black stones set in the paving of the Roman Forum during the High Empire to mark the spot, according to widely accepted tradition, where Romulus was buried.[15] The fact that one of the few words read by all scholars in the truncated inscription, which is written in bafflingly archaic Latin, was *rex* (king) became a powerful weapon in arguing for the reality of the Rome of the kings. In fact, in the early twentieth century there was developing a compromise position among historians, associated particularly with the names of Beloch and De Sanctis, less critical of the received tradition than Niebuhr and Pais and willing to accept much of it in a reconstruction of early Roman history.[16] Some scholars, encouraged by archaeological discoveries, went further. At the end of the 1920s Mrs Ryberg wrote of the "Essential correctness of the Romans' own traditions concerning their earliest history."[17] And in 1936 G. Pasquale was riding the crest of the historical wave when he published his essay "La grande Roma dei Tarquinii" (The Great Rome of the Tarquins).[18]

Two years later a discovery was made which seemed to reveal regal Rome in all its splendor: the early levels (seventh to fifth centuries) underlying the twin temples discovered in 1937 below and beside the church of Sant'Omobono just below the Capitoline Hill and along the road from the Roman Forum to the Tiber and the cattle and produce markets located on the river bank (Forum Boarium and Forum Holitorium) (fig. 1.1). The excavator, A. M. Colini, immediately identified the twin temples of the later ancient phase of the site as the temples of Fortuna and Mater Matuta (Aurora) known to have stood in the Forum Boarium and often mentioned together.[19] When an archaic temple was discovered beneath one of these shrines, its first phase datable before 550, this was assumed to be the temple of Mater Matuta of King Servius Tullius.

Finally, the grand work of archaeological synthesis carried out by Einar Gjerstad accepted the new interpretation, differing from it only in the dates assigned to the various phases.[20] The general movement to revise Gjerstad's "low chronology" has cancelled even his modifications of the ancient tradition and has now given us works in which archaeology marches hand in hand with the annalists from Romulus to Tarquin the Proud.[21]

One of the most important archaeological discoveries bearing on early Roman history also brings out the nature of the problems connected with these traditions with great clarity. In 1857 the explorer of Etruscan cemeteries Alessandro François discovered the tomb at Vulci that now bears his name.[22] The frescoes from the François Tomb passed into the collection of the Villa Albani in Rome and have never been on public view. They belong to the fourth century and are composed of two sections, which were displayed around the walls of a single chamber. Both serve to satisfy the Etruscan need for blood to honor the dead, a desire which encouraged the repetition of the most gory episodes from the repertoire of Greek mythology in their funeral art. On one wall and part of another the hero Achilles is seen slaughtering the Trojan captives at the grave of Patroclus, while Eteocles and Polyneices, among other scenes, engage in their mutually destructive duel. The corresponding paintings are similarly sanguinary but are not drawn from Greek mythology. Rather, their subjects are Etruscan. A figure labeled as Cneve Tarchunies Rumach (Gnaeus Tarquinius Romanus) is being attacked by Marce Camitlnas (Marcus Camillus?). Then across from the Homeric sacrifice to Patroclus a warrior labeled Macstrna (Mastarna) is found freeing one Caile Vipinas (Caelius Vibenna) from chains. Next come three duels to the death. Larth Ulthes runs through Laris Papathnas Velznach (Volsinii?). Rasce comes against Pesna Arcmsnas Sveamach (Sovana?) and Aule Vipinas kills Venthicau . . . plsachs. Despite the reference to Rome and Etruscan cities the significance of these encounters between Etruscan and at least one Latian champion would be lost on us were it not for the appearance of Mastarna and the brothers Vibenna, who were also known to Roman history.

The sources for early Roman history to whom we now turn are unusual but important. They include some of the best minds of the late Republic and Empire: Varro, the pioneer student of the Latin language and Roman institutions (116–27), the Emperor Claudius (10–AD 54), who was plucked from a life of scholarship to assume the Imperial purple and whose specialty was Etruscan antiquity, and finally, Tacitus, the Roman Thucydides (ca AD 56–post AD 113). According to Tacitus (*Ann.* IV, 65) the Caelian Hill, once known as the Querquetulanus (from the oak trees growing there), had been renamed when Caelius Vibenna, an Etruscan captain, settled there in the time of Tarquin the First or perhaps under another of the kings. Claudius, whose remarks come down to us in an inscription which gives the text of a speech by the Emperor, noted that King Servius Tullius was an ally of Caelius Vibenna (*CIL* XIII no. 1668). After the latter's death the king brought the remnants of his followers to Rome and settled them on the hill renamed in his honor. Servius himself had formerly borne the Etruscan name Mastarna. Varro (*LL* V, 46) transports Caelius Vibenna back to the reign of Romulus. And to complete this array of conflicting opinions we may note that Verrius Flaccus (tutor of Augustus' grandsons) seems to have said that Caelius and his brother aided King Tarquin (in the fragmentary epitome of Festus p. 355 M).[23] The pair also appear on an Etruscan mirror in the British Museum attacking Cacus, the demon of the Palatine or a transmutation of Tarcun/Tarquinius.[24]

Returning to the François Tomb, we find still further variations on the theme. The Tarquin of Rome falling before Marcus Camillus is not Lucius (like the two Roman kings) or Lucomo, the Etruscan title thus transformed into a Roman name, but Gnaeus.[25] Mastarna, as Claudius maintained, appears as the ally and rescuer of Caelius Vibenna. And Aulus Vibenna is also known to the Etruscan story depicted in the tomb. Indeed Claudius, not surprisingly given his interests, seems to repeat the Etruscan version. But what happened in Rome? There is complete uncertainty about the relations of Caelius and Aulus Vibenna to the Romans and their kings.[26] Aside from a topographical association, there was confusion. The normal narrative of Rome's history, moreover, as put together in the late Republic and retold by Livy and Dionysius, had eliminated such troublesome figures as the brothers Vibenna and the question of Servius Tullius' real name. If more records such as those of the François Tomb and Claudius' oration were preserved we would undoubtedly meet similar contradictions and missing figures at every turn in the story of early Rome. The problem that confronts the historian is to determine how far he may develop his narrative from the single name. Although the personalities and places are recorded, the relations between them are obscure. Such questions, already occupying many volumes, are not the subject of this book. But we must still face the use that has been made of archaeology to encourage faith in the common narrative of early Rome.

In 1973, Ferdinando Castagnoli, professor of topography in the University of Rome (now La Sapienza) and distinguished successor of the great figures of two centuries of research into the history and monuments of the city, published a study entitled (in translation) "Roman Topography and the Historiography of Archaic Rome."[27] Castagnoli cited excavation in three principal areas of Rome which, in his opinion, confirmed the tradition regarding the regal period and the early Republic. The first was the Temple of the Castores, Castor and Pollux, the Greek Dioscuri, in the Roman Forum. The temple stands today at one side of the Basilica Julia in the form given to it at the end of the first century AD (fig. 1.3). Its three surviving columns and the entablature above them have been a landmark throughout the centuries.[28] The temple was established, Livy tells us (II, 20, 2), following the battle at Lake Regillus (Gabii) in 496 when the young Republic confronted and defeated her sister cities of the Latin League. The temple was dedicated in 484. After the battle the Dioscuri were seen watering their horses at the spring of Juturna in the Forum. They had aided the Romans; their cult was brought to the city.[29] For Castagnoli the temple and the tradition of the cult weighed heavily in favor of the historical account. Recently excavations have been made inside the podium of the existing temple. The first temple on the site can now be restored as a large structure 27.5 m (90.2 ft) on its front and 37–40 m (121–131 ft) on the flank.[30] From the fill of the late Republican temple of the Castores overlying the first temple there come fragments of antefixes (covers masking the joint between tiles at the edge of the roof or ornamental developments of the same) of the Juno Sospita type (fig. 11.10).[31] If these belonged to the earlier building, they would support a general date in the early fifth century, but such antefixes were commonly used at the time and the pieces from the Forum may have belonged to another structure. Two examples of the type come from the Palatine as well as another from below the Basilica Julia. Other antefixes of a type current at the same time and found in the surrounding area have also been attributed to the temple. They are the familiar type of consorting satyr and maenad (fig. 11.12).[32] To these have been added crest tiles for the ridgepole of the building and other fragments of disc *acroteria*, placed at the apex of the roof on either end of the ridgepole, and gorgon antefixes, the last items typical of a somewhat earlier period not wholly consonant with a building date of the early fifth century.[33] On the whole, the evidence of excavation cannot be said to prove that a temple was dedicated on the spot in the early fifth century.[34]

The second monument considered by Castagnoli was the Temple of Jupiter Optimus Maximus. There is, he noted, "almost unanimous belief" in the tradition of the erection under the Tarquins (First and/or Second) and its dedication during the first year of the Republic (509). The great temple rose on the foundations outlining its podium which underlie the Caffarelli Palace (the Imperial German Embassy until, following the First World War, it was made part of the Capitoline Museums in 1925): figs 1.1 and 1.2. The foundations, impressive in themselves, rise to fifteen courses in height and outline a podium 62 × 53.3 m (203.3 × 174.8 ft).[35] If the building occupied the entire space thus provided it was a behemoth among the temples of Etruria and Latium. It was rebuilt on this scale after the fire of 83, and despite the suggestion that the original temple may have occupied only part of the podium,[36] it is difficult not to believe that the restoration followed the lines of the preexisting building.

The Temple of Jupiter Optimus Maximus might thus seem to have been the grandest monument of the Great Rome of the Tarquins. But before adopting this conclusion we must deal with one aspect of the foundations. Above the twelfth course of the foundations the dimensions of the tufa (*cappellaccio*) blocks change from a height of 30–32 cm to 40 cm (1 to 1.31 ft).[37] It is definitely stated that the foundations of the temple were not rebuilt after the fire of 83.[38] And they surely were not rebuilt when the temple was again restored after the fire of AD 69 since by that time *cappellaccio* stone was no longer used as building material. And what reason is there to think that the foundations of the temple below the level of the paving would have been affected by a fire? Perhaps another hypothesis may be advanced: that the difference in construction was due to a suspension of work on the building. The work was begun, suspended, and taken up again at a later time. The Romans knew that a Marcus Horatius had dedicated the temple. But in addition to the consul of the artificially contrived first year of the Republic, we know of a consular tribune of the same name of 378 or 376 (Livy VI, 31, 1, 5), although the calendar year of his office may be inaccurate.

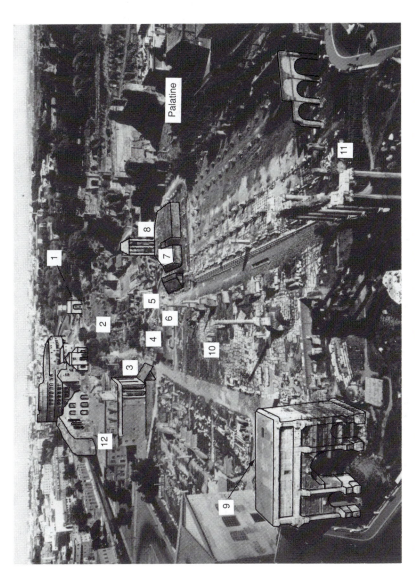

Figure 1.3 Rome, Forum seen from the Capitoline. Arch of Titus; 2, Sacra Via; 3, Sepulcretum; 4, Regia; 5, Temple of Vesta; 6, Arch of Augustus; 7, Temple of Castor and Pollux; 8, Spring of Juturna; 9, Lapis Niger; 10, Base of an Equestrian Statue (Domitian); 11, Temple of Saturn; 12, Basilica of Maxentius

But still, if one so desires, there would be a M. Horatius available to dedicate the Temple of Jupiter Optimus Maximus during the fourth century, at a time far enough removed from the beginning of Roman historical writing that an inscription with his name could be misinterpreted as that of the consul of 509 – to the greater glory of Rome and of the Horatii.[39] In its completed form the Temple of Jupiter Optimus Maximus would thus be the monument of the fourth century and of a city well on its way to a dominant position in the Italian peninsula.[40]

It follows that much of the tradition surrounding the building cannot be accepted. Vulca of Veii, the master coroplast (sculptor in clay) supposedly called to execute the cult statue and architectural terracottas (Pliny *NH* XXXV, 157), never existed. The sculpture of Jupiter triumphant in his *quadriga* on the roof (Livy X, 23, 11) was not set up until 296 and the date of the installation of this final element in the decoration of the temple is suggestive of the date of the building.[41]

There remains the problem of dating the first stage of work on the foundations before the interruption. Here archaeology can be of no help. Any of the original fill against the foundations has long ago been lost in the continual rebuildings to which the site has been subjected since antiquity. The project for the temple may well belong to the kings of the sixth century. But even so, their resources were not sufficient to carry the work forward.[42]

Archaeologically, the most vivid reminder of Rome of the sixth century is to be found in the Sant'Omobono sanctuary, the early levels (seventh to fifth centuries) underlying the twin temples situated below (and beside) the church of Sant'Omobono (figs 1.1, 5.1, 5.2). Although Colini's identification of the twin Republican temples with those of Fortuna and Mater Matuta and his assumption that the underlying archaic shrine was Servius Tullius' temple dedicated to the latter goddess is widely accepted, the evidence on which it rests is not convincing.

The most important texts are those of Livy (to which the evidence of Plutarch, *Life of Camillus*, Dionysius of Halicarnassus, and Ovid, in the *Fasti*, is, in every case, of secondary importance).

Writing of events in 396 during the siege of Veii Livy says (V, 19, 6) that Marcus Furius Camillus "vowed that if Veii fell and the senate gave its approval he would hold large-scale games and would dedicate a remade temple of Mater Matuta which had in the past been dedicated by King Servius Tullius."[43] There was, clearly, an archaic temple of Mater Matuta, but Mater Matuta alone.

Now to the year 213, again Livy (XXIV, 47, 15–16): "At Rome a fire raged for two nights and a day. Everything from the salt pans to the Gate of Carmenta was levelled to the ground together with the Vicus Aequimaelius and the Vicus Iugarius and the Temples of Fortuna and Mater Matuta. And outside the gate the fire cut a wide path burning many shrines and nonsacred buildings."[44] The temples of Fortuna and Mater Matuta are mentioned together. But one should note that they are two of four points of reference cited, with the intention, it seems, of showing the extent of the destruction.

Finally, for 196 Livy (XXXIII, 27, 4–5) recounts the following concerning Lucius Stertinius after his return from Spain: "L. Stertinius . . . erected from his share of the booty two arches in the Forum Boarium, before the temple of Fortuna and the temple of Mater Matuta, and one in the Circus Maximus and he placed gilded statues on these arches."[45]

It is this last passage that provides the principal support for what has been called Colini's "happy intuition."[46] But in order to accept his identification of the twin temples as those of Fortuna and Mater Matuta one must envisage two arches cheek by jowl outside the *area sacra* (there is no trace of the two arches inside the enclosure) in addition, of course, to the arch in the Circus Maximus. This is possible, but not necessary, and without doing violence to Livy's text we may equally well envisage the two arches placed before two temples located in different parts of the Forum Boarium. Certainly in the latter case the effect of Stertinius' monuments would have been no less imposing and possibly more so. Furthermore, if the two temples were separate landmarks of the Forum Boarium area, Livy's mention of them, together with the Vicus Aequimaelius and the Vicus Jugarius, in connection with the fire of 213 makes sense as a means of defining the extent of the devastation. To sum up: the temples of Fortuna and Mater Matuta were not necessarily situated one beside the other, and there is no concrete evidence to identify either with the remains in the Sant'Omobono sanctuary.[47]

Castagnoli placed little emphasis on the fortifications of archaic Rome as evidence for the size and importance of the archaic city. The existence of such fortifications, enclosing an area approaching in any way the 246 hectares (608 acres) within the existing Republican walls, is extremely dubious.[48]

This review has shown how difficult it is to cite archaeological evidence in support of the annalists' accounts of the history of early Rome. The early temple of the Castores in the Forum is still a matter of mystery.[49] At some time during or after the regal period work began on a grand temple to Jupiter on the Capitoline, but the work was suspended and in the process of completion of the building the last element of architectural decoration was not installed until 296. A sanctuary did exist in the Forum Boarium and excavation has shown that it was visited by Etruscans, who left objects carrying their graffiti, and by importers of Greek and oriental wares. But identification of this temple with the temple of Mater Matuta supposedly erected by King Servius Tullius is unlikely.

Archaeology deserves better than to remain a crutch for the tales of the annalists and their followers. Its own tale is no less fascinating, and it has one supreme advantage over the written tradition as we have it: its evidence is direct and uncontaminated. The following pages are an attempt to answer the call to turn archaeology into history.

A BRIEF OUTLINE OF ROMAN HISTORY

By tradition the history of Rome begins in the eighth century with the foundation of the city by Romulus. The date 753 is often cited but the ancient sources have dates as early as 814 or as late as 729. In the thinking of the Romans this event marked the true beginning of the city while the stories of Evander, the Greek settler of Rome, and Aeneas the Trojan, the progenitor of Romulus through the line of the kings of Alba, belonged to a distant and separate past. According to ancient reckoning the Trojan War and Aeneas' flight to Italy would have taken place well before 1000.

Romulus' settlement was thought to have been little more than a refuge for the restless or fugitives from the surrounding area. It required a fusion with the neighboring Sabines, led by their king Titus Tatius, to create a true city, an event remembered in the tale of the abduction of Sabine women by the Romans. Romulus and Titus Tatius were followed first by Numa Pompilius, next by Tullus Hostilius and then by Ancus Marcius. These early kings were succeeded by a dynasty of Etruscan origin, the Tarquins. The first of the family, Lucomo and his wife Tanaquil, came to Rome from Tarquinia. Their son Tarquin the Elder was the chosen successor of Ancus Marcius, confirmed as always by election. The sons of Ancus subsequently assassinated Tarquin, but his son-in-law Servius Tullius seized power. The last king of Rome, Tarquin the Proud, came to power by a palace coup instigated by his wife Tullia, daughter of Servius Tullius. At last in 509, in a revolution set in motion by the rape of the noble lady Lucretia by Sextus Tarquin, son of Tarquin the Proud, the Romans expelled the king and his family. Although the city was attacked, and possibly taken by the Etruscan leader Lars Porsenna, this was merely a final episode of the Etruscan period. It gave rise to some of the most famous tales of Roman heroism, on the part of Horatius Cocles (the lone defender of the bridge), Mucius Scaevola (who held his hand steady in the fire to prove the courage of a Roman) and the maiden Cloelia (the intrepid leader of the escape of the Roman hostages from Porsenna's camp). The city and its growing territory was henceforth led by magistrates elected for a year or less (under various titles: consuls, dictators, praetors, and military tribunes – in one period a board of ten magistrates, the decemvirs, was instituted). The major force in the government, however, was the senate, a council of elders drawn from a circumscribed group of families, the patricians.

The patrician families, originally thirty in number, were represented in the curiate assembly, thus forming "the Roman people." The patricians exercised an effective monopoly of religion through their priesthoods, of government through the senate, and of law through magistracies which they in fact dominated and often claimed to hold by exclusive right. They wielded further power through their clients, individuals bound to patrician families by formal traditions of dependency and protection. Distinct from the patricians and their clients were the plebeians: citizens but citizens enjoying nothing of the power and privileges of the patricians. In tradition the plebeians first achieved a measure of political importance under King Servius Tullius, who was thought to have instituted a reform of the army, ordering it by classification on the basis of wealth and investing the army so ordered with the standing of a political assembly (*comitia centuriata*). The patricians in command of the young republic, however, were opposed to plebeian rights and between 494 and 449 it required five secessions of the plebs (mass withdrawals of the plebeians to a location outside the officially established boundaries of the city from where they could treat with the patricians as with a foreign state) for them to begin to achieve political recognition. The tale of the wicked decemvir Claudius and the innocent virgin Virginia reflected the plebeians' complaints in popular romance. The core of the protection won by the plebeians was the institution of the office of tribune of the plebs and the right of appeal from a capital sentence on the part of a magistrate to the body of the people. These political reforms were not completed until the third century, when finally laws passed by the plebeian assembly were recognized as binding on the entire community (287). Plebeian admission to the highest magistracies of the city had become accepted over the previous two centuries and more.

Tradition credited the kings with the beginning of Rome's territorial expansion. The Republic was quickly drawn into war with Rome's Latin neighbors, who, after 493, however, were held to be bound to Rome by treaty. In the fifth century we hear of continual wars against the Sabines to the northeast, the Aequi and the Volscians to the south. From these decades, the tale of the appeal of the Roman mother and of the repentant patriotism of her exiled son immortalized the name of Coriolanus, while the response of the patriot to the call of duty has ever recalled Cincinnatus leaving his plow in mid-furrow to lead his country. The century ended with war against Veii, Rome's Etruscan neighbor across the Tiber, and the capture of Veii in 396. Soon thereafter, however, in 387, Rome fell victim to the Gauls, whose progress southward through the Italian peninsula was felt no less intensely by the Etruscans, by the Latians, and by the groups speaking related Italic languages. Rome's recovery after the Gallic sack, and the weakness of her neighbors in the aftermath of the Gallic invasion, paved the way for Rome's emergence as the leader of the Latians (338). Rome immediately embarked on the three great Samnite Wars (343–290). Thereafter Rome faced the south Italian Greeks led by King Pyrrhus of Epirus (280–275) and, with Italy secured, entered the long struggle with Carthage (264–146) from which she emerged as the dominant power in the Mediterranean.

A BRIEF OUTLINE OF LATE ITALIAN PREHISTORY

Before the excavations in the Sant'Omobono sanctuary it would have been possible to write as if the archaeology of Rome began in the Iron Age. Latium, however, has been inhabited since paleolithic times, and more recent evidence has demonstrated that there was a settlement at Rome in the second millennium BC.[50] The Capitoline was one hill inhabited at this time, as shown by the Bronze Age (Apennine) sherds found there and also recovered from the great fill over the sixth-century temple in the Sant'Omobono sanctuary at the foot of the Capitoline toward the Tiber.[51] Further material, of later date but still belonging to the period before 1000 BC, has been identified in the Forum.[52]

The Italian Bronze Age has little of the brilliance of its counter-part in Greece, and there was no Italian Homer to sing its praises. More than any other part of Italy Sicily was drawn into the orbit of the eastern Mediterranean. Eastern traders built warehouses at Thapsos just north of Syracuse and at the end of the Bronze Age local kingdoms arose which may have been pale reflections of the states of Mycenean Greece.[53] The mainland shows less political influence from the east, but eastern craftsmen set up workshops to make local versions of Mycenean pottery and local versions of Aegean faience in Italy. The exploitation of natural resources, especially the development of copper mining in Sardinia, fed an eastern market and was very possibly organized by miners and metalworkers from abroad. Phoenicians may already have been involved in this commerce.[54] One part of the mainland witnessed a precocious development in the growth of large settlements. This was in the Po Valley, where the so-called Terremare mounds represent the remains of well-organized cities beginning toward the end of the second millennium.[55] South of the Po Valley the Middle and Later Bronze Age is a shadowy period. This is the so-called Apennine culture for which settlement information is slight and tombs uncommon. On the basis of the information available now the Apennine groups may be envisaged as peoples living in scattered farmsteads and gathering from time to time at sanctuaries generally associated with springs and caves.[56] Mycenean pottery reached central Italy in the thirteenth and twelfth centuries.[57] In this apparently stable sphere of the Apennine culture there appear within a century or two before 1000 cemeteries of cremation urns which signal the appearance of a new element in the culture of the peninsula. These burials, which are also characterized by new styles of pottery and pottery decoration and new types of bronzes, the violin bow fibula (safety pin), simple arch fibulae, curved-sided knives and straight and curved-sided razors, are referred to as belonging to the "Proto-Villanovan" culture.[58] This term comes from the Iron Age cremation cemeteries of central Italy, the first of which came to light at Villanova near Bologna in 1853, and which begin their life in the ninth century BC.[59] The Proto-Villanovan culture, the predecessor of the classic

Villanovan, is widely represented in Latium.[60] The Proto-Villanovan epoch also witnessed the accumulation of reserves of metal found in increasingly large and frequent hoards (fig. 1.4). The sites of the Latian coast participated in the distribution of metal and finished metal objects that reached from Etruria to southern Italy.

The culture of the Latian Iron Age develops directly from its Proto-Villanovan predecessor. The first remains of Iron Age Rome, the cremation tombs from the Forum, belong to the same culture as that represented in the Alban Hills and in southern and central Latium by similar burials (figs 1.5, 1.6, 1.7).[61] These tombs show firmly established funeral practices. Among the earliest tombs the pottery and implements of the tomb group are frequently miniature models of real objects. The offerings are made up of a model table service and a lance, where appropriate, for a grown man. There are also instances of figurines, possibly representing a man in the guise of priest. Miniaturization of this kind is found only rarely outside Latium.[62] The hut urn for the cremated remains, although known in Etruria and Campania as well, is typical of Latium. Although the documentation of the early Alban and Latian tombs is scattered, it still shows that the Roman tradition that their founders were descendants of the Alban kings reflects a true bond between the Romans of the early Iron Age and the Alban Hills. The Alban/Roman type of burial is not found outside Latium. It belongs to the *nomen Latinum*, the speakers of the Latin language.[63]

In Etruria the cremation cemeteries of the Proto-Villanovan type develop into the classic cremation burials of the full-fledged Villanovan type

Figure 1.4 Monte Rovello-Allumiere, hoard of raw metal and bronze axes of the Proto-Villanovan age, Museo Nazionale Preistorico ed Etnografico "L. Pigorini."

Figure 1.5 Rome, Forum, Tomb Y, drawing of the remains as found. The hut urn for the cremated remains and other offerings are contained within a large vessel or *dolium*.

Figure 1.6 Grave goods from Iron Age tombs of the Alban Hills, Rocca di Papa and Marino.

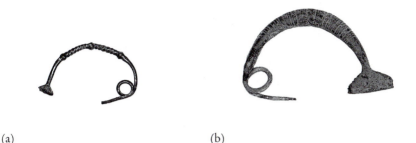

(a)   (b)

Figure 1.7 Bronze fibulae, (a) twisted bow type, (b) thickened bow type, Rocca di Papa and Marino.

(fig. 1.8). Beginning with the Villanovan cemeteries in the ninth century, Etruria also witnessed a marked concentration of population in the centers that were to develop into the Etruscan cities of later centuries. In Latium, although there is less archaeological evidence, it seems that a similar process was under way.[64] None of the Latian cities, however (with the possible exception of Rome, where much of the evidence is forever lost), seems to have reached the size or population of the major Etruscan centers.

In the eighth century southern Italy was opened to colonization from Greece. Within a century most of the coast of Sicily and the region surrounding the Ionian Sea between Tarentum and the Straits of Messina had been colonized.[65] Farther north Greek traders had established themselves on the island of Ischia in the Bay of Naples (even before the main colonizing effort began) and provided a conduit of commerce to willing Italian clients.[66] It is clear that Semitic people were resident there at the same time, and through these eastern contacts oriental imports began to reach Etruria and Latium.[67] It has been argued that the Phoenician presence in Sardinia goes back to this period.[68]

The impact of Greek and Phoenician colonization on Latium and her neighbors has always been evident. It is only recently, however, that the force of influence and perhaps colonization from Etruria south of the Tiber has been realized in considering the evidence of the "Villanovan" cemeteries in Campania, specifically those of Capua, inland from Naples, and Pontecagnano, now a suburb of Salerno.[69] The Etruscans, thus enveloping ancient Latium, were destined to be a major force in the cultural development of the early city of Rome.

17

Figure 1.8 Barbarano Romano, ash urn and pottery helmet of the Villanovan type, Museo Nazionale Preistorico ed Etnografico "L. Pigorini."

BUILDING STONE IN EARLY ROME

Beginning in the seventh century the Romans employed volcanic stone (tufa) from various quarries in building.[70] Initially, and probably well into the fourth century, only stone quarried in Rome (the so-called *cappellaccio*) was used for building, although isolated blocks of stone for inscriptions (such as the famous *cippus* beneath the *lapis niger* of the Forum, a block of *Grotta Oscura* tufa) might come from farther away. Gradually, as Rome extended her authority over her neighbors, the quantities of stone needed for building could be sought from quarries in the territory of Veii (*Grotta Oscura*) and in the Anio Valley as well as from beyond the Janiculum Hill across the Tiber. The three tufas of major concern to the study of early Rome are *cappellaccio*, *Grotta Oscura* and *Peperino*.

Cappellaccio from Rome is a lamellar tufa. It weathers badly and its poor qualities as a building stone explain why the Romans, as soon as their resources and territorial control permitted, brought stone from farther away. It is the stone used in the podium of the Temple of Jupiter Optimus Maximus.

Grotta Oscura tufa is a pale color sometimes described as "yellow." It comes from quarries near the Tiber but originally controlled by Rome's enemy Veii. *Grotta Oscura* tufa is the major component of the surviving sections of the ashlar defense wall on the Esquiline (the "Servian Wall"). The stone from Fidenae, notable for large inclusions of volcanic debris, was used alongside *Grotta Oscura* tufa.

Peperino is a grey tufa from quarries at Marino in the Alban Hills. The first secure instance of its use at Rome (trophy of Marcus Fulvius Flaccus in the Sant'Omobono sanctuary in the Forum Boarium) belongs to the third century (264).

The tufas from Gabii, the *lapis ruber* (red stone), from various quarries in the Anio Valley, and Monteverde tufa from beyond the Janiculum Hill and other quarries of the lower Tiber are associated with building of the later Republic.[71]

2

TOMBS OF THE FORUM AND ESQUILINE

The Arch of Titus stands at the crest of the Sacra Via, which makes its ascent toward the arch from the Forum. The head of the Sacra Via is a saddle which originally connected the Palatine with the Velia (to the northeast) (figs 1.3, 1.4). The latter hill was leveled in the early 1930s to make way for the grand allée which now unites the Colosseum to the Altar of the Fatherland and the Piazza Venezia in eight lanes of rushing traffic. Another landmark, the Basilica of Maxentius, was built against the slope of the Velia which thus occupied a position between it and the Colosseum.

When Giacomo Boni began his activity in the Forum there was already speculation that the early inhabitants of the Romulean city on the Palatine and the adjoining hills might have used the edges of the Forum Valley as a burial place. This was the notion in particular of Luigi Pigorini, who was the leading figure in Italian prehistory for a half century and who was at Boni's side as the search for an early cemetery in the Forum began. Pigorini (1842–1925) was a boy of 11 when the first cremation cemetery of the Italian Iron Age was discovered at Bologna (Villanova) in 1853. He began his career in the epic years of the discovery of the Bronze Age towns of the Po Valley (the Terremare). At 28, in 1870, the year of Italian unification, he was in Rome, Section Chief in the General Direction of Museums and Archaeological Excavations. In 1875 he founded the *Bollettino di Paletnologia Italiano*, which remains the principal journal of Italian prehistory. In 1876 he assumed both the directorship of the National Prehistoric Museum, which now bears his name, and the professorship of Paleoethnography at the University of Rome. For fifty years, until his death in 1925, in a career spanning the most fruitful years of the discovery of man's antiquity and development in Europe, Pigorini was the leader of Italian prehistory.

The search for the tombs proceeded down the Sacra Via from its summit, at first without result. But at the foot of the descent from the Arch of Titus beside the Temple of Antoninus and Faustina, there came success. Pigorini was on hand that April morning in 1902 and with him Christian Hülsen, the student of the topography of ancient Rome. The excavation was being made through a tangle of drains of the Republican period intercepted by larger sewers of Imperial date, numerous wells of all periods and medieval cesspits. Some 3.5 m (11.5 ft) below the surface, excavating in a probing shaft slightly more than 1 m (3.28 ft) wide, one of Boni's workmen came on a tufa slab. The slab was raised. Below it could be seen the top of an ash urn. The first cremation grave of the Roman Forum had been found.

Let us leave Boni, Pigorini, and Hülsen in the first euphoria of discovery and confirmation of Pigorini's intuition[1] and recall earlier discoveries of tombs of the first Romans.

The discovery of the cemeteries of early Rome began soon after the city became the capital of the United Kingdom of Italy in 1870 (fig. 2.1). The establishment of the capital of the new nation with its burgeoning bureaucracies and expanding population was reflected at once in land speculation and building. One of the new quarters was on the Esquiline Hill, and its buildings destroyed a large Roman necropolis. There are practically no records of the tombs found below the nineteenth-century palazzi that now pack the area southwest of Santa Maria Maggiore on the Esquiline plateau. The earlier part of the cemetery was concentrated on the plateau beyond the Cispius and Fagutal/Oppius ridges.[2] The work on the Esquiline was not left unsupervised by the city of Rome, which in May 1872 constituted an Archaeological Commission whose secretary was Rudolfo Lanciani, later professor of topography at the University of Rome, best known for his edition of the archaeological map of Rome (including the information from the surviving elements of the marble plan dating from the early third century AD) and author of books on Rome across the centuries written in English which added to the tone of innumerable parlors in England and America of their day. This Commission promptly founded a periodical, the *Bullettino della Commissione Archeologica del Comune di Roma*, and has continued its work ever since, caring for the municipal monuments and museums (whose origins go back to the first papal donations in 1472) and recording discoveries and excavations within the city. The *Bullettino* is one of the world's major archaeological journals. Thus, in 1872, the Commission had far more to contend with than the graves coming to light on the Esquiline. By and large inscriptions, sculpture, and remains of the Imperial Age crowded protohistory out of the reports in the pages of the *Bullettino*. Lanciani's one report on the Esquiline cemetery gave only the generalities of the tombs found in the first four years, illustrating no more than a score of individual items, although it is clear that Lanciani had made his observations on the spot.[3] The same is true of the reports of M. S. De Rossi, who was subsequently inspector.[4] How supervision on the Esquiline was exercised is difficult to say. According to Giovanni Pinza, who in 1905 published a large monograph on the prehistory of Rome and Latium, in which he included all available information concerning the Esquiline tombs, the day-to-day supervision was negligible.[5] It is essential to remember that these were not archaeological excavations. They were the collection of archaeological material from workmen making the cuttings for streets and sewers. Before 1870 the Esquiline in the area of the future Piazza Vittorio Emanuele and its surroundings had a decided hump which reached 5–7 m (16.4–23 ft) above the present-day street level. The hump was largely composed of debris of the Imperial Age. This area had remained unoccupied during the Middle Ages, the Renaissance, and later times, save for several churches which all now occupy elevated terraces that came into being during the general lowering of their surroundings. The work of making the new quarter of post-unification Rome proceeded as follows. First a street grid was laid out. Next the city excavated the streets down to the desired level, installing sewers at an even greater depth and thus excavating below the ancient ground level and encountering the tombs lying below the modern streets. Finally the individual lots along the streets were excavated by their owners before buildings were erected. The responsibility and supervision of the Archaeological Commission extended only to public land, the streets. With the rarest exception, what was found on the building sites has disappeared. The fate of many tomb groups from the streets was little better because both to some extent on the site and then in changing storage in 1882, the tomb groups became hopelessly confused. The record is less faulty, though hardly perfect, thereafter.

Despite the manner of its recovery, the information from the Esquiline necropolis is of the highest value. The recorded tombs belong to three groups. First there are early graves (all inhumations in a *fossa* or trench) of the type also found in the Forum and of approximately the same time, the eighth and seventh centuries.[6] To judge from the imported Greek (Protocorinthian) and Etruscan pottery in the Antiquario Comunale, in the seventh century there must have been tombs in the Esquiline cemetery whose contents rivaled that of most lavish tombs of Latium, from Castel di Decima, Acqua Acetosa, Laurentina and even Praeneste.[7] Among the important discoveries made by Dr Anna Sommella Mura during her recent work on this material are pieces of the body of the Corinthian *olpe* with a Greek graffito previously known only from fragments of the base. The inscription gives the name of the owner, Ktektos, apparently a Greek resident at Rome (fig. 2.2).[8] Second, there were chamber tombs cut into the soft tufa bedrock. The chamber tomb is common in Etruria and Latium after the seventh century. At its most elaborate the archaic chamber tomb in Etruria faithfully mimics a portico house, details of construction and furniture carved in place. The Latin chamber tombs are less elaborate but in the chamber funeral couches are frequently represented by benches of stone left in place.[9] The burials themselves could be made in tufa sarcophagi or cinerary urns, a category including burials from the sixth to the second century. Because of the almost complete absence of Greek black figure and red figure pottery, or their Italian derivatives, among the grave goods, the best chronological guides were absent from the Esquiline tombs and the manner in which the

22

inventories were made does not help. Furthermore, it seems almost certain that burials were often made without grave goods of any sort. It is only recently that the handsome marble ash urns buried inside tufa sarcophagi have been recognized as belonging to tombs of the fifth century (figs 2.3, 2.4).[10] The notion that whole centuries of Roman burials have never been found (or never existed) must be given up, although the work on the Esquiline permitted hardly a glimpse of the remains of these periods. The final form of burial documented on the Esquiline was the cellular *puticoli* in which mass burials were made at the end of the Republic and which gave the Esquiline such an unsavory reputation until this dumping ground of mortality was covered by the gardens of Augustus' friend Maecenas.

The Esquiline burial ground, in its later Republican phase reaching beyond the so-called Servian Wall, thus spans a period of time from the early Iron Age to the third century and later.[11] Thanks to the excavations of the last twenty years at other Latin sites near Rome, especially Castel di Decima and Acqua Acetosa, Laurentina, one can also appreciate what is missing from the material of the Esquiline cemetery dating to the seventh century. What are missing are objects easily sold on the antiquarian market. Two small silver rings are preserved.[12] There are beads, bronze fibulae, even fibulae with amber decoration. But there is no armor save one bronze shield and one pectoral. Yet surely there was much more of antiquarian value. Among the material from the early excavations there are eight bronze cauldron stands (they are made in easily crushed bronze sheeting and so were probably badly deformed when excavated). From tombs excavated below Palazzo Brancacci at the corner of Via G. Lanza and Via Merulana, there is a handsome bronze sword.[13] But where is the gold, the arms, the metal vessels that we now know from Decima and other contemporary necropolises and whose presence is suggested by the elegant imported Corinthian pottery from the cemetery? Under the conditions of recovery on the Esquiline in the 1870s and 1880s their flight to the antiquarian market is all too probable.[14]

Although their existence has not been generally recognized, it is certain that tombs comparable to the cremation graves of the Forum had been found on the Esquiline near the church of Sant'Eusebio.[15] To this extent the discovery made by Boni in the Forum was not new to Rome, although the relation of the Forum cemetery to the Velia and the Palatine was of paramount interest. Nevertheless, Boni's discoveries in 1902 and subsequent campaigns revolutionized archaeology in Rome.[16] Much nonsense has been written about the practice of excavation. The kernel of these discussions is usually that the genius of the piece "discovered" the logic of stratigraphy, i.e. the temporal sequence of superimposed layers whether natural or manmade. Some of these culture heroes, like Heinrich Schliemann, have sought their own laurels. Some, like Thomas Jefferson (another American since we must remember that Schliemann became a United States citizen in 1849)

Figure 2.1 Rome, showing early cemeteries.

Figure 2.2 Corinthian *olpe* with graffito from the Esquiline cemetery, Rome, Antiquarium Comunale – Musei Capitolini.

have won applause for the passing application of common sense to the situation of ancient remains. Not every excavation must be a stratigraphic exercise. In my younger days I once drove my more experienced foreman almost to despair by faithfully recording the stratification of the fill of an ancient theater which had finished its days as a garbage dump for the residents of the hill above. The garbage had nothing to tell us about the theater and nothing new to tell us about the folk on the hill, remains of whose existence were in place in their dwellings. But when the relation of the remains to their earth covering is important, excavation requires more than common sense about accumulation and an eye to the sundry tricks that pitting, robbing of building material and backfilling in an inverted sequence can produce. It requires a keen eye to see what is in the dirt, ability to record what is seen in word and image so that others will understand the record, and most of all it requires the imagination to understand the remains, restoring them to their original form and mutual relationship and imagining, if possible, the activity that produced them. Like many of the great archaeologists of his generation Boni was an architect, and both his talent for architecture and his training gave him that sense of three-dimensionality

Figure 2.3 Marble ash urn in the form of a sarcophagus, Rome, Antiquarium Comunale – Musei Capitolini.

Figure 2.4 Tufa container for the same marble ash urn, Rome, Antiquarium Comunale – Musei Capitolini.

26

with which a good excavator must look in the bottom of his trench and look at the section of dirt in its walls. He thought clearly and immediately, leaving notes that are still invaluable. He recorded his work meticulously. The drawings executed for Boni's excavations are a pleasure to see and an education to use. He photographed constantly and took planimetric coverage of the Forum excavations with a camera suspended above the subject (fig. 2.5). To Boni are also due early aerial photographs of the Roman Forum (1910).[17] He understood what physical science had to tell about material remains. Boni consulted physical anthropologists even for cremated remains.[18] Because of his consultation with botanists and zoologists we know what species of fish and domesticated animals were offered as food to the dead, as well as the grains and beans that accompanied them.[19] Fifty years before the advent of dating archaeological materials on the basis of physical properties (especially the dating of organic material by C14 analysis) Boni proposed dating pottery from magnetic variation. The theory is a simple one. Since the magnetic constituents of clay are frozen in position at the time of firing (above a certain temperature) and since the earth's magnetic field has a cyclical variation, the measurement of the deviation from the current magnetic field of the magnetic particles in an ancient vase will place the date of manufacture of the same vase along the path of cyclical variation of the earth's magnetic field. Unfortunately for Boni's experiments, to carry out such an age determination it is necessary to know the position in which the vase was fired. Boni's theory was excellent, although he lacked the circumstances for its application. Boni was also what today would be called an experimental archaeologist. He recreated the process of forming and firing the handmade pottery from the Forum tombs, showing that it had been fired not in a kiln but in an open brushwood fire. Finally, Boni did not hesitate to press the interpretation of his discoveries. It is true that he exhibited a streak of theatrical antiquarianism that led him to stage costumed revivals of Roman festivals and shared the spirit of exaggerated nationalism common at the time. But Boni, unlike some fumbling excavators, had a clear mental picture of what was in the ground and how it got there. His work has had its equals, but his standard remains unsurpassed.

Boni and his scientific consultants set to work immediately to extract the most information possible from the first Forum tomb (Tomb A in Boni's sequence) and its surroundings (fig. 2.6).[20] The burial was the cremation of a robust man of above 30 years of age whose remains were contained in a jar which, together with eight other vessels, was placed in a still larger vessel (the *dolium*). The burial, covered by a conical tufa cap, was set into the ground some 0.6 m (almost 2 ft) below the ground level of the time. The tomb was not dug into sterile soil. Fragments of pottery were found to a depth of an additional 3 m (10 ft) below the lip of the *dolium*. The pit (*pozzo*) was refilled with the earth removed in making the grave, a few rocks thrown in to avoid settling. A denser rock packing was often encountered both over

Figure 2.5 Rome, Forum, view of the Sepulcretum during Boni's excavations. Visible in the center of the photo is a trench or *fossa* grave lined with small stones and three well or *pozzo* graves still retaining the stone fill above the large jar or *dolium* containing the ash urn and other funeral gifts.

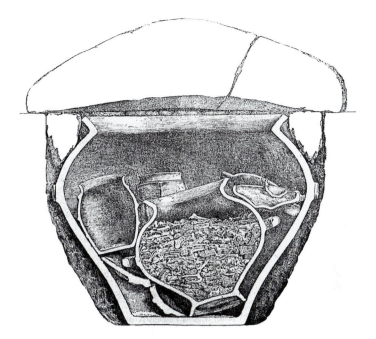

Figure 2.6 Rome, Forum, Tomb A.

the *pozzo* and over the *fossa* (trench) graves. The vases of grave group A are both normal size and miniatures. They are handmade. The pottery is undecorated save for a ribbed checkerboard pattern on two handleless beakers.

The second of Boni's discoveries was an inhumation grave in a *fossa* (B) (fig. 2.7). The digging of this tomb showed Boni as an excavator at his best. Identifying the trench of the tomb by the difference in the consistency of the soil – softer in the fill of the trench, more compact surrounding it – he covered the area of the trench with a tarpaulin, whitened the surrounding soil with plaster dust, removed the tarpaulin and made an overhead photo-graph to document the tomb before excavation. In the tomb the body of a mature man, 30 to 40 years old, had been placed extended supine and then covered with a fill of rock. The meticulousness of Boni's excavation is immediately visible in a photograph. The pottery of the grave had simple decoration in the form of knobs on the body of two vessels, a cup and amphora; one cup has a handle in the form of two rings one above the other. The burial garment was fastened on the chest by a large fibula (safety pin) with a disc catch plate (fig. 3.2).[21]

Tomb C was once again a *pozzo* cremation tomb, of a young adult male.

29

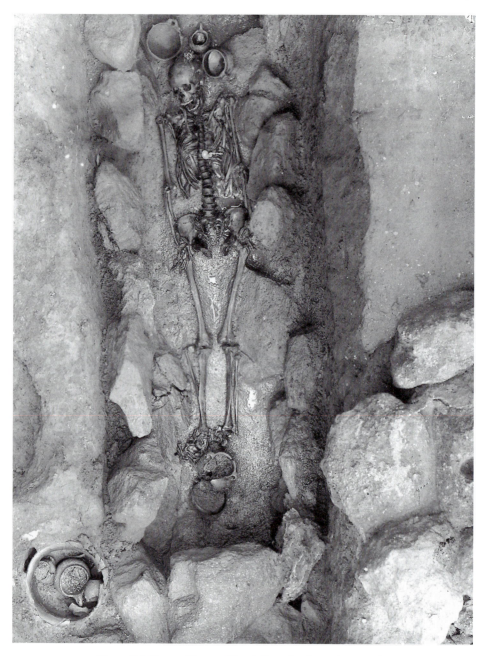

Figure 2.7 Rome, Forum, Tomb B at the time of excavation.

Figure 2.8 Rome, Forum, hut urn from Tomb C, Antiquario Forense.

The *dolium* contained a hut urn in which the cremated remains had been placed (fig. 2.8). These faithful models of contemporary oval huts are especially common in the cremation burials of the Alban Hills and seem to have represented the abode of the dead. With the hut urn there were both miniature and normal size vessels.[22] Three of the miniature vases contained food. One held part of a catfish, one portions of sheep and pig, the third salt. One of the larger vessels contained a spongy mass that Boni conjectured could have been the remains of *far*, the traditional Roman porridge. All the elements of a meal were thus present. A small jug could have held honey and three jars possibly water, milk, and wine. This is a hypothetical but not improbable interpretation of the set.

Nearby was Tomb D, the *fossa* grave of a child.[23] In this tomb there was the first of the oak coffins for which the Forum cemetery is famous. The coffin was made by splitting a trunk lengthwise and hollowing out the cavity. Wood preserves well in waterlogged conditions. But once removed from saturation it quickly dries out, cracks, twists, and is lost. Boni, drawing on the experience of his excavations in the Terremare of the Po Valley and his first stratigraphic dig in the foundations of the Campanile of St Mark's in Venice, acted quickly and consolidated the wood by immersing it in a

celluloid/acetone bath. The pyrox-
ylin of the celluloid, containing
cellulose, which is the chief component of the solid framework of
plants, is thus conveyed into the
wood, where it replaces water.
After a sufficient time the piece can
be removed from the bath and it
becomes a solid once more.[24]

Tomb G, the grave of a child of
about one to one-and-a-half years
old, was of the same variety.[25] The
fossa was larger than necessary for
the small coffin, leaving room to
one side for a rough box of tufa
slabs in which there were placed
two jars, two bowls, three cups,
and a perfume pot. The pottery
shows that this tomb was later in
date than those burials with handmade black-surfaced pottery de-

Figure 2.9 Rome, Forum, Greek (Protocorinthian) small perfume jar from Tomb
G, Antiquario Forense.

scribed heretofore. The pottery is wheelmade, light-ground and painted
(before firing) to make contrasting colors on the surface. The perfume pot,
an imported Greek (Protocorinthian) vessel, belongs to the mid-seventh
century (fig. 2.9).

Tomb I was another inhumation of a small girl of about two years whose
body was covered by a dress or shroud ornamented by a profusion of glass
paste beads. She also wore a bracelet of ivory and another of vitreous fruit
and had with her an amber disc. Her tomb dress thus included materials
from Africa or the Near East (ivory) and northern Europe (amber). The
glass beads may also have been imported. This tomb of the seventh century
clearly illustrates widening horizons and an ability to acquire exotic imports.
The little girl was also given food to take with her into the beyond, a mullet
cooked, we may hope, to her liking.

Altogether Boni excavated forty-one tombs in an area slightly larger than
20 × 10 m (65 × 33 ft). Of these, thirteen were cremation burials in *pozzi*
except for one (Tomb U) which was a cremation placed in a *fossa*. Twenty-
four were inhumations.[26] As we have already noted, inhumation graves
show the appearance for the first time in the Roman Forum of vases made on
the potter's wheel, imported Greek pottery of the seventh century, and
light-ground pottery influenced by such Greek wares. It seems probable,
therefore, that the inhumation tombs were generally more recent in date
than the cremation tombs, particularly since cremation is the dominant
tradition of the Proto-Villanovans and what appear to be the earliest graves

of the Italian Iron Age both in Etruria and in Latium (see the further discussion of chronology in Chapter 3). There is, however, a considerable overlap between the two groups.[27]

The tombs discovered by Boni in what has become known as the Sepulcretum were part of a far more extensive burial ground in the Forum. In 1952 four cremation tombs were excavated some 60 m (197 ft) away near the Arch of Augustus (the precise find spot is on the south side of the podium of the Temple of Divine Julius) and more recently an early burial has come to light nearby below the Regia.[28] Two additional cremation tombs had been found previously just inside the Forum Transitorium by the south hemicycle of the Forum of Augustus. As we have noted above, it is certain that there were early cremation graves in the Esquiline cemetery. And on the Palatine a single early cremation grave was found in 1953. In general this distribution of graves suggests that there were settlements on the Palatine Hill, on the Velia and others extending further along the Fagutal. This is the core of early Rome.

There is evidence of early burial in the central area of the Forum too. Boni made a stratigraphic sounding beside the foundation of a monument which until recently has been identified as that of an equestrian statue of the Emperor Domitian. Boni never published an account of the work, although the material was presented by Gjerstad, who made a second stratigraphical excavation on the site.[29] But an account of the highpoint of the excavation is preserved by Boni's biographer Eva Tea.[30]

All digs attract visitors. But Boni's work, bringing to light the vestiges of early Rome, had a worldwide following.[31] And so on the morning of March 20, 1904, in addition to the ever-present Hülsen, the correspondent of the London *Times* was on hand. As the morning wore on, King Victor Emmanuel, whose residence was at the Quirinal Palace, strolled down to the site for a look. It was just then that a travertine block which had been fitted into the Imperial concrete statue base caught the attention of the excavators. Upon removal it proved to have been hollowed out to receive a group of five vases, a jar, an amphora, two cups, and a jug, all whole and together a homogeneous group of the seventh century. Boni and the King together removed the vases from their hiding place. Why were they there? The best surmise is that they were the offerings from a tomb that was disturbed during the erection of the Imperial monument, whose builders piously recomposed the group in its new resting place. The later Romans knew that the Forum had eerie things underground. They laid a black paving over the reputed tomb of Romulus and they called the area just beyond Boni's sepulcretum the *doliola*, where it was forbidden to spit because there were tombs underground or, as others had it, because certain taboo objects belonging to the second king of Rome, Numa Pompilius, had been buried there.[32] As usual with such traditions, doubt mingles with superstition, but when faced with a tomb in their foundation trench the workmen of the first century AD took precautions that the spirits might remain calm by reburying the offerings.[33]

Further down at the bottom of his sounding Boni found two tombs, both inhumations without grave goods. Although chronologically perplexing, these tombs are important for questions relating to the use of the central Forum as a burial ground.

A more thorny problem arises with respect to the earlier inhumations, i.e. inhumations belonging to a time before the appearance of vases made on the potter's wheel and the manifestation of Greek influence in the form of light-ground (*figulina*) pottery. Such tombs are known in the Sepulcretum and constitute all of the documented graves of the early Esquiline necropolis, save for the group of cremations near the church of Sant'Eusebio. There is no easily established typological boundary separating the material from the Forum tombs from that of the Esquiline necropolis. A distinctive shape in the Forum, the sack-shaped jug, does not occur on the Esquiline. The traditional bowl with a low horizontal handle is similarly absent there too. The footed amphorae of the latter necropolis are unknown in the Forum. The cups with two-part handles are different in the two cemeteries. The character of the incised ornament is different, finer and more complex in the Forum, rougher on the Esquiline. Among the bronze fibulae there is greater harmony, the simple thickened bow type (a woman's fibula) predominating in both (fig. 3.2). Bronze-working, however, is different from vase-making. It deals in more expensive materials and with a higher level of technology. The centers of production are fewer. Uniformity exists over a wider area.[34] To judge from the Forum and Esquiline tombs, pottery production must have been very local. The differences between the two cemeteries mean one of two things. Either the potters had independent traditions or there is a temporal difference between the two. It is a question either of style or of chronology. And a difference of style may be interpreted as a difference of tradition or even as a sign that the two groups involved would have seen themselves as unrelated.

This last, and audacious, interpretation was put on the Roman tombs because early Rome, according to the traditions drawn on by the ancient historians, had both a Latin and a Sabine element in the population.[35] The tales begin with Romulus' men kidnapping wives from their neighbors (the Rape of the Sabines). Soon, however, harmony is established and one nation is led by Romulus and the Sabine king Titus Tatius.[36]

It was Hermann Müller-Karpe who shifted the discussion onto the chronological plane.[37] He demonstrated that in the period of the thickened bow fibula the pottery shapes and decoration of the Esquiline were simply not present in the Forum. Following an initial period in his sequence represented by cremation burials with house urns, miniature vases and associated material (Period I) there followed the Forum group of the subsequent (thickened bow fibula) period (Period IIA) and the Esquiline Group thereafter (Period IIB). It was his contention that Period IIB was absent in the Sepulcretum only because the small area investigated did not provide an adequate sample of the cemetery.[38]

Renato Peroni, who published a similar but more detailed discussion of the tomb groups of Periods I and II two years before Müller-Karpe, still entertained the Latin/Sabine theory, although in a much attenuated form.[39] Peroni saw different traditions but a rapid assimilation of the two ethnic elements.

Both Müller-Karpe, who had earlier treated the epoch of the hut urns in a separate monograph,[40] and Peroni were reacting consciously to the very different periodization of the Forum tombs made by Einar Gjerstad.[41] Gjerstad's system rested on the attempt to establish a sequence of fabrics among the handmade pottery of early Rome on the basis of very limited stratigraphic sequences from the Forum. This was amplified by the application of a somewhat abstract set of concepts, "normal," "expansive," and "contracted," to distinguish the evolution of vase shapes in a single potting tradition. The system has not won favor (we shall return to it in Chapter 3). Gjerstad's organization of tomb groups by period was consequently very different from that of scholars like Peroni and Müller-Karpe who pursued a formal and typological approach. Gjerstad believed that there were tomb groups from the Esquiline belonging to Period I, that is comparable to the earliest material from the Forum. He emphasized the independence of the two cemeteries and championed the Latin/Sabine interpretation of the differences between them.

The interpretation most generally favored at present was put forward by Giovanni Colonna in 1974.[42] This scholar, whose grouping of the tombs followed that of Müller-Karpe and Peroni, took seriously the absence of tombs attributable to Period IIB in the Forum. He also emphasized, as had Gjerstad, that in the following age of wheelmade pottery and Greek contact (Period III) only children were buried in the Forum Sepulcretum. For Colonna the Forum cemetery effectively went out of use with Period IIA. There was room from that point on only for children's graves, which were exempt from whatever custom or regulation now prevented adult burials. With Period IIB the Romans moved their burial ground, for adults at least, to the Esquiline cemetery.

This theory is not free from difficulties. First, like other studies of the subject, it does not take into consideration the early cremation tombs of the Esquiline. Burials were taking place there, cremations with hut urns, in Period I as defined by Müller-Karpe and Peroni. The meagerness of the sample in the Forum is also a constant danger to generalization. It is clear that the early Romans tolerated burials within the community not only of infants but of children. Such is shown by two children's tombs (occupants 2 to 4 years old) from the Palatine belonging to the period of wheelmade pottery and Greek influence in the seventh century (Period III).[43] The same consideration was evidently at work in the old cemetery of the Forum.[44] But when the Forum was closed to adult burial one cannot say.

At present one must still admit that the differences between the Forum and the Esquiline cemeteries of Period II may be due either to style or to date. They are less likely to be due to cultural differences between Romans and Sabines. They do not represent an expansion toward a previously vacant burial ground on the Esquiline.

3

CHRONOLOGY

Without dates archaeological discussions provoke a kind of giddy weight-lessness that is the result of the inability to reason sequentially or, in the crudest sense, to reason historically. Pinza distinguished two periods in the tombs of the Forum and Esquiline: Period I before the appearance of light-ground pottery and Greek imports or direct imitations thereof; Period II marked by the presence of light-ground pottery and imports.[1] As in almost every archaeological chronology, Pinza's system makes an assumption: that the period of Greek influence followed and did not precede the period lacking it. There are many good reasons for the assumption: the continued presence of Greek influence in the development of early Latium, traditions in Period I which look back to the beginning of the Iron Age. But the sequence still remains an assumption, and we shall find assumptions behind each and every chronological scheme.

Pinza's scheme is still valid today, although his periods have been sub-divided in the following way:[2]

Pinza I	I	1000 – 900
	IIA	900 – 830
	IIB	830 – 770
	III	770 – 730/20
Pinza II	IVA	730/20 – 630/20
	IVB	630/20 – 580

As discussed in Chapter 2, the subdivision of Period II is essentially between the Forum tombs (IIA) and the Esquiline group (IIB), although some doubts concerning the validity of the distinction have been expressed above. Greatly simplifying the question, one may say that Period I is the time marked by cremations, the use of the hut urn (and if not, an ash container as the house of the dead) and generally undecorated pottery. In addition to the appear-ance of decorated pottery, in Period II the thickened bow fibula becomes typical in women's tombs (fig. 3.2). In Period III the influence of imports is felt (although none is present in the Forum tombs) and in Period IV the imported vessels and their imitations are evident.

37

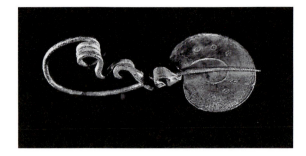

Figure 3.1 Latian bronze fibula, disc type.

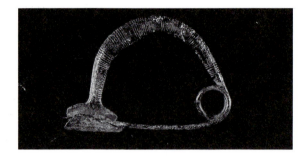

Figure 3.2 Latian bronze fibula, thickened bow type.

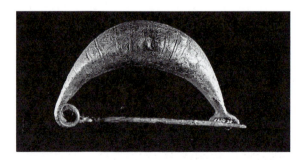

(a)

Figure 3.3 Latian bronze fibulae, (a) bulbous bow type, (b) bulbous bow made with bone elements.

(b)

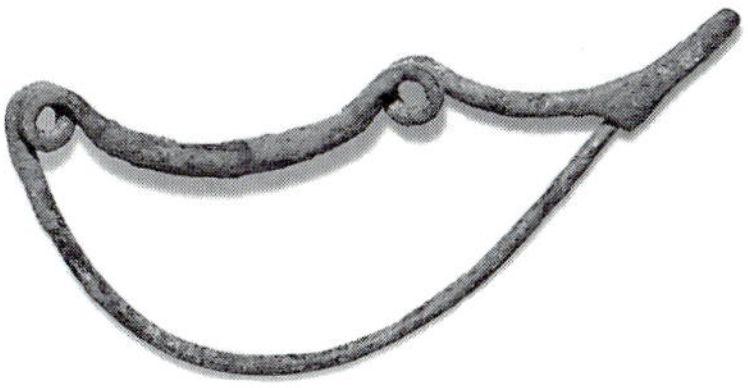

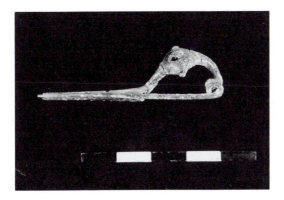

Figure 3.4 Latian bronze fibula, bent bow type.

Figure 3.5 Latian bronze fibula, lengthened pin type.

The fundamental revision of Pinza's original two periods was made by Hermann Müller-Karpe and Renato Peroni, working at almost the same time and with very similar results.[3] We shall examine Müller-Karpe's solution because it was presented with more easily understood graphic detail. It also embraced both the Forum and Esquiline graves. The solution takes the form of a table displaying the tombs in a vertical column and the elements composing the tomb groups arranged horizontally. The construction of any such table requires using certain specific types of objects as the nuclei around which to construct groups of associated tombs, and it requires making other assumptions about the chronological sequence of these same guiding typological elements. Studies of the Italian Iron Age have long relied on the fibula as a major tool of this sort because the typology of these objects is clearly defined and because the geographical distribution of each type is widespread. In Müller-Karpe's organization of the Forum and Esquiline tombs the twisted-bow fibula and the fibula with hammered-out spiral catch plate are the guides to Period I (figs 1.8, 3.1) and together with the miniature vases they encompass all the tombs of the period. The hut urn does not belong exclusively to Period I but makes an appearance in one of the Forum tombs (Tomb GG) of Period II. Once again it is the fibula, of the thickened bow type, that defines Period II (fig. 3.2). The bulbous bow or leech type (fig. 3.3 together with the same form achieved with amber discs on a wire bow) and the bent bow (or serpentine type, fig. 3.4) blocks off Period III, although there is some overlap with tomb groups where the pottery is more characteristic of the types found with the thickened bow fibulae of Period II and therefore attributed to that period. Finally, the fibula with lengthened pin gives us Period IV (fig. 3.5). In this phase, of course, there are Greek imports, and the fibula with long pin goes comfortably with them since this is the fibula type that appears regularly in the earliest graves of the Greek colonies in Sicily. Once the skeleton is established by means of the fibula or other characteristic items the process of constructing the table proceeds with few decisions on the part of its assembler (fig. 3.6). Müller-Karpe's table does not take into consideration decorative patterns as independent elements nor does it use cremation versus inhumation burial as a criterion, though both of these aspects of the tombs and tomb groups were used by Peroni in his analytical table.

The virtue of Müller-Karpe's table is clarity. Its defect is that it emphasizes discontinuity between periods. Other methods of constructing association tables exist which emphasize progression rather than discontinuity by disposing the elements on either side of a median line or by grouping them smoothly on one side but against the median line (fig. 3.7).[4] The construction of such smooth flow below the median line would require the displacement of a good number of tombs from their position in Müller-Karpe's system to obtain an even line on the right side of the graph.

The association graph, therefore, is only a way to see the evidence, not a

Figure 3.6 Chronological table (association method) of Iron Age tombs in Rome by H. Müller-Karpe. Numbers on the horizontal axis denote artifact types: 1, twisted bow fibula; 2, disc fibula; 15, hut urn; 24, thickened bow fibula; 32, bulbous bow fibula; 33, same form achieved by amber or bone discs on a wire bow; 34–35, bent bow fibula; 47, fibula with lengthened pin.

final solution to the problem of chronological succession. This point has been made by Susan S. Lukesh, who organized the data from the Forum tombs with the aid of the computer and a standard statistical program.[5] In the analysis each element of all tomb groups is compared with every other tomb group resulting in four possibilities: presence in both tomb groups, absence from both, presence in "a" but not in "b," presence in "b" but not in "a." The result for each comparison receives a numerical equivalent which becomes the basis for calculating a coefficient of similarity/dissimilarity for each pair of tombs. It is how this coefficient is calculated that determines the shape of the sequence that is finally achieved for the entire group of tombs. While Lukesh's analysis in general supported Müller-Karpe and Peroni, it too is only one way to organize the data and indeed the application of different expressions for calculating similarity/dissimilarity produces different results. Such different coefficients represent judgments as to the relative importance of the four factors recorded for each pair of items examined. For example, one may debate whether absence in both cases of a specific attribute/object is a valid measure of similarity/dissimilarity. Clearly, if the attribute/object did not exist at the time when the two tombs being compared were made, its absence from them is no measure of similarity.

Another challenge has come from Anna Maria Bietti Sestieri, whose work on the large cemetery of Osteria dell'Osa enabled her to show that still other criteria must be considered in reconstructing the chronology of an ancient cemetery (see Chapter 8).[6] The excavator of the Osa cemetery has demonstrated the importance of family groups in the topography of the cemetery and of the individuality of family customs. The association chart of the whole cemetery is no longer sufficient in itself without taking into account the groups of families represented and the microtraditions represented in these units: differences in status, differences in the funeral equipment of adult men and women and the separate treatment of children and adolescents according to sex. As a result, she suggests that in the Roman Forum Period I and Period IIA may in fact represent different aspects of the same time span, and similar questions could be posed for the later divisions of the Müller-Karpe and Peroni chronological system.

The absolute chronology of the Roman tombs is anchored only in Period IV, by imported Greek pottery. The dating of the earlier phases is a matter to which both Peroni and Müller-Karpe made contributions. Müller-Karpe's work took the form of a comprehensive study of chronology of the Late Bronze and Iron Age cremating groups both in Italy and north of the Alps.[7] The starting point for an absolute chronology was provided by the Bronze Age (1400–1100) pottery from Mycenean Greece found at sites in southern Italy and in Sicily. Mycenean pottery was a largely standardized product made in industrial workshops. Its phases for two hundred years after 1400 can be dated with some precision because of exports from Greece to the Near East and especially to Egypt. For example, the Mycenean

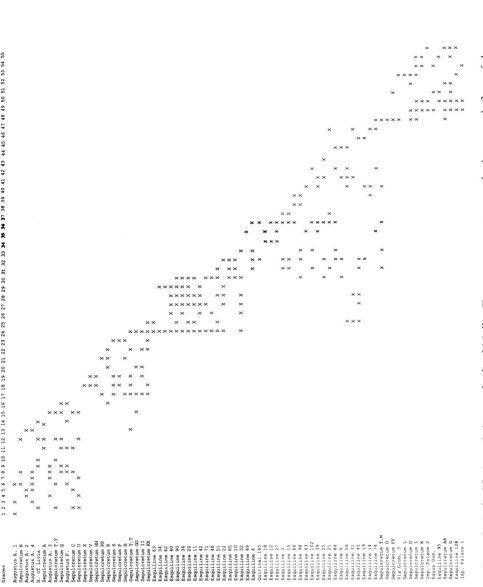

Figure 3.7 Chronological table (association method) of Müller-Karpe rearranged to emphasize smooth flow of the sequence of tomb groups. Numbers for artifact types as in preceding figure.

pottery from Tell El Amarna, the short-lived capital of the pharaoh Akhnaten, must have been exported to Egypt in the second quarter of the fourteenth century. Beginning with the association of local material with Mycenean pottery in southern Italy and Sicily Müller-Karpe built up a sequence stretching from Sicily to Slovenia, Croatia, and Bavaria. Renato Peroni for his part exploited the discovery of Bronze Age pottery closely related to that of mainland Italy on the island of Lipari (off the north coast of Sicily), where it too was associated with Mycenean imports, and from this starting point made an important study of the later Bronze Age in Italy. Both Peroni and Müller-Karpe saw the earliest cremation tombs of the Forum, distinguished by simple arched fibulae, as not far distant from the earliest cremation cemeteries elsewhere in the peninsula which belong to the Proto-Villanovan phase, so-called to distinguish it from the cremation cemeteries of the developed Iron Age first discovered at Bologna in 1853. Proto-Villanovan is typical of Etruria and well represented in Latium.[8]

The earliest Roman tombs were very closely related to the Iron Age cremations of the volcanic hills that rise at the southern edge of the Latian plain, the earliest of which was found in 1817.[9] The same bronze objects – hut urns, beakers with rectangular ribbed decoration and warming stands, and the use of miniature copies in place of full-size vessels, to mention only the most characteristic features – were common to both. This relationship has always seemed important because of the legends of Romulus and Remus and their native city Alba Longa, situated, according to common belief, in the Alban Hills. However, this was of little help in fixing the date of the Forum cemetery. For that, an estimate that Period I was a later phase of Proto-Villanovan had to suffice. If the Proto-Villanovan could be dated beginning in the twelfth century, and if it endured until some point following which an entire phase of the first true Villanovan had to take place before any Greek influence (datable in the eighth century) was felt, then a date midway through the span 1200–900, perhaps somewhat before 1000, would be appropriate. Such a date, of course, is mere convention. However, it represents the conviction that the Roman tombs stand in an unbroken succession from the Bronze Age. This conviction has been reinforced by the increasing number of sites in the neighborhood of Rome with Bronze Age/Proto-Villanovan remains, including Rome itself. In Rome late Bronze Age (sub-Apennine) material comes from the excavations of the Regia in the Forum.[10] The calendar dates for Period II are equally vague, especially at the beginning. It is divided into two subphases, A and B, each receiving a duration of fifty to seventy-five years. These dates are another useful archaeological fiction.

Greek, or imitation Greek, sherds with decorative circles or semicircles were discovered in the secondary fill over the early temple in the Sant'Omobono sanctuary (fig. 3.8). Such decoration is characteristic of Greek geometric pottery dating before the last quarter of the eighth century.

Figure 3.8 Rome, Sant'Omobono sanctuary, Greek or imitation Greek sherds, Antiquarium Comunale – Musei Capitolini.

Figure 3.9 Veii, Middle Geometric Greek cup, Museo Nazionale di Villa Giulia.

No such vases were found in the Forum tombs, but there is one pendant semicircle cup from a tomb at Veii (fig. 3.9).[11] In Etruria and so at Veii the sequence of periods is numbered differently, beginning after Proto-Villanovan (while Rome I is part of Proto-Villanovan). Consequently Veii II = Rome III. The tomb with the pendant semicircle cup belongs to Veii Period IIA. Since the pendant semicircle cups were made from before 850 until close to 700, the general type itself has only a limited chronological value. Closer study of the cups, however, places this one well along in the sequence. A date of 750 or after has now been proposed for the cup from the Veii tomb.[12] Although one cup alone cannot justify the displacement of the dates of Latian Period IIB downward by twenty or thirty years, the same message is repeated by a second class of early Greek imports at Veii, cups with chevron decoration, again post-750 (fig. 3.10).[13] The new chronological chart for Rome, allowing for some displacement downward in Periods III and IV, would read:

I	1000 – 875
IIA	875 – 800
IIB	800 – 750
III	750 – 700
IV	700 – 580

One cannot emphasize too strongly that the chronology of Greek geometric pottery is itself built on tenuous evidence. It rests in large part on material from the cemeteries of the Sicilian Greek colonies. Thucydides gives approximate dates for the foundations of the eighth century; the later historian, Diodorus Siculus, gave a precise calendar date for one colony, Selinus (differing from Thucydides). Since the Greek chronologies were founded on calculations by generations, their accuracy is very low.[14]

A consequence of the revised dating of the pendant semicircle and chevron cups is that they become the contemporaries, not the predecessors, of the so-called "Thapsos" cups that accompanied the early wave of Greek colonization in Sicily, also in the mid–late eighth century.

The chronology derived from Müller-Karpe's and Peroni's studies does not hold the field alone. A second system, based on radically different

Figure 3.10 Veii, Late Geometric Greek cup, Museo Nazionale di Villa Giulia.

criteria, has fewer adherents but should not be dismissed for that reason alone. In fact the reconsideration of the Greek cups just discussed has revived the premises of the dating advocated by Einar Gjerstad (1897–1988), whose *Early Rome*, published over a twenty-five-year period (1948–1973), is the *summa* of the archaeology of the beginnings of the city. It is impossible to overstate the lasting value of Gjerstad's six volumes. He examined everything, he obtained photographs of everything, he organized everything, and then, in an achievement approached only by Pinza's monograph of 1905, he published everything.

Gjerstad's dissertation, from 1926, was based on field work in Cyprus. With one or two exceptions, the history of prehistoric pottery on Cyprus is made up of a sequence of readily distinguishable fabrics and equally individual, and occasionally bizarre, vase shapes. Gjerstad left his Cypriote studies, which were prolonged during his leadership of the Swedish Cyprus Expedition in the 1930s, convinced that analysis of fabric and vase shape could unlock any pottery chronology. (Naturally, stratigraphic data from excavation, if available, could add invaluable evidence.) Coming to Rome as director of the newly founded Swedish Institute, Gjerstad put his convictions to work on early Rome. Before examining his conclusions, it would be worthwhile to take account of his objections to the system of Müller-Karpe and Peroni, which touch points also raised from a different perspective by Bietti Sestieri.[15]

Association analysis, Gjerstad pointed out, is a very generalizing exercise. As practiced in the case of the Forum and Esquiline tombs, it is based largely on a group of standard vase forms abstracted from the actual objects. Müller-Karpe's and Peroni's tables exaggerate discontinuity. The continuity of the "style" in which a vessel is made – that is the dialogue between generations of artisans and the objects they produce, which unquestionably reduplicates types but which adds the personality, if not of the individual then at least of the generation or workshop – is completely forgotten. In the process of establishing a universal chronology based on typologies, there is no place for local cultural history.

These were Gjerstad's general objections to what has become the standard treatment of the early Roman cemeteries. But the Swedish scholar had specific objections as well. The first has to do with the eighth-century graves

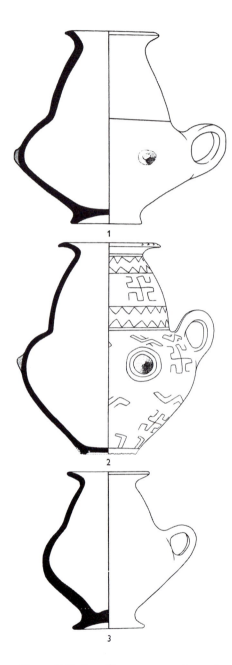

at Cumae. This Greek settlement just north of the bay of Naples was reputed to have been the oldest Greek colony in Italy. Its beginnings certainly belong to the mid-eighth century. But there was a pre-Hellenic Cumae, and in tombs attributed to the pre-Greek town, because of the large quantity of Italic Iron Age pottery they contain, there were two Greek cups, pieces with chevron decoration similar to those from Veii; thus the tomb is eighth century too.

Gjerstad's theory of the development of pottery vase form is illustrated by three jugs from the Esquiline cemetery (fig. 3.11). The three vessels come from a single cemetery and so should represent the work of a single potting tradition, yet we find an "expansive" version, the "normal" type and finally the "contracted" form. There must be, according to Gjerstad, a temporal factor in the development of these stylistic changes. In fact "expansive" forms are characteristic of Gjerstad's Period I (including what he considered the oldest tombs of the Roman Forum), "normal" forms appear in Period II (while some "expansive" pieces are still encountered) and "contracted" forms are distinctive of Period III. The Cumean pre-Hellenic tombs of the eighth century show a similar development in a pottery which is comparable to that of the Esquiline cemetery, belonging as it does to the general group of the *fossa*

Figure 3.11 Esquiline cemetery, jugs of (top) expansive, (middle) normal, and (bottom) contracted shape.

graves of central Italy. The Esquiline tombs, therefore, also belong to the eighth century and the Forum tombs no earlier. The Iron Age at Rome began in the eighth century.

Further evidence leading to the same result, according to Gjerstad, comes from the stratigraphic soundings of the Roman Forum, especially those beside the Temple of Divine Julius. It was here that four tombs were excavated in 1952, long after Boni's discoveries. The tombs are early cremation graves which stand at the head of Müller-Karpe's and Peroni's sequences in Period I. These tombs were found dug into Stratum 11 of the excavation. But Stratum 12 below them already belongs to Period II, according to Gjerstad, because of fragments of "normal" impasto cups from it. The tombs, according to Gjerstad, can be no older than Period II, to which they conform also because of the position of their pottery in the developmental sequence "expanded," "normal," "contracted."

This stratigraphic argument bears a heavy weight in the debate. The fragments from Stratum 11 and 12 are those of sharply angled (so-called carinated) cups.[16] This is a form with a long history. Gjerstad had no reason to consider the possibility that the stratum into which the cremation tombs were dug had originated in the Bronze Age when such cup profiles already existed. But in view of the material found nearby under the Regia,[17] and until the fragments from the Divine Julius sounding have once again been examined with care, Gjerstad's interpretation of the evidence must remain in doubt because the fragments in question may be of Bronze Age date.

The parallels cited by Gjerstad with the Cumean tombs are damaging to the chronology based on the association method only if the Cumean material must implicate Rome I and IIA as well as Rome IIB and III, the later two periods entering the time when the chronology derived from Greek pottery becomes germane to the Italian tomb groups. But did the evolution of form from "expansive" to "contracted" happen throughout Italy at the same time and only once? If it happened at Cumae in the eighth century, is it so sure that Rome followed the same timetable? Gjerstad himself argued against neglecting the individuality of local craft history. Müller-Karpe and Peroni would reply that the Cumean evidence is valid but only in comparison with material of Rome's Period IIB and Period III.[18]

To sum up: the majority of students of early Rome and related matters look at the Iron Age tombs of the Forum and Esquiline through the eyes of Peroni and Müller-Karpe. Gjerstad and Gierow, who applied Gjerstad's methodology to the tombs of the Alban Hills in an exhaustive publication performing the same archival service for this material that Gjerstad had done for Rome,[19] have not been able to produce inconfutable evidence to prove the results of the typological chronology wrong. But the arrangement by types is still open to the criticisms of the Swedish school; it simplifies and it may distort. And Bietti Sestieri has opened a new perspective on treating

49

chronology as a function of the family group topography of cemeteries.[20] Finally, as long as there remains any doubt as to the chronological limits of the Proto-Villanovan cemeteries, there must remain doubts about the age of the Roman tombs of Period I.[21]

Polemic surrounded the publications of Gjerstad's volumes, much less in regard to protohistory than in regard to Gjerstad's treatment of Roman history of the later kings. In brief, Gjerstad espoused the theory that the Roman Republic did not come into being until about 450 and that the existence of regal Rome in the early fifth century was apparent from various archaeological contexts, the Sant'Omobono sanctuary, for example, where, Gjerstad believed, the second phase of the archaic temple should be dated in the half-century after 509. But as Massimo Pallottino, the dean of Italian etruscologists, pointed out, none of the issues brought up in the debate was direct evidence for the historicity or chronology of any figure, political or military event in Roman history.[22] Historians, Pallottino wryly noted, had shown very little interest in Gjerstad's interpretations; it was the archaeologists who had rushed into the debate. Gjerstad's dating of the earliest tombs of the Sepulcretum to the eighth century made the beginning of Rome contemporary with the ancient dates for Romlus' foundation. But this apparent confirmation of the annalistic tradition rests, as we have seen, on a much contested chronology.

4

HUTS AND HOUSES

During the winter of 1961–1962 I attended the course in archaeological air photography offered by the Italian Air Force to members of the Italian antiquities service and guests from the foreign schools in Rome at the airport of Guidonia just east of the city. Within a few hundred yards of the airfield and its Bell and Howell helicopters, from which we had an opportunity of surveying the lower Tiber Valley at the end of the course, there were the huts of shepherds from the mountains of the Abruzzi, who were wintering with their flocks in the Roman Campagna. Oval structures with walls of reed chinked with mud and roofs of the same material, they would have provided a welcome sight for the shade of Aeneas or Evander, whose Roman house would not have been substantially different. This simple shelter had a long history behind it, even in the early Latian Iron Age (fig. 4.1).

The hut urn of the Latian tombs of Period I and II is simply a model of the buildings of the time. The most completely documented such structure was excavated at Fidenae, located atop the Tiber's left bank on the outskirts of modern Rome (fig. 4.2). The Fidenae house, like all houses of the Iron Age known in Latium, belongs to the eighth century (Period III).[1] It is 6.2 × 5.2 m (20 × 17 ft), a good-sized room, but not a good-sized house. There was a doorway with a small porch on one of the short sides. The walls were made of pisé (compacted clay) pressed between wide boards. This method of construction has not been documented heretofore in Latium. Elsewhere the walling appears to have been made of interlaced branches covered with clay. Like the more common form of construction, however, the Fidenae structure was reinforced by uprights set in the wall line at irregular intervals. On two sides there was an artificial bench of loose tufa rocks set against the exterior. There was a further line of posts set 1.5 m (5 ft) out from the two long sides of the oval, evidently intended to carry the extension of the roof which would thus make a portico along the building. The roof, of which some traces could be identified in the collapse on the floor of the building, appears to have been sloped. It was made of branches and straw over a skeleton of rafters. Channels in the rock some 2.5 m (8 ft) away from the building to the south and east have been interpreted as drainage channels but may have been made at an earlier time.

Although post-reinforcing of walls and post-supported porches are typical of Latian architecture of the Iron Age, post holes in themselves do not make a house. They may belong to sheds or enclosures of all sizes. Sheds measuring 2–2.5 × 2.5–3 m (6.5–8 × 8–10 ft), their floors sunk about 0.5 m below ground level, have been documented among the early houses at Satricum (fig. 4.3). A number of these have now been convincingly interpreted as cook huts.[2] The huts in question contained many pieces of cooking stands, bowls, jars, trays, and casseroles. There were meat bones. Table wares were absent, as were the common spools, weights, and whorls used for spinning and weaving. The larger units were also sunk below ground level. The resulting house had advantages. It required less walling and provided some insulation. The village at Satricum grew up around a pond, which must have cult associations (like the Spring of Juturna in the Roman Forum) from an early time. Subsequently, when a temple was built on one side of the pond it exactly covered one of the huts. At Ardea, too, the temple at Colle della Noce was placed over preexisting huts.[3] In both cases the earlier buildings must have had religious significance.

In Rome a group of huts is known on the Palatine Hill. The best-

Figure 4.1 Gabii, thatch huts in the crater of Lake Castiglione, photographed by Dr Esther Boise Van Deman ca 1900.

documented was excavated in 1948 (fig. 4.4).[4] It was an oblong building 4.9 × 3.6 m (16 × 11.8 ft) with slightly bulging sides. Like the hut at Fidenae, it had a porch and its walls were reinforced by posts. In photographs it appears set down into the bed rock, but this is true only on two sides, the cut probably having been made to level the floor. Two neighboring huts were uncovered in 1907. Channels are visible around all three, possibly for drainage, but not surely made for these houses. The hut excavated in 1948, and presumably its neighbors, belongs to Period III.

The Palatine Hill is in fact composed of two heights and a depression between them. The high ground to the west where the huts just described are located is called the Germalus. Traces of similar buildings have been found below the Imperial Palace on the Palatine proper.[5] It is in the depression between the two groups of dwellings that the Period I tomb was found below the House of Livia.[6] Clearly at the time the tomb was made this depression lay outside what was considered the settled area. Infant burials in jars were also associated with the huts.[7]

The most important group of these early buildings, now numbering some thirty, has been brought to light at Lavinium (fig. 4.5). The buildings are either oval or rectangular. Post-reinforcement is again evident. The oval

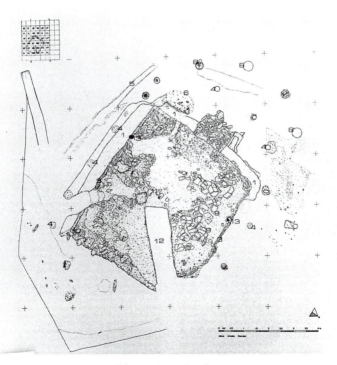

Figure 4.2 Fidenae, Iron Age house.

53

buildings reach a diameter of 10 m (33 ft). Once again children's burials were made within the settlement.[8] At Lavinium the rock-cut channels are for the emplacement of walls, not for drainage. Other groups of such buildings are known at Ficana (oval and rectangular) and Ardea.[9]

In the excavation of the Sepulcretum Boni identified small mounds of earth with carbonized wood and bits of wattle and daub in the stratum above the tombs as the remains of huts.[10] However, there were no foundations or consistent series of post holes, and the *tumuli* remain an enigma. Post holes have been noted elsewhere in the Forum: in the stratigraphical excavations of Boni and Gjerstad beside the foundation formerly identified as that of the Equus Domitiani (Equestrian Statue of Domitian), in the excavations beside the Arch of Augustus (Temple of Divine Julius) and in the lowest strata of the excavations under the Regia.[11] In the first two cases the area excavated is too restricted to draw definite conclusions. In the third, the excavation has not been completed and published, although some remarks can be made.[12] Ten structures have been identified. In the stratum beneath them there is a child's burial of Period IIB/III.[13] The structures are oval, measuring approximately 3.5 × 3 m (11.5 × 10 ft). There are traces of hearths within them. A road bordered the huts on the south.

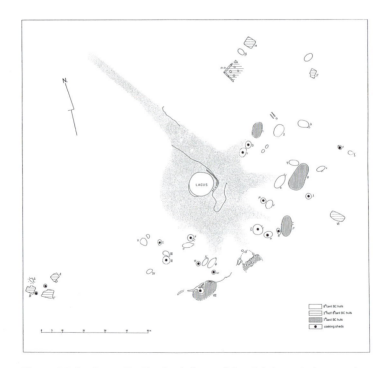

Figure 4.3 Satricum (Le Ferriere), huts of the eighth to sixth centuries.

In these circumstances a succession of cooking huts on this site would not, perhaps, be unusual. Ten over a span of two centuries before the construction of the first permanent structure of the Regia would give each a life of twenty years or so, not overly short if one considers the ever present danger of fire in such structures of reeds and timber. The question whether the hearths of these huts are early manifestations of the cult of Vesta, whose temple later stood a few meters away, and in any way connected to the later Regia, cannot be considered until the final publication of the excavations appears.[14]

At the end of the seventh century a revolution occurred in building at Rome, a revolution not only in materials but also in scale. In the excavation of the Sepulcretum Boni already had discovered the remains of a building constructed, at least partially in its lower courses, of square-cut tufa blocks. The plan shows a rectangular structure 10 m (32.8 ft) wide (fig. 4.6).[15] The most likely plan, on the basis of similar buildings reviewed below, would be that of a central block, possibly with three rooms side by side fronted by a courtyard across the full width.

In size the Forum building is not greatly enlarged compared to its predecessors. The block of rooms give ca 50 sq. m (538 sq. ft) interior space, about the size of the interior of the largest house at Lavinium (Hut D). The Fidenae house, by contrast, had 32 sq. m (344 sq. ft). Nevertheless, the new material, squared stone blocks used almost certainly with heavy terracotta roof tiles and the timber to support them, represents an enormous change.

It was at the end of the seventh century that the original gully between the Palatine and the Velia was filled in. The street leading from the Forum up to the ridge at the Arch of Titus could not have existed before that time.[16] But as soon as the gully was closed and the street opened the area was occupied by large houses that gave the noble character to this district that it maintained throughout the Republic. Two of these patrician *domus* have now been excavated and we shall return to them below.

Until very recently there was little to compare with the Forum house. But within the last decade it has become apparent that the seventh century in central Italy witnessed the building of great country houses and city mansions. The first evidence of these structures came from the excavations at Murlo near Siena. Here a very large rectangular complex (approximately 60 m, 197 ft square) has been unearthed consisting of four blocks of rooms surrounding a central courtyard (fig. 4.7). An interior colonnade ran around three sides of the court, and at one side of the courtyard there was a small structure, framed by the interior colonnade, which might be a shrine. The building as one sees it today belongs to about 575, but it had a predecessor of the seventh century. Together the two illustrate the importance and architectural character of the place. From the lower building there is a wealth of fine pottery, ornaments of various sorts and ivory. After the fire which destroyed the first structure, its successor made a

Figure 4.4 Rome, Palatine, hut foundations.

brilliant architectural display. Common terracotta roof tiles, the flat pan tiles and the curved cover tiles that seal the joint between them, may seem humble objects, but they deserve attention. Such roofing requires investment in the kilns and fuel to produce it. It is heavy and requires costly support. The Murlo building had some 3,000 sq. m (32,800 sq. ft) of roof tiles, representing something like ten times the roof area of a large temple in central Italy of the sixth or fifth centuries. Along the border of the roof there were terracotta friezes: (1) a banqueting scene, (2) a horse race, (3) a marriage procession, the bride and companion seated on a cart under an umbrella and followed by serving girls carrying gifts, and (4) an assembly of seated and standing figures. This last frieze is generally interpreted as an assembly of gods, as pictured in Greek art, but there is no reason why the figures (holding a budding branch, an ax and a *lituus* – the crooked staff of augury) could not be interpreted as mortals. The iconography of the decoration would thus be wholly secular.

Along the apex of the roof of the Murlo building in its second phase there was placed a series of large terracotta statues. This is an Etruscan practice well known from the Portonaccio temple at Veii built some half century or more after the Murlo structure. The statues at Murlo are both human and

Figure 4.5 Lavinium, foundations of early oval and rectangular buildings.

animal (real and imaginary). To the latter category there belong sphinxes, horses, lions, a wild boar, a goat, and a seahorse. Beside them were stiffly seated human figures, both men and women, accompanied by standing attendants. The building was thus protected both by the bestial troop, also known in Greek architecture of the period (and marshaled for protection against various unseen dangers), and by grander versions of the dignitaries of the assembly frieze below. These must be divinities, but among them there may well be heroized ancestors – and the building over which they presided no other than the hall of the clan and the clan chief. The origin of such clans, the Roman *gens* and its Etruscan counterparts, is a subject of debate.[17] But whether the *gens*, with its single family name borne by all the members of its various family branches, had deep roots in prehistoric Italy or whether, as is more likely, it was a phenomenon of the social changes of the ninth and eighth centuries, it was in full flower by the time the Murlo building was erected.[18] This consideration clarifies much about Murlo, but not everything. The building seems to have sported towers suggesting a residence and the need for defense. Initially the debate over the building turned on the roof terracottas. These, it was supposed, could only have been for a "temple." No private house had decorated roof terracottas – not in Greece at least or in

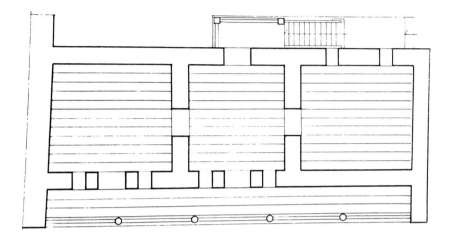

Figure 4.6 Rome, Forum, reconstructed ground plan of building over the Sepulcretum.

Italy as far as it was known.[19] But soon it became clear that Italian houses were so decorated. This was due to discoveries at Acquarossa in southern Etruria near Viterbo.[20]

In the sixth century Acquarossa was a developing community very much like an American village of the eighteenth century with plenty of room for buildings and open space. The most conspicuous house now excavated at Acquarossa has similarities with the great complex at Murlo. There is a courtyard with colonnades and blocks of rooms beyond facing inward to the court. However, the size is more modest, the plan is irregular, and the building possibly not all of a piece. This is clearly a town house. But it had roof terracottas, friezes of the type found at Murlo and elsewhere. The subjects are unlike the Murlo friezes. One set has a banquet, the other comes in two parts, the first a stylish couple in a light chariot drawn by winged horses and then behind them Hercules struggling with the Cretan bull. Had I been a visitor to Acquarossa when this house was new I would have been inclined to see both scenes as Hercules stories, first the struggle with the Cretan bull and then the hero at the house of Eurytos in the company of the fair Iole, the scene from a fine Corinthian *crater* that had been imported to

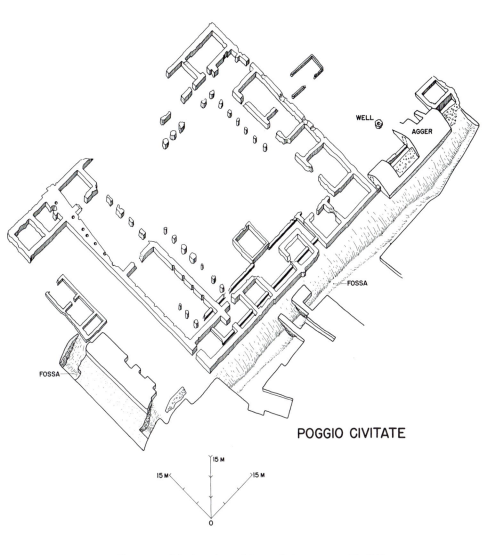

WELL

AGGER

FOSSA

FOSSA

POGGIO CIVITATE

15 M

15 M

15 M

0

Figure 4.7 Murlo, plan of the archaic courtyard building.

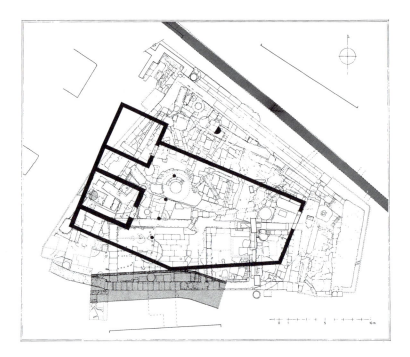

Figure 4.8 Rome, Forum, plan of the Regia, first phase.

Etruria from Corinth somewhat earlier and which, together with other Greek decorative arts, provided the iconography from which these banquet scenes were taken (the adaptor remembering to include the ladies in the party after Etruscan custom).[21] The building at Acquarossa may no more have been exclusively a "private" house in our sense of the word than the Murlo complex was only the headquarters of a clan. In a world in which the head of every family was a priest the line between private and sacred is hard to draw.

The excavations at Acquarossa illustrated the development of Etruscan architectural decoration in another way. Finds from a second location on the site showed that there was a period at the beginning of the use of architectural terracottas in the seventh century when the idea of such covering for buildings had been introduced and the technique of production as well but when the decoration, including open-work finials on the roofs, was strikingly central Italian. And these open-work finials take us once again to Rome.

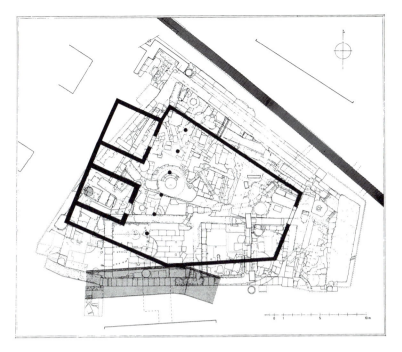

Figure 4.9 Rome, Forum, plan of the Regia, second phase.

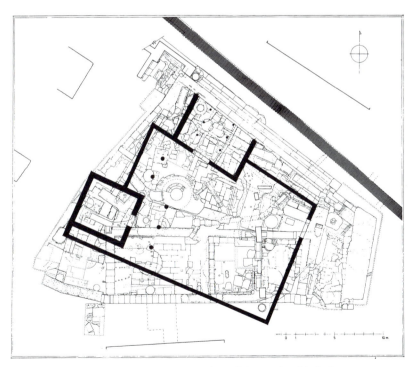

Figure 4.10 Rome, Forum, plan of the Regia, third phase.

61

Recent excavations in the Temple of Castor and Pollux in the Forum led to the reconsideration of architectural terracottas from work by Boni in the same area. Among the fragments from Boni's excavation was a similar open-work roof ornament of the seventh century.[22] Roof terracottas, which we may now recognize as typical of the Acquarossa type, were thus in use at Rome well before the erection of the house near the Sepulcretum and well before the building of the single most significant house-like structure in the Forum, the Regia.

The Regia bore the name of the office belonging in tradition to the seven kings of Rome and subsequently to their priestly successor, the *rex sacrorum*. From the Regia there has been preserved the floor of a *bucchero* cup of the last quarter of the sixth century with the graffito REX, a vessel thus reserved for the use of the political or priestly king.[23] In the Regia, moreover, were kept the *sacra* of Ops Consiva and Mars, including the shield fallen by miracle from heaven and the copies created to conceal it among so many facsimiles.

The Regia had a complicated history.[24] The first moment after the end of the period of small huts on the site saw the erection of a marker, and presumably more than the one surviving marker, indicating that the area had been isolated for some purpose. Soon afterward the first Regia came into being (fig. 4.8). The plan consists of a courtyard and behind a portico at one end two chambers with a space intervening between. One thinks immediately of the shrines of Ops and Mars. In its second phase the Regia changes little, merely extending the courtyard to include fully both rooms behind the portico (fig. 4.9). In the third phase, of the mid-sixth century, one of the rooms was eliminated and its place taken by a hall reached by a door in the north wall of the courtyard (fig. 4.10). Architectural terracottas are attributed to this phase of the building: the unusual frieze plaques with lions, panthers, birds, and minotaurs, disc *acroteria* to crown the gable peak and possibly terracotta sculpture for display at the corners of the roof (fig. 4.11).[25] Antefixes of gorgons and female heads may have decorated the roof of the new hall.

Following a fire which destroyed the third Regia about 540–530 (the date is based on Attic black figured pottery from the destruction layer) a new Regia was built with a new orientation (fig. 4.12). The portico and chambers behind it were transferred to the east side of the building from the west. There were again two chambers separated by a vestibule giving both onto the courtyard and onto the exterior. A new set of architectural terracottas is attributed to the building. They form a *sima* (the cresting of the gutter along the eaves) strigilated with ribbing along its exterior and further decorated with feline and female heads, whose mouths were open to serve as rainwater spouts.

At the very end of the sixth century the building once again was subjected to radical transformation (fig. 4.13). The group of rooms was placed on the south side of the complex. (The portico now ran along the opposite side of the courtyard.) The entrance to the complex remained in much the same location as in the preceding period. This plan was scrupulously maintained for the remainder of the history of the building, one replacement in the third century, the other by Cn. Domitius Calvinus in 36.

The architectural vicissitudes of the Regia are one of the great puzzles of the archaeology of Rome. In the light of the discoveries at Murlo and Acquarossa, however, one can appreciate how closely the essential elements of house design, courtyard, portico, and chambers behind it are repeated in each phase of the building. Despite the graffito REX, which testifies to the king's presence, the Regia tells us very little about the Roman kingship or the king's functions, political or sacred.[26]

The courtyard and *porticus* house is now widely documented in Latium at Ficana, Torrino, and most clearly at Satricum.[27] The *porticus* house is not the end-point of house development in archaic Rome. Recent discoveries along the Sacra Via in the direction of the Arch of Titus suggest that the next stage of development of the well-to-do town house, the *atrium* house, was introduced into Rome at this time. The *atrium* plan remained dominant for town houses throughout the Republic. From an entrance hall, the *fauces* or jaws, one passed into a central room, the *atrium*, which, however, must often have given the effect of a court because it was open to the sky, an arrangement which brought light and air into the house while rainwater from the roof was conducted into a cistern below the floor.[28] At the rear of the *atrium* there was originally the master bed chamber, the *tablinum*, with wings, or *alae*, to the right and left. During the morning the master of the house received his clients and visitors in the *tablinum*, which also contained the memorabilia of the family, including, in the case of old and successful lineages, the collection of portraits of illustrious ancestors. Cooking was banished to the rear. On the sides of the *atrium* there opened secondary chambers.

The plan of the buildings uncovered beside the Sacra Via in excavations, where the extraordinary depth of fill has given great hope of further important discoveries, is slightly more ample than the basic *atrium* house (fig. 4.14). Shops open off the facade, there is a vestibule leading to the *atrium* proper, the *tablinum* has been extended in depth, and a dining room (*triclinium*) has been added off the *tablinum*. As restored, the buildings have two floors. Like the Regia, these houses were long-lived, remaining in use until the end of the Republic. The Sacra Via was a fashionable neighborhood. Tarquin the First was supposed to have lived here, as did Publicola, according to tradition consul during the first year of the Republic.

The *atrium* house is only the end result of the adaptation of the courtyard house to increasing urban congestion. When there is little feeling of crowding not even courtyards are necessary. The Acquarossa house is the first

Figure 4.11 Rome, Forum, terracotta frieze attributed to the Regia, third phase.
Antiquario Forense.

stage of adaptation to urban conditions, as are the courtyard houses of
Greek Megara Hyblaea in Sicily. The *atrium* house shows compression
advancing to the point that the courtyard, which has lost whatever agricul-
tural functions it may have served earlier, has become vestigial, no more than
a light well.[29] There are traces of houses of the archaic period on the Palatine
Hill.[30]

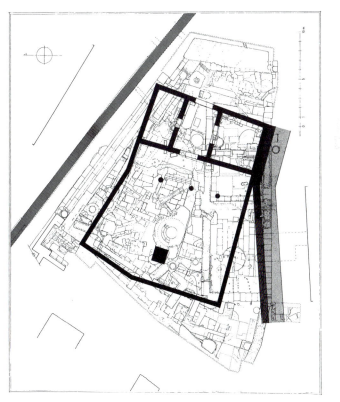

Figure 4.12 Rome, Forum, plan of the Regia, fourth phase.

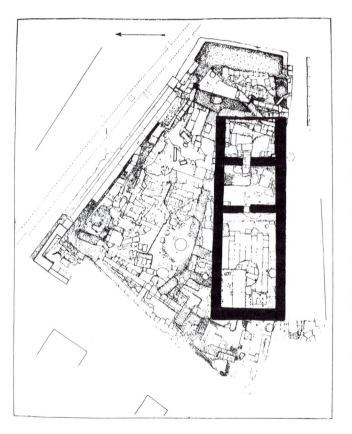

Figure 4.13 Rome, Forum, plan of the Regia, fifth phase.

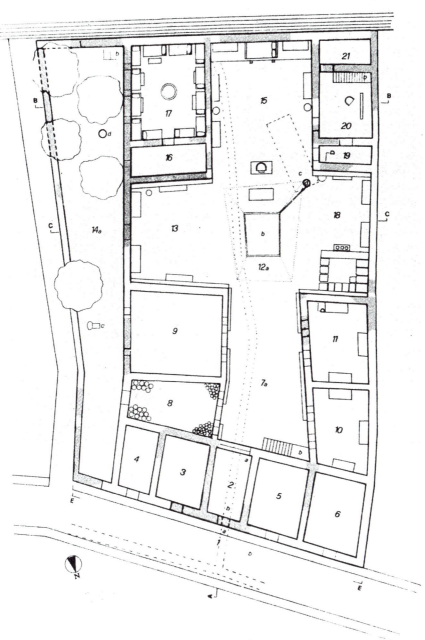

Figure 4.14 Rome, atrium house of the Sacra Via.

5

THE SANT'OMOBONO
SANCTUARY

At the foot of the Capitoline, where the valley of the Velabrum (the depression between the Capitoline and the Palatine) begins its descent to the river bank, there stands the church of Sant'Omobono, patron of the Roman tailors (fig. 1.1). Sheathed in a modern brick exterior and isolated from its surroundings, the church is incongruously ugly. Its interior, however, is still the work of the sixteenth century AD and the history of religion on this site is far older than Christianity. The church is built over a Roman Republican and then Imperial temple, one of two, as has become apparent, that stood here side by side within an enclosure. (Remains of an archaic temple and its altar have been found situated partially beneath the eastern member of the pair of temples.) The complexity and importance of the remains around the church became apparent only in 1937 when construction began on an office building for the city of Rome. The building project had to be cancelled. The archaeological excavations begun the next year were interrupted during the Second World War but resumed in 1959. The most recent excavation took place in 1986.[1]

The twin Republican structures have been identified as the temples of Mater Matuta (Aurora) and Fortuna, which according to tradition were built by King Servius Tullius in the sixth century.[2] Although, as is so often the case, epigraphical evidence for the identifications is lacking from the excavations, these temples were located in the Forum Boarium, the cattle market beside the river. The twin structures below Sant'Omobono are unquestionably temples, as shown by their reconstructed ground plan, by the two altars on the plaza in front of them (both facing east although the temples face south), and by the long history of cult on the site (fig. 5.1). Although the discoveries of the twin temples and of their archaic predecessor have been widely hailed as confirmation of the annalistic tradition concerning the kings, the fit is not without difficulties, some of which emerge directly from the stratigraphy of the site, others of which concern the general credibility of what the ancient sources say about early Rome. History in the sense of reference to specific recorded events does emerge strikingly at

Sant'Omobono from the inscribed base of the trophy set up here by Marcus
Fulvius Flaccus after the sack of Volsinii in 264.[3]

The section through the excavated area illustrates the sequence of phases
and structures on the site (fig. 5.2). The ancient street, the Vicus Jugarius,
occupying a terrace along the side of the Capitoline, was some 6 m (almost
20 ft) above the ground level around the early temple. Before the archaic
temple was built seven strata accumulated on the spot. One must note that
the stratigraphy shown on the general section should not be taken to
represent excavation of the entire area. Work below the level of the paving
fronting the twin Republican temples has been restricted to (1) limited
trenches around the podium of the archaic temple and immediately south of
it, (2) excavation within and just behind the podium of the eastern member
of the pair of twin temples, and (3) an excavation around the well situated
between the altars of the twin temples. The stratigraphy is complicated by
the presence of fragments of Apennine pottery which almost certainly came
from deposits further up the Capitoline slopes, and similar uncertainty
surrounds the fragments of Greek and Greek imitation pottery of the eighth
century from the same fill. It is also unclear to what extent fragments of daub

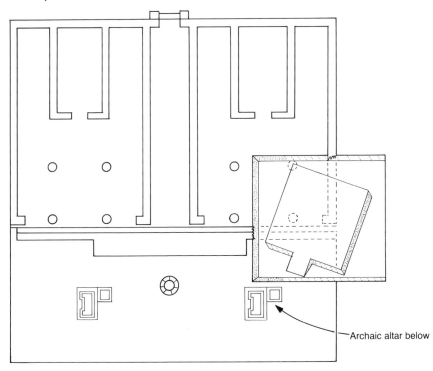

Figure 5.1 Rome, Sant'Omobono sanctuary, plan of sanctuary of the archaic and
Republican periods. The depth of fill above the early temple (about 6 m, approximately 20 ft) is much foreshortened.

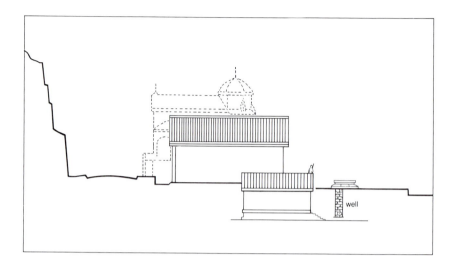

Figure 5.2 Rome, Sant'Omobono sanctuary, section through sanctuary of the archaic and Republican periods.

Figure 5.3 Rome, Sant'Omobono sanctuary, graffito, Antiquarium Comunale – Musei Capitolini.

and roof tiles in the lower stratum can be taken to represent architecture on the spot before the sixth century, although there is no reason to doubt that the cult antedates the first temple. Indeed below the altar of the first temple there was uncovered a compact level composed of sand, clay, and tufa chips and marked by the presence of carbonized material and bones of sheep, goats, and cattle. Between the altar and the temple podium at the same level there was found what may be the earliest inscription from Rome, a graffito on a small pot sherd reading UQNU(S), apparently Etruscan (fig. 5.3).[4]

The first temple rose in the first

half of the sixth century. The evidence for this date is set out by Dr Anna
Sommella Mura as follows:

> The pottery and in particular the numerous fragments of Laconian, Ionic
> and Attic cups [fig. 5.4] recovered in the strata connected with the
> destruction and abandonment of the archaic temple offer useful elements
> for placing the two phases of the temple's life within the sixth century.
>
> Indeed, the upper limit that can be placed on the cult of the sanctuary is
> offered by Laconian pottery, found in stratigraphic context which places
> the initial phase of the temple around the second decade of the sixth
> century, while the lower chronological limit is offered by the latest "eye
> cups" datable no later than the last decade of the sixth century.[5]

Figure 5.4 Rome, Sant'Omobono sanctuary, Attic black figure cup ("Little Master
Cup") of the sixth century, Antiquarium Comunale – Musei Capitolini. The Greek
dipinto reads "Hail and drink well!"

The podium of the temple was crowned by a simple half round molding.
It was only slightly smaller than its successor which measured 36 Roman feet
square (1 ft = 29.6 cm), and, in respect to the podium, represents no more
than an additional casing over the first structure. Enough remains of the
support for interior walls to suggest a plan with a single *cella*. It was
presumably fronted by columns, possibly two flanking the stairway which
led up to the front of the temple. To the revetment for the cornice of the
gabled roof over the front (and rear) of the building (the raking cornice) is
attributed a fragmentary terracotta plaque with a lion below and a half-
round crowning molding decorated with a scale pattern.

Two further inscribed sherds were discovered at levels which may be attributed
to the period of the first temple. On one only two letters of the inscription remain,
AL. The other, certainly Latin, reads OUDUIOS (written right to left). To the
rear of the podium in a stratum thought to represent debris from the first temple
there was found an ivory plaque in the form of a crouching lion (figs 5.5, 5.6). The
smooth back of the plaque has an Etruscan inscription ARAZ SILQETENAS
SPURIANAS read as Araz Silketena of Spuriana.[6] The same deposit yielded
further evidence of the richness of votive gifts to the sanctuary. This consists of
carved amber (fig. 5.7) and figurines and figurine pendents in bone (figs 5.8,

Figure 5.5 Rome, Sant'Omobono sanctuary, ivory plaque in the form of a crouching lion, Antiquarium Comunale – Musei Capitolini.

Figure 5.6 Rome, Sant'Omobono sanctuary, reverse of ivory plaque, Antiquarium Comunale – Musei Capitolini.

Figure 5.7 Rome, Sant'Omobono sanctuary, amber pendents and amber and bone disc, Antiquarium Comunale – Musei Capitolini.

Figure 5.8 Rome, Sant'Omobono sanctuary, ivory figurine, Antiquarium Comunale – Musei Capitolini.

Figure 5.9 Rome, Sant'Omobono sanctuary, ivory figurine, Antiquarium Comunale – Musei Capitolini.

73

Figure 5.10 Rome, Sant'Omobono sanctuary, figurines cut out of bronze sheeting, Antiquarium Comunale – Musei Capitolini.

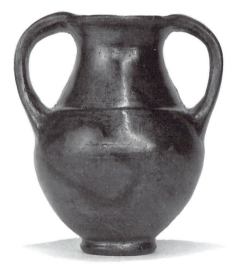

Figure 5.11 Rome, Sant'Omobono sanctuary, Etruscan *bucchero* amphora, Antiquarium Comunale – Musei Capitolini.

Figure 5.12 Rome, Sant'Omobono sanctuary, Etrusco-Corinthian perfume flask in the shape of mother and baby monkey, Antiquarium Comunale – Musei Capitolini.

5.9), together with worked bone that came from furniture or objects decorated with bone plaques.

The sanctuary in general contained objects familiar from other ritual contexts in Rome and Latium. Cut-out figurines (fig. 5.10), terracotta models of bread, miniature vases, *bucchero* pottery (5.11), and Italic imitations of Greek wares (especially Corinthian, fig. 5.12), bronze fibulae, and unusual bone objects consisting of a stand and upright plaque or spear. Weaving implements, loom weights, and spindle whorls (or weights) are present, suggesting women's role in the cult as do the alabaster unguent vases and the amber and bone already mentioned.[7]

The animal remains from the sanctuary show the sacrifice of cattle, sheep, goat, pig, and dog. The large majority of animals were sacrificed soon after birth. Various species occur sporadically: dove, goose, turtle, and fish. Vegetal remains are those of cereals, wheat, barley, olives, figs, and large quantities of hazelnuts. Wood samples come from conifers, oak, olive, hazel, and vines.

At the end of the sixth century the temple was rebuilt. A new podium was decorated with a double molding (half-round above the typical archaic Latian bed molding). Interestingly enough, the new podium was carried around only three sides of the structure. There are numerous terracotta elements attributed to the building. The columns were of wood. They may have had terracotta capitals, although the terracotta elements in question may belong to the base of a votive offering (fig. 5.13). These are a form of Aeolic capital, a type also documented from the Greek west by its use on the treasury of Massilia (Marseilles) at Delphi. In the Sant'Omobono temple the capital crowned a fluted column shaft, another Greek characteristic. The lateral *sima* (a vertical barrier placed along the roof on the long sides of the building to mask the edge of the final row of roof tiles) was furnished with alternating female heads and lion's head spouts; the pantiles of the roof were also decorated with a diamond pattern. On the facade the raking cornice, below a *sima recta* crowning molding decorated with a scale pattern and a strigilated hawksbeak, carried a frieze in relief of chariots drawn by winged horses, in each a charioteer and woman passenger accompanied in some instances by a youth on foot (fig. 5.14). The same subject appears on a cornice at Veii and Velletri and is common at Rome, as shown by fragments from the Forum, the Palatine, the Esquiline, and the Capitoline.[8] The scene, therefore, must be

Figure 5.13 Rome, Sant'Omobono sanctuary, terracotta capital or base, Antiquarium Comunale – Musei Capitolini.

considered generic rather than specific to any cult. The frieze is endlessly repetitive, each section representing an impression from the same mold. It is the style of this frieze that offers frequently cited evidence for the date of the rebuilding.[9]

The excavations in the sanctuary brought to light further important terracottas that may be related to the second temple. Prominent among these are two felines each restored as 1.54 m high and 1.31 m long (5 × 4.25 ft) (fig. 5.15). There are fragments of two such beasts, both plaques and posed antithetically. The most convincing hypothesis for their use places them as a pedimental group, perhaps flanking a gorgon or gorgon mask, of which a possible fragment has also been identified. A partition wall of flat terracotta panels, which in large part survive, would have closed the pediment. The reminiscence of the Temple of Artemis on Corfu of the beginning of the sixth century is unmistakable. In the pediment of that building, too, a gorgon is flanked by felines executed as relief plaques. Because of the date of the Corfu decoration it would seem more logical to attribute a similar pedimental group to the first half of the sixth century, and thus to the first phase of the Sant'Omobono temple rather than to the second phase.[10]

The most striking and unusual architectural elements from the sanctuary are the great terracotta volutes, which stood 1.24 m (4 ft) high (fig. 5.16). Although the exact arrangement on the roof of the temple is uncertain, I prefer to see these finials as the direct descendants of the horns which are found on Italic hut urns of the ninth and eighth centuries. It is therefore tempting to attribute them to the first phase of the temple. A terracotta

Figure 5.14 Rome, Sant'Omobono sanctuary, terracotta *sima* and frieze from the archaic temple (second phase), Antiquarium Comunale – Musei Capitolini.

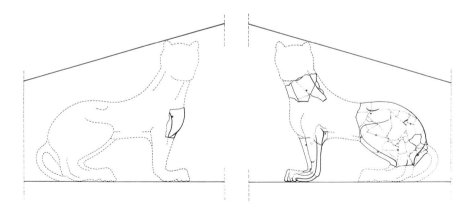

Figure 5.15 Rome, Sant'Omobono sanctuary, terracotta felines restored as part of pedimental decoration from the archaic temple (first phase), Antiquarium Comunale – Musei Capitolini.

Figure 5.16 Rome, Sant'Omobono sanctuary, terracotta volutes from the archaic temple, Antiquarium Comunale – Musei Capitolini.

sphinx may be an *acroterion* (a figure for the angles or peak of the roof) of a later phase when Greek influence had supplanted the old Etrusco-Italic traditions.

Finally, two life-size figures (1.45–1.50 m, 4.75–5 ft original height) in terracotta and fused along the arm constitute a group of Hercules and Minerva (fig. 5.17). The hero is identified by his lionskin, the goddess by her helmet. The generally accepted identification is unlikely to change despite attempts to use the similarity of Cypriote images of Hercules (also with belted jacket) to suggest that the goddess is an armed Aphrodite or Venus[11] or to identify the armed goddess as Fortuna Virilis.[12] The work is of the highest quality, pleasant but not mannered archaic. The eastern Greek parallels for Hercules' dress and Minerva's facial style point to artistic influences, less certainly to the ethnic origins of the artist. The group stood on a handsome base with a decorated torus molding. Part of a second base and some fragments of sculpture show that there was a second group of the same type. These would have been the *acroteria* of the second-phase temple, although one cannot exclude the possibility of their being a non-architectural votive group.

Figure 5.17 Rome, Sant'Omobono sanctuary, terracotta group of Hercules and Minerva, Antiquarium Comunale – Musei Capitolini.

The statuary group of Hercules and Minerva is mirrored in a similar group, of the same date, from the Portonaccio sanctuary at Veii.[13] This group of Hercules and Minerva was found in a part of the sanctuary where the evidence of graffiti shows that Minerva was worshipped. We have already reviewed the evidence against connecting the cults of the Sant'Omobono sanctuary with Fortuna and Mater Matuta. But judging from the evidence from Veii, it may well be that the archaic temple, at least, was dedicated to Minerva, who as patroness of weaving would have been the logical recipient of the spindle whorls and loom weights associated with the archaic sanctuary.[14]

After the archaic temple in its second phase was destroyed or dismantled, the sanctuary area was covered by a vast artificial fill, requiring possibly 30,000 cubic m (1,059,480 cubic ft) of earth, which raised the level of the area by almost 6.0 m (19.68 ft).[15] Although this fill has a preponderance of archaic material, it contains fragments of pottery that bring its date down to at least the late fourth century or after.[16] The date thus required for the creation of the terrace supporting the later temples agrees with the date for their building suggested by the material used in their construction. In their initial phase their walls were made of *Peperino* tufa, stone from quarries at Marino in the Alban Hills.[17] The twin temples were certainly built in or before 264 when M. Fulvius Flaccus took Volsinii and erected a monument to his conquest on the paved area before the temples (paving of Monteverde tufa on *cappellaccio* foundations). This monument is the earliest dated instance of the use of *Peperino* tufa at Rome, and the very distance of the quarries from the city would make it unlikely that *Peperino* was used at any significantly earlier date.[18] Apparently the fill over which the temples are set came from an archaic deposit somewhere in the neighborhood, presumably on the slopes of the Capitoline.

A second Monteverde tufa paving resting on *Grotta Oscura* tufa foundations was installed above the first. This new paving has been connected with reconstruction work presumably following the fire of 213 which caused widespread damage in the Forum Boarium area.[19]

One of the more striking anomalies of the sanctuary is the orientation of the two altars, in *Peperino* and connected with the lower paving of Monteverde tufa, which face east rather than south as do the twin temples. The history of cult on this spot was clearly complicated, both in spatial arrangements and possibly because of a long hiatus between the archaic phase and the structures of the third century.[20]

6

THE *LAPIS NIGER* AND
THE ARCHAIC FORUM

The Comitium was an open area at the foot of the Capitoline Hill bordering the Forum at its northern corner (figs 1.3, 1.4). It was an assembly place where judicial actions were also heard.[1] But in the Comitium, or more precisely above the speakers' loggia which faced the Comitium from the base of the Capitoline (the rostra), there was a place of ill omen marked by "the black stone" (*lapis niger*). In one version of tradition the black stone marked the spot set aside for the tomb of Romulus but occupied by another figure from the dawn of Rome, Faustulus, the shepherd who rescued the exposed infants Romulus and Remus; others said that the tomb of one Hostilius, grandfather of the third king of Rome, Tullus Hostilius, was there.[2] Others still, forgetting that Romulus had been assumed bodily to join the divinities on high, said that the black stone paving covered the founder's grave.[3]

At the very beginning of Giacomo Boni's excavations in the Forum the paving of Imperial times was cleared in the area just in front of the Arch of Septimius Severus on the Forum side, immediately above and to the south of the Comitium.[4] In the travertine paving there appeared one area, 3 × 4 m (9.84 × 13.12 ft) paved in black stone. The black paving was also fenced around with an enclosure wall of upright slabs. Further excavation showed that the *lapis niger*, as the black paving was immediately identified, covered one end of the Republican rostra.[5] At a lower level, and partially covered by the *lapis niger*, were three monuments that were all truncated to a similar height (figs 6.1, 6.2). One of them was an altar of the type now so well documented at Lavinium (especially Altars 8, first phase, and 13). The altar has the familiar U-shape, its two arms surrounding a corridor. On its wider side it measures 3.6 m (11.80 ft). What remains is two courses of foundation and the lowest course of the altar proper, the latter finished with the robust molding characteristic of Latian and Etruscan altars.[6] Adjoining the altar to the north, but occupying separate foundations, are two other monuments. One is a monolithic column 0.77 m (2.5 ft) in diameter at its base. Beside the column stands the most remarkable surviving monument of the early Forum, a stone block (*Grotta Oscura* tufa from Veii) 0.47 × 0.52 m (1.54 × 1.7 ft) and preserved to a height of 0.61 m (2 ft) (not counting the foot of the

81

stone set into the paving) (fig. 6.3). All four sides of the *stele* or *cippus* carry the bold letters of an early Latin inscription. The text is written vertically. The direction of the lines alternates between bottom to top and top to bottom. The removal of the top of the *cippus* has robbed us of the beginning or ending of each line. The letters are deeply cut and perfectly legible. But the sense of the inscription cannot be made out. It is generally taken to be a text of regulations connected with a cult (a *lex sacra*) but only the following nouns and adjectives are agreed on: *recei* (to the king), *sakros* (cursed), *kalatosem* (possibly herald), *iouxmenta* (oath), *iouested* (just).[7] Since the *cippus* could have been examined down to the end of the Republic, this is most likely the very inscribed stone over the supposed tomb of Hostilius mentioned by Dionysius of Halicarnassus. The historian's remark that the inscription named Hostilius and extolled his accomplishments shows us what the Late Republic made of the text of the inscription. It is unlikely that even the most learned men of the day could have really understood it. And this also suggests why there were so few scruples shown in cutting down and burying this and the neighboring monuments.

When the three monuments in question were covered over, the fill employed for the purpose contained a quantity of material typical of a cult place. At the bottom of the stratum there was a layer of burnt material. In it were the remains of several score of sheep, goat, and pigs. These remains have been taken to be evidence of expiatory sacrifices made at the time the monuments were buried, but, as we shall see below, consideration of the stratification as a whole casts doubts on this interpretation. With the animal remains and composing a stratum 0.4 m (1.3 ft) thick around and reaching just over the top of the truncated remains of the altar, *cippus*, and column were a hundred or so (*centinaia*) vases, many of them miniature jars and cups certainly intended for ritual use.[8] There were also tiny pottery discs imitating loaves of bread. Notable is a group of round, oval, or flat river pebbles found with others on which a neck is distinguished from the body and the neck is pierced for suspension or in one case has a channel for the same purpose. There were glass paste beads and pottery spindle whorls. There were 164 knucklebones, precursors of dice and widely employed for divination together with two dice, one showing traces of gold foil. There was a wide selection of Italic–Etruscan pottery of the sixth century. There were some outstanding fragments of Greek decorated pottery, both Ionian and Attic black figure. One of the Attic pieces shows Hephaistos mounted on a donkey and raising a *cantharus*, part of the scene of the return of the bemused smith god to Olympus and his reconciliation with the divine family. This fragment came from a master vase of the mid-sixth century from the circle of the vase-painter Lydos.

In the deposit there were eleven small bronze male and female figures of the Greek *kouros* (standing nude male) and *kore* (standing draped female) types. Another male figure holds a curved augur's staff (*lituus*). There is a *kouros* and a *kore* in ivory. Among the fragmentary bronzes there are pieces of fibulae, discs and hooks, and fragments of weapons. Moreover, there were twenty pieces of cast bronze, which the early Romans used as money (*aes rude*). A few terracotta figurines (some, such as a male head and a lion's head, of high quality), architectural terracotta fragments, a plaque with a rider and two gorgon antefixes complete the material from what has been called a votive deposit of the sixth century. Whatever the origin of these objects, however, it is certain that they were not found in their original location. The deposit surrounding the archaic monuments was mixed with later pottery extending down possibly as late as the first century BC. There were also fragments of Greek marble, a material which was not in wide use at Rome until the late second century BC. It seems clear that the fill was brought in from elsewhere to cover the archaic remains at the time they were hidden from view. The slabs of the *lapis niger* were first installed in a paving resting on this fill; fragments of the same stone, presumably chips from working the slabs on the spot, were found in it. The *lapis niger* would then have been raised and reset for the Imperial pavement. In its final position it is not centered over the archaic monuments and does not cover them fully but takes its orientation from the Curia at the other side of the Comitium. There is no way of knowing whether the orientation was changed when the Imperial paving was laid.

The sequence in which the archaic monuments were built is shown by their relation to their foundations.[9] The *cippus* originally stood alone at the head of the three steps which approached it from the north. Next a long kerbing (only a single course high) was laid on the side facing the Comitium and, probably at the same time, a pebble paving was laid in the Comitium itself.[10] The altar comes next: one corner of its foundations rests on the kerb. The rectangular paving on the far side of the altar was intended for the altar and must have been laid down when the altar was built. The columnar monument, resting on foundations also encroaching on the kerbing, implies the same ground level as the altar. The sequence of their building is not clear. The column, however, must, like the altar, have been set up after the *cippus* and the kerbing.

Those working with the evidence of Boni's excavation could date this complex only from the inscription of the *cippus*, its archaic character and the reference to a king, assumed to mean the kings who ruled, according to tradition, down to 509. Even if valid for the expulsion of the Tarquins, the date was not absolutely binding for the dating of the *cippus* because the title *rex* survived for priests (the *rex sacrorum*). As seen above, no appeal to the archaic character of the material in the fill over the monuments can be made as a chronological guide. A reliable basis for dating was provided by Romanelli's excavation of 1955. Extending Boni's work, Romanelli discovered that the altar and the paving on its south side were built over the side of an open pool. Beside the pool there was an artificially cut basin, apparently made to assist in drawing

Figure 6.1 Rome, Comitium, monuments below the *lapis niger* drawn at the time of excavation.

Figure 6.2 Rome, Comitium. The altar below the *lapis niger* is visible in the upper right-hand area of the photograph. Immediately above and to the right, the *lapis niger* is visible in the upper right-hand corner.

water. Both pool and basin were filled in at some time in the sixth century, judging from the Corinthian pottery in the fill. Thus it appears that the altar was built at the end of the "regal" period. The *cippus*, being earlier, belongs to the same era.

Romanelli believed that the pool might have already been the site of an early cult, a conclusion suggested but not substantiated by the presence of the later monuments around it. There is no trace of a tomb. It has been hypothesized that this was the site of the cult of Vulcan, which was in the area of the Comitium.[11]

There is almost no evidence concerning the development of the Forum during the "regal" period. In the stratigraphic sounding by the base of the large imperial monument often identified as an equestrian statue of Domitian in the center of the Forum, Gjerstad, reopening Boni's unpublished excavation of 1903–1904, found a sequence of pebble pavings. By means of his *impasto* pottery chronology (which, however, has not been widely accepted)[12] Gjerstad dated the first paving about 575.[13] According to others it may be fifty years older. Gjerstad was quick to identify this as part of a general paving laid down in the Forum.[14] He interpreted the stratigraphy at the equestrian statue of Domitian site to suggest that at this point the paving was laid down over the strata made up of the remains of a community of huts that had stood on the spot. His identification of post holes for buildings in the small surface area exposed by his trench has been called into question, most recently by A. Ammerman, who has been making a series of borings to determine the early ground level of the Forum and adjacent areas.[15] It is Ammerman's contention that the debris found in Gjerstad's sounding came from fill intentionally carted into the Forum to raise the ground level in preparation for laying the pavement. The need for such a considerable fill arose because the central Forum and Velabrum, extending down to the Forum Boarium, were subject to flooding from the periodic inundations of the Tiber. In addition run-off from the surrounding hills and springs at the base of both the Palatine and the Capitoline Hill, of which the Lacus Juturnae remained a reminder throughout antiquity, created generally soggy conditions, particularly in rainy periods of the year. In this situation, Ammerman reasons, no one would have put a house in the central Forum. If there was a project in the "regal" period to raise the entire level of the Forum approximately 2 m (from 7 m above sea level, the original height according to Ammerman's researches, to 9 m above sea level, the elevation of Gjerstad's earliest pebble paving), then, Ammerman calculates, it would have required between 10,000 and 20,000 cubic m of fill (approximately 350,000–700,000 cubic ft). This is an astounding quantity of earth, and before accepting the implications of this calculation to estimate the resources and power of organization of Rome midway through the "regal" age, one must await the results of Ammerman's future borings and their analysis. It is quite possible that, rather than a general paving having been

Figure 6.3 Rome, Comitium, *cippus* with archaic inscription below the *lapis niger*.

laid at one moment, various parts of the Forum were filled and covered with pebble surfaces at different times.

That major operations of the sort were undertaken to eliminate, if only partially, the inconvenience of periodic flooding, is clear from the fill brought in to raise the level of the Sant'Omobono sanctuary from the level of the archaic temple to that of the subsequent twin temples. But this fill was made in the third century.[16]

Finally, one may note that the Cloaca Maxima (the Great Sewer), which carries water from the Argiletum (the thoroughfare which climbed the valley between the Viminal and the Esquiline) first across the Forum, collecting the water of other drains on its way, and then through the Velabrum to the Tiber, remained an open ditch down to the later Republic (fig. 1.1).[17] It could not have been part of a flood control project since it facilitated rather than hindered water backing up through it from the Tiber.

APPENDIX: Archaic votive deposits in Rome

The votive material from the fill surrounding the archaic monuments below the *lapis niger* came, almost certainly, from a *favissa* or underground cache of votive objects. The *favissae Capitolinae* in particular are known from an exchange between the jurist Servius Sulpicius and Varro, the student of Roman antiquities.[18] Varro gave the following definition: "These are cells or cisterns found underground in that location, in which it has been customary to place old decorational elements which have come off that temple and other things that have been consecrated by dedication." Such *favissae* were to be respected, as Q. Catulus found when he proposed cutting down part of the Capitoline to give the new Temple of Jupiter Optimus Maximus greater prominence. But, as the material from the Comitium shows, such scruples were not always so carefully observed.

A votive dump came to light on the Capitoline during construction work in 1925–1927.[19] The material from this deposit had none of the exceptional items found in the Comitium but it was similar in general composition. The same miniature cups and jars and the same models of loaves of bread were present (figs 6.4, 6.5). It contained Italo-Corinthian pottery of the sixth century (fig. 6.6). Instead of the *kouros* and *kore* figurines it had miniature figures crudely cut out of bronze sheeting (fig. 6.7).

A small deposit is also known from the foot of the Capitoline near the Temple of Concord.[20] Its composition is identical to the deposit just described, although the fragments of bronze sheeting are not large enough to identify cut-out figures with certainty.

The essential features of these deposits are also repeated in the find made at S. Maria della Vittoria.[21] None of the bronze objects from the *favissa* survives (there were originally six hundred of them), but the same miniature vessels, Italo-Corinthian alabastra (flasks for scented oil) and the miniature

Figure 6.4 Capitoline *favissa*, miniature vases, Antiquarium Comunale – Musei Capitolini.

Figure 6.5 Capitoline *favissa*, model loaves of bread and tray for small vegetable offerings (seeds etc.), Antiquarium Comunale – Musei Capitolini.

Figure 6.6 Capitoline *favissa*, Italo-Corinthian pottery, Antiquarium Comunale – Musei Capitolini.

Figure 6.7 Capitoline *favissa*, figurines cut out of bronze sheeting, Antiquarium Comunale – Musei Capitolini.

loaves of bread are present. The representation of sixth-century pottery, Etruscan *bucchero* and Italo-Corinthian, is notable, and there were a few pieces of Latian Period III material pointing to an early origin of the cult or a mixture of material from nearby tombs on the Quininal and Viminal.

On the right bank of the Tiber a votive deposit with numerous bronze figurines of the type from the deposit below the *lapis niger* was found in 1888.[22]

These deposits illustrate the generic character of Roman votive religion in archaic times. The miniature vases and model loaves which are numerically the largest part of the material seem to have been appropriate for any divinity. The figures, cut-outs or small-scale reproductions of the Greek *kouros* and *kore*, are also typically present. Inscriptions are rare. The most important one comes from the otherwise dispersed deposit from the Quirinal, Villa Hufner. It is a long graffito on a vase formed of three joined bowls, a not uncommon form for offering first fruits (the Greek *kernos*). The vase is now in Berlin. Although complete and entirely legible, the Duenos inscription, as it is called, has resisted all attempts at understanding it.[23]

These deposits lack any of the specificity we associate with Greek votive terracottas and bronzes, whether in regard to the worshipper or to the divinity. This is a sphere of long-lived tradition, recalling the miniature vases and figurines of the Latian Period I tombs.[24] Despite the Italo-Corinthian vases and the occasional imported pieces, this is a closed and Latin world.

The votive material from the Sant'Omobono sanctuary, already discussed above,[25] stands in sharp contrast to the other Roman votive deposits. The cut-out figurines, miniature vases, and model loaves are all represented, but they are part of a much richer context. There are objects in amber, bone, ivory, and Egyptian alabaster, imported Greek pottery, weaving tools (the latter present, although not in significant numbers, in the Comitium deposit). The Sant'Omobono sanctuary was apparently more international than the cult places of the Capitoline, Forum, or Quirinal. The graffiti found there show that it was frequented by Etruscans, and very possibly by the Greeks and other foreigners who came up the river to Rome. This deposit has something of the character of the harbor town sanctuaries at Pyrgi, the port of Caere, and Graviscae, the port of Tarquinia, where foreign cults flourished. The cult of the Sant'Omobono sanctuary may possibly have been foreign too, that of the Etruscan divinity Minerva.

Still incomplete is the excavation on the Oppius where an *area sacra* has been interpreted as belonging to one of the shrines from which annually chaff was removed, fashioned into human figures and then thrown into the Tiber.[26] As revealed up to now, the remains consist of an enclosure, 2.8 m (9.18 ft) on its longer side, within which there is a paving and the base of a *cippus*. Material from the area does not follow the standard composition of offerings at Roman shrines in archaic times. There is a bronze *kouros*, an incense burner, bobbins, and loom weights.

7

WALLS

During the campaigning season of 211, Hannibal, the invader of Italy and for seven years the undefeated antagonist of the Romans, rode up to the walls of Rome and calmly studied them.[1] But like the advance columns of the German army that came within sight of Moscow in November, 1941, Hannibal retreated, never to see Rome again. When he looked toward the walls of Rome, "What," we may ask, "did Hannibal see?" Two impressive sections of the walls of Republican Rome are still to be seen (fig. 7.1). The first is the section preserved beside the entrance to the main Rome railroad station, 94 m (308 ft) long, curving slightly toward its eventual junction with the fortifications along the summit of the Quirinal (fig. 7.2). Seventeen courses of *Grotta Oscura* tufa are preserved for a total height of some 10 m (33 ft). The wall is 4 m (13 ft) thick. Impressive as it is in isolation, the curtain that we see today is only part of a far grander defense work. As reconstructed by H. Riemann the wall, reaching a height of 40 Roman feet, faced an earth mound or *agger*, while to the far side of the wall a moat or *fossa* reached a depth of 55 Roman feet (fig. 7.3).[2] (The retaining wall along the inner slope of the *agger* is also partly preserved.) The *fossa*, as observations made at various points make clear, extended along the entire Esquiline plateau from the Porta Esquilina to the Porta Nomentana, almost 1.5 km (slightly over 0.9 mi.).[3]

This concept of defense, ditch and mound, is an old one, as the defenses of Ardea, Decima, Acqua Acetosa, Laurentina, and Gabii demonstrate. But the system was also well adapted for protection against attack in the centuries after 400 when machines revolutionized siege warfare. Protection now lay first in keeping the rams and towers away from the wall and next in devising upper works capable of absorbing the impact of stone-throwing artillery. The *fossa* met the first requirement. The earth mound, the *agger*, met the second. There is nothing necessarily primitive or archaic about the walls of the Esquiline.[4]

The late Imperial defenses of the city, originally erected by the Emperor Aurelian (AD 270–275) to meet the threat of barbarian invaders, are in brick-faced cement. The earlier walls in masonry have traditionally borne the name of King Servius Tullius.[5] It was the American scholar Tenney Frank who undermined King Servius' claim by observing that the stone of the Esquiline walls was, with the exception of a few blocks, *Grotta Oscura* tufa, a stone which is quarried near Veii.[6] It was thus unlikely that before the conquest of Veii (396) the Romans would have had access to the *Grotta Oscura* quarries for the quantity of stone needed to build the Esquiline wall. The walls, therefore, would belong to the fourth century, at the earliest.[7]

Subsequently, the walls have been dated to the years immediately after 378 on the evidence of Livy's statement that in that year a tax was levied for building a masonry defense wall laid out by the censors (VI, 32, 1).[8] Whatever the results of this work, and other work by the legions in 353 (Livy VII, 20, 9), they were insufficient to allay the fears of the populace over the weak state of Rome's defenses in the face of the Umbrian threat of 308 (Livy IX, 41, 11).

Another body of evidence bears on the dating of the Esquiline *agger*. This is the quarry marks on individual blocks of the wall. These are frequent in the Esquiline section of the *agger*. Säflund lists over one hundred blocks with quarry marks and notes 140 instances seen earlier but obliterated by the time of his investigations around 1930.[9] There are eighteen different signs. Except for the curved Roman *C* all are angular letters or signs (including the Greek *pi*) indicating the quarry or quarry gang to be credited for the individual block. The visible quarry marks all appear on the interior (hidden) face of the wall. They were originally hidden by the earth mound of the *agger*. In the section at the railroad station, where the construction can be studied best, there is an obvious break in work resulting in two vertical seams across which the courses are not bonded. This must indicate boundaries between crews executing the work. The quarry marks are independent of such divisions. Evidently the various contractors or units drew on a common supply of building material. The chronological value of the quarry marks in limiting the construction to any particular period after 387 is doubtful, although to judge from similar walls and similar marks on their blocks at Rhegium and Bolsena, this group of signs would seem more characteristic of work in the third than in the fourth century, although the earlier date cannot be excluded.[10] The other *Grotta Oscura* blocks with quarry marks found elsewhere in Rome are generally reused.[11] One instance, however, in the foundations of the Basilica Aemilia in the Forum has three signs of the same type as those of the "Servian Walls." This part of the basilica was attributed by T. Frank to the building of 179.[12]

The quarry marks lead us to the second major surviving section of masonry fortifications, situated on the south side of the Aventine (fig. 7.4). There are two sections of wall here, the first 42 m (138 ft), the second 43 m (141 ft) in length. The height of the two sections is twelve and fourteen courses respectively. The material of these blocks is *Grotta Oscura* tufa. The dimensions of the individual blocks vary from 50 to 60 cm (1.6–1.95 ft),

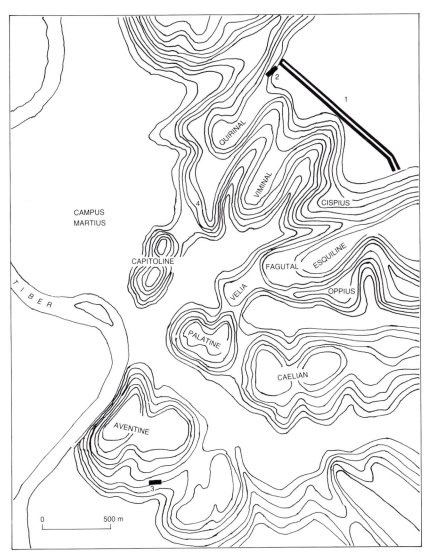

Figure 7.1 Map of the circuit of the Servian Walls of Rome. 1, Esquiline *agger* and *fossa*; 2, Via Salandra; 3, Aventine wall; 4, Piazza Magnanapoli.

Figure 7.2 Rome, the Servian Walls on the Esquiline. Note the quarry marks K and E visible on blocks at the right of the photograph.

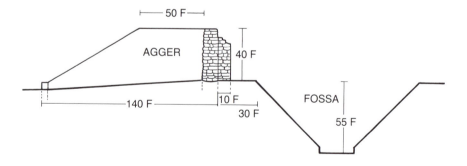

Figure 7.3 Rome, section of the Servian Walls of the Esquiline. Measurements in Roman feet (F).

comparable to those of the Esquiline *agger*. The westernmost section (not illustrated here), reaching 4 m (13 ft) in thickness, faces an *agger* much as does the Esquiline wall. The eastern section, however, which boasts an arched embrasure, evidently intended for a small catapult or ballista, is backed not by an earth but by a cement fill. If the cement backing were original it would preclude dating the section of the wall before about 200. Cement construction is mentioned by Cato the Elder writing in the second century (*De Agric.* IV, 1 and 4, XVIII, 7). Its first known appearance at Rome is in the Porticus Aemilia, the large warehouse beside the Tiber built after 197.[13]

Roman cement is not like modern poured concrete. The *pozzolana* stone powder, which once mixed with water dried into such a durable bonding material, was employed with quantities of loose rock so that the desired volume could be achieved economically. Other debris could find its way into the mix. Imperial cement walls are full of sherds and tile fragments. (Broken tiles were used as facing in Imperial times while earlier builders employed small pieces of tufa, either untrimmed, producing an effect described as *opus incertum* or trimmed into cubes and set in a diamond pattern, *opus reticulatum*. The latter began to be used in the first century BC.) In the

Figure 7.4 Rome, the Servian Walls of the Aventine.

cement fill of the Aventine section of the Servian Wall I have observed (April 19, 1992) a fragment of marble, a material which did not find common use in Rome until Augustan times. The cement work backing the defense wall is probably not original. It is difficult to determine when it replaced the original earth fill, but it has no bearing on the date of the fortifications.

The artillery embrasure is made in Anio stone, the so-called *lapis ruber*. One might think that this was an addition made well after the building of the wall. This may be, but not only around the embrasure but elsewhere in the fabric of the wall there occur blocks of the same material (they wear better than the *Grotta Oscura* tufa and stand out sharply in our photograph).

Some limits on the date of the fortifications represented by the Esquiline and Aventine walls can be established on the basis of the tenuous but important evidence from the extensive cemetery which originally covered much of the plateau of the Esquiline and which extended, possibly in a discontinuous fashion, over the Quirinal as well. The history of the excavation of these tombs has been reviewed already. It is now time to return to the graves of the fourth century BC, some of which were unquestionably found inside the Servian circuit. To this end I shall let Giovanni Pinza put the case that he developed from patient study of the records of the recovery operations of the end of the nineteenth century. Writing of the Quirinal at its southwestern end toward the Forum and the Capitoline, that is at a point where there is not only a slope on the two sides of this ridge but also a general rise of ground in the direction of the Esquiline plateau, which the Quirinal joins not far from the railroad station and the Esquiline section of the Servian Wall, Pinza says (in translation):

> Within the masonry wall near the Porta Fontinale [a conjectural identification], which stood at the base of the funnel-like reentrant of the defenses – one side of which is preserved in the little planted plot [today a traffic circle] of Via Magnanapoli and the other, preserved in part, has the usual ballista embrasure visible in Palazzo Antonelli (wrongly identified as a gate) – there were found the remains of a cemetery of the Third Period, that is with tomb groups made up of Hellenistic and Etrusco-Campanian material.

"Etrusco-Campanian" refers to common Italic black glazed pottery, largely of the third century. Pinza's use of the word "period" is not to be confused with the periods of early Rome now employed for the tenth to sixth centuries; see above, Chapter 3.

> Moving up the hill [that is away from the Capitoline] there were single *fossa* graves and one *a buco* as the excavators in Tuscany would have described it [equivalent apparently to *pozzo*], with an Attic red figure vase of early type serving as an ash urn. Downhill on the slope, there opened the entrance to one of the usual chamber tombs dug in the rock. This tomb, closed by the part of the defense wall which can still

be seen in Piazza Magnanapoli, was brought to light in the excavations for the street. It was found full of earth in which Etrusco-Campanian vases were recovered. The uncertain character of the report leaves open two possibilities. One might suppose that the vases belonged to the burials made in this chamber. But one cannot exclude the possibility that they were mixed with earth that was later used to fill the chamber. The first is the more probable hypothesis. It fits with the evidence of the single, and presumably contemporary, burials found higher up the slope, as I have mentioned, near the church of Santa Caterina di Siena. The tomb in question, however, had had its entry cut off or at least blocked up with a fortification wall of blocks of yellowish tufa stone, which still must be considered later than the burial chamber and thus no earlier than the period of common use of Etrusco-Campanian pottery. There remains the alternative hypothesis, which, however, does not change any conclusions regarding the chronology of the fortification walls in relation to the tomb, because the earth fill in which the Campanian-type vases were found came into the tomb before and certainly not after the fortifications were built. The latter were constructed backing up on the door of the tomb and to contain the earth dumped for the terracing of the slope on the inside of the fortification where the necropolis was situated. They must, therefore, have made any further change to the tomb impossible. Thus even admitting the second possibility, which is in fact less probable than the notion that the dirt mixed with the Etrusco-Campanian material was dumped into the burial chamber during the work of terracing carried out on the inside of the fortifications, it follows that this earth fill with material from tombs or other sources included Etrusco-Campanian pottery, the introduction of which must be earlier than the construction of the wall in granular yellowish tufa.

Further still, it can be demonstrated that the Esquiline section of the wall was not built before the beginning of the Third Period, because inside its circuit was found Tomb LXI which contained, according to the reports of the inspector of the Commission, an "ordinary Etruscan cup with ornament in black on the concave part, without foot." Ornament in black on an "Etruscan" cup, notwithstanding the imprecision of the description, presupposes painted decoration. Moreover, the description of the piece by Marsuzi shows that it was acquired by the city of Rome. There is no doubt, therefore, that it should be found among the five or six small plates of southern Italian production [Pinza here corrects Marsuzi's term "Etruscan"; more recent research has returned to a central Italian attribution] decorated in black on a clear ground among which, once we have excluded those decorated with a woman's head, which the Report would certainly have mentioned, and those retaining their foot, one can identify with certainty the small plate of the Report as the one illustrated here. This is sufficient to demonstrate that the tomb group of Tomb LXI, certainly that of a single burial, belonged to Period III.[14]

Figure 7.5 Plate of the Genucilia group similar to the piece from the Esquiline Tomb LXI, collection of the Center for Old World Archaeology and Art, Brown University.

The vase from the Esquiline Tomb LXI belongs to the so-called Genucilia class, so named from the inscription of P. Genucilia occurring on such a plate in the Museum of Art, Rhode Island School of Design, Providence, R.I. (USA) (fig. 7.5). The Genucilia group was discussed in detail by Mario A. Del Chiaro in 1957.[15] Del Chiaro attributed the Esquiline plate to a workshop at Caere active, in his view, over the entire fourth century. The evidence now accumulated in respect to the simpler kinds of Genucilia plates, such as the piece from the Esquiline, makes it appear that Del Chiaro may have tended toward dating them somewhat too early. Certainly tomb groups now published from Caere with star-decorated Genucilia plates belong to the end of the fourth century or the beginning of the third.[16] It has also been pointed out that examples from the Roman colonies of Alba Fucens (founded in 303) and Cosa (founded in 273) further suggest that production of plates of Del Chiaro's Caere type continued into the third century.[17] A group of these plates from a well, at the Regia in the Roman Forum, which went out of use about 240, further strengthens the case for attributing much of the Genucilia class to a date after 300.[18]

At the time that this chamber tomb on the Quirinal and Tomb LXI on the Esquiline were made, they cannot have been within the city. And the Servian Wall, as we know it today, did not yet exist. On the subject of burial within the city Roman law was unequivocal. "Do not bury or cremate a corpse within the city" ("Hominem mortuum in urbe neve sepelito neve urito," *XII Tabulae*, X:1). It is useless to argue that this is the grave of one of the few outstanding individuals (*clari viri*) for whom an exception was possible (Cicero, *De Leg.* II, 58). With this tomb we are not moving in the class of Romulus or Julius Caesar. It is equally desperate to hold that the tomb (and the other tombs of the Quirinal and, of course, Tomb LXI of the Esquiline) were covert violations of the law. One has only to think of how many tombs of the same type and same date must have been lost during the boom of the

1870s and 1880s, and how many others cannot be identified because of the faulty record of what was recovered, to realize that burial must have been common within the circuit of the Servian Walls into the fourth, and very likely into the third century. But let us suspend final judgment as to the date of the masonry fortifications because not all the evidence has been considered.

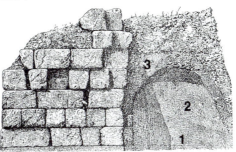

Figure 7.6 Rome, the Servian Walls in Via Salandra.

Not far beyond the northern end of the Esquiline section of the wall another unit of fortification exists which has been attributed to an earlier date. This is the wall excavated in the grounds of the Ministry of Agriculture in Via Salandra in 1907 (fig. 7.6). The wall is *cappellaccio*.[19] It had the thickness of the other sections already examined and was backed by a mound. To the exterior the steep slope of the Quirinal Hill at this point made a *fossa* unnecessary. Excavational evidence, so rare in connection with the walls of Rome, was obtained here. The earth behind the wall was not a uniform deposit. The excavator, none other than Giacomo Boni, interpreted it as a series of fills laid up against the rising wall by its builders.[20] It has also been interpreted by Einar Gjerstad as a preexisting *agger* against which the *cappellaccio* wall was built and which, finally, was covered by new fill piled over it and against the wall.[21] The lower mound is made up of Strata 1 and 2; the last fill over it and against the wall is Stratum 3. The material from both Stratum 1 and 2 was archaic (that is, before the early fifth century). Stratum 2, in particular, produced one imported black figure sherd belonging probably to the sixth century.[22] No such useful evidence was noted from Stratum 3.[23]

The result is: Strata 1–2, after about 500; fortification wall and Stratum 3, unknown. But does the initial mound (or *agger*) belong to the fifth century? One must be on one's guard in respect to a stratigraphy of this nature. This is not a domestic deposit recording activity down to its cessation on the spot. Rather it is a deliberate fill removed from its original location and possibly brought from outside the immediate vicinity according to the needs of the work. The same problem arises here that arises in the Sant'Omobono sanctuary regarding the fill below the twin temples: the contents of such a fill may be much older than the time of its deposit in the new location. There is no reason, furthermore, to insist on a chronological stratification of the tufas used in the defenses of Rome. *Cappellaccio* walls are not necessarily early. The retaining wall of the inner face of the *agger* on the Esquiline, for example, is *cappellaccio*.[24] It is therefore possible that the section of wall in the Ministry of

99

Agriculture is no older than the Aventine or Esquiline walls. It is impossible to say when the fill made up of archaic sherds was deposited on the spot. It could have been deposited as late as the third century. And this is the date to which better evidence, from masons' marks and the tombs within the walls, seems to point.

When the city of Rome felt it necessary to fortify a territory of 246 hectares (608 acres) within the circuit of at least 8 km (5 mi.) enclosed by the Servian Wall, the Republican city had reached its greatest extent.[25] Its size far exceeded that of any other city of the Republican age in Etruria, Campania, or Latium.[26] It places Rome in the category of the Greek metropoleis, Sybaris, Agrigentum, and Syracuse.[27] This is surely the Rome of the time of Hannibal. Perhaps it is Rome of the time of Pyrrhus and the First Punic War (280–240), but not earlier.

It is quite within the realm of possibility that the massive *fossa* that existed across the Esquiline is a widened and deepened successor of earlier defenses in the same location. Similarly, the mound behind the *cappellaccio* wall discovered in the Ministry of Agriculture could have been part of a defense system put in place in the century between Rome's suppression of the Latin League (338) and the end of the First Punic War (241). But in the region from the Oppius to the Quirinal one must admit that there is no evidence of fortifications belonging to any period before the second half of the fourth century, if then. The early defenses of a primitive settlement on the Oppius or Fagutal must also remain conjectural, although Säflund was certainly justified in indicating a hypothetical *fossa* across the neck of the Oppius where some such defense would surely have been needed.[28]

Along the Quirinal there are several traces of fortifications, as noted above.[29] At the foot of the Capitoline toward the Quirinal a portion of the enceinte is visible. But of the fragmentary walls existing on the Arx, none is surely anything more than a terrace wall or foundation, or a defense limited to the top of the hill.[30] In the dip between the Arx and the Capitolium there are elements probably of fortification but in *Grotta Oscura* stone and so probably no older than the fourth century. Below this, at the foot of the hill, a fine stretch of wall was brought to light in 1930. It is built of *cappellaccio* but is evidently a later addition to the defensive works.[31]

The situation on the Palatine is complicated by the fact that the fragments of masonry walls discovered on the west corner of the hill have all become part of subsequent construction. Only one piece of *cappellaccio* walling has any claim to be part of an early defense.[32]

The wall extending along the Vicus Jugarius behind the twin temples of the Sant'Omobono sanctuary has been interpreted, although not without reservations, as a spur wall from the Capitol to the river. The opening in the wall may be the Porta Carmentalis. It is built of *Grotta Oscura* and Fidenae stone and associated with pottery of the fourth and fifth centuries.[33] Much less convincing is the wall in Piazza Bocca della Verità. Consequently the

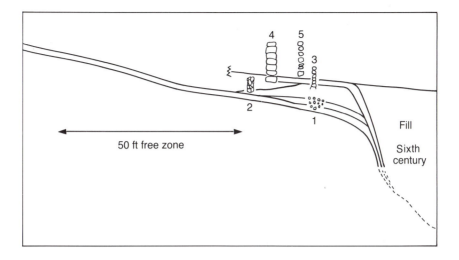

Figure 7.7 Rome, north slope of the Palatine, early structures. The sequence of walls is indicated by the Arabic numerals.

existence of fortifications of any period along the Tiber must remain in doubt.[34]

The walls of archaic Rome that have become so elusive in our discussion up to this point have once again become the subject of attention in the excavations on the east side of the Palatine facing the Velia, at the edge of what appears to be the lower slope of the hill immediately above a sharp drop into the gully at the head of the Forum Valley.[35]

The first in this series of walls girdling the lower slope of the Palatine was a small rubble construction bedded into a trench cut in the clay subsoil (fig. 7.7). The pottery associated with the fill of the foundation dates the wall about 725. Either at the time of building or immediately thereafter a young girl was buried here. If the tomb was made subsequent to the construction of the wall, the wall would have been partially dismantled for the purpose. The alternative, that the tomb existed before the wall, is thus a stronger possibility.

Soon the low rubble wall was replaced by a new rubble structure which endured until about 675 when it was succeeded by a third wall of the same character that remained in place until 600. None of these walls could have been a defense wall. They were too low and too lightly built for the purpose. They may, however, and do in the interpretation of the excavator, represent a ritualized boundary surrounding the Palatine. This view finds support in the fact that for a distance of 50 Roman feet inside the walls an open zone was kept free of building. This circumstance increases the possibility that we have to do with the primitive *pomerium* (ritually defined boundary) of the

Palatine. The inner limit of the pomerium was marked by a line of stakes of which the post holes remain.

In the sixth century the outer line of demarcation was maintained by a masonry wall which was rebuilt during the course of the century. The excavator stresses that these walls did not support a terrace on the uphill side; they were freestanding. Being only one course thick, they are not fortifications but seem to have prolonged the life of the line of demarcation originally set out in the eighth century.

About 530 the gully below these early walls was filled in and the area was given over to the building of *atrium* houses (see Chapter 4). The area above the former gully now carried a street running down to the Forum. This street was provided with a covered drain. It follows the line of what is generally considered to have been the Sacra Via.

APPENDIX: The walls of Veii

Any treatment of the Servian Walls must take account of the walls of Veii, studied during the British research on the site. The masonry tufa walls backed by an *agger* are similar to the Servian Walls and are dated by the excavators to the late fifth century on the basis of the excavation of one section at the northwest gate of the city.[36] Here the wall was built across the remains of houses. The interpretation of the excavators is that the building of the walls followed closely on the destruction of the houses. The same walls, moreover, were "The walls that defied the armies of Camillus" (referring to the ten years' struggle between Rome and Veii leading to the victory of the Romans under M. Furius Camillus in 396). One may wonder, however, whether this conclusion, natural though it is, has not been reached with a subconscious desire to see the great events of history reflected in the remains of the excavation. Archaeologically, we know that the walls belong to the end of the fifth century or possibly later. Town life at Veii did not come to an end in 396, as the work of the British team so amply proved. What if the burnt houses below the walls at the northwest gate, rather than the walls built over them, are the witnesses to the Roman conquest? Certainly the material associated with the building of the walls does not exclude a date after 396.

The fortifying of satellite communities of Rome at a later date has now been shown by discoveries at La Rustica.[37] Here stout defense walls were erected around the small community of the fourth century, in the face of danger, possibly the Umbrian threat of 308. One must not exclude such a later situation as the occasion for the building of the masonry defenses found at Veii.[38]

8

OSTERIA DELL'OSA

The road to Praeneste 17.5 km (11 mi.) east of Rome passes between the basins of two lakes: to the south Lake Regillus, drained in the seventeenth century but still memorable as the site of the battle between Romans and Latins reputed to have taken place in 496; to the north Lake Gabino (Castiglione) which occupied a volcanic crater until it too was drained for farm land in the nineteenth century. The waters of the lakes fed the Fosso dell'Osa and the Fosso di San Giuliano, which, in turn, drain into the Anio midway in its course between Tivoli and the Tiber.

The isthmus between the two lakes was the site of ancient Gabii, where the walls of the late Republican temple still form a conspicuous landmark. Controlling the road to Praeneste and so south to the Sacco–Liris Valley before the creation of the Via Casilina (running south of Lake Regillus), Gabii was an important place. Its early development is now known from reconnaissance and from the excavation of two cemeteries. On the isthmus there are six areas of presumed Iron Age habitation and others extending along the rim of the cliffs above the crater of Lake Gabino.[1] The two cemeteries are located at the extremities of this arc of settlement. The Castiglione cemetery, situated within the depression of Lake Gabino, is rather close to the last of the Iron Age hamlets along the arc of the cliff.[2] The cemetery of Osteria dell'Osa, on a ridge beyond the opposite side of the Lake Gabino depression, is divided from the nearest traces of settlement by almost 0.5 km (0.3 mi.).[3]

Sixty tombs are known from the Castiglione cemetery. In the main group, comprising twenty-four tombs, there are three cremations, the others inhumations, mostly of women, together with two children. The tomb goods are made up exclusively of handmade vessels; the bronzes are few. All the tombs belong to Latian Period IIA, extending perhaps to the very beginning of IIB.

It is the Osteria dell'Osa cemetery that has provided the outstanding evidence for the Iron Age from Gabii. The excavation was carried out between 1971 and 1986 during which time six hundred tombs were brought to light. They span the period from Latian IIA to Latian IV, beginning with cremation and inhumation graves of the ninth century and ending with chamber tombs of the early sixth century. The major part of the tombs and the importance of the cemetery is in the Latian Periods II and III, the ninth and eighth centuries, for it is at Osa, as in no other site or excavation from ancient Latium, that one can appreciate the swift and far-reaching changes in the structure of a community of the time. This excavation, therefore, is a great step forward, transforming the archaeological record into an historical document. It is the first major cemetery of ancient Latium to have been published since the end of Boni's reports from the Roman Forum in 1911.[4] This achievement is due to the tenacity and vision of the leader of the major series of campaigns, Dr Anna Maria Bietti Sestieri. The exhaustive and searching fashion in which she has treated her discoveries reminds one of Boni, but with a great difference. The point of view of her distinguished predecessor was founded in nineteenth-century natural science, both Pigorini's paleoethnography and the biological sciences, allied with the traditional view that the archaeologist's first duty was to interpret the remains as an illustration of ancient tradition and a sense of honor in the face of the grand ancestry of ancient Rome and modern Italy. Indeed Italian archaeology, both of the classical world and of its protohistory, like archaeology in Germany to which it has a long-standing debt of influence, has remained intellectually anchored to an outlook with which Boni would feel at home. Dr Sestieri's work is part of a new trend centered on the interest in social organization and its manifestations that has animated American and British archaeology since the 1960s. It is the fate of historical studies, and especially archaeology, to react to intellectual stimuli only after some delay. If Boni and his contemporaries, with their nationalist zeal and desire to further the application of empirical science, were children of the French Revolution, today's "New Archaeology" is the heir of Proudhon and Karl Marx. In the United States there is a direct line of descent to the "New Archaeologists" through Friedrich Engels, writing in English, and the nineteenth-century American anthropologist Lewis Henry Morgan, whose *Ancient Society* touched early Rome by showing the similarity between the expanding Roman commonwealth and the confederation of the Iroquois.[5] For all the reluctance of most elements in the United States to register anything but suspicion, if not hostility, toward European socialism, one should not forget that the same country has a polemical social conscience and a long tradition of distrust of social distinctions and privileges. The founders of the "New Archaeology" were by and large children of the Great Depression when the economic issues that became paramount in their studies were matters of daily survival. Both the aggressive tone and populist tinge of the "New Archaeology" come from these sources. Dr Bietti Sestieri's approach to Osteria dell'Osa has profited from the stimulus of this American-born movement without falling prey to its excesses, notably the tendency to put theory before the evidence (producing suspiciously consistent confirmation of preconceived ideas). Her work is solid and reliable.[6]

At Osteria dell'Osa the cemetery can be divided into fourteen clusters. Two of the earliest, belonging to the ninth century, are located in the northwest area of the cemetery (fig. 8.1). For convenience they may be referred to as the "northern" and the "southern" group. In both the tombs are evenly spaced and rarely disturb a neighboring grave. Inhumation and cremation are both present. The cremations, exclusively of men, are usually *pozzo* graves with a large vessel (the *dolium*) containing the ash urn and grave goods. This is the type of tomb which we have already seen in the Roman Forum and which is characteristic of early Latium. Occasionally the *dolium* was placed in a small rectangular pit. The *fossa* graves once again recall the situation in the Forum. The pottery of the cemetery is exactly what might be expected of a town midway between Rome and the Alban Hills. A tomb such as no. 131, a man's cremation grave,[7] has a hut urn and group of miniature vessels that would have been at home either in the Forum or in the Alban Hills. At Osteria dell'Osa in the portion of the cemetery under consideration all the male cremations were given miniature fittings (with four exceptions, Tombs 103, 138, 152, 154). In Tomb 131 we find miniatures reproducing three storage jars, a two-handled vessel on a high foot (for wine or other liquids), a cup, bowl, and condiment jar. The bronzes with the burial comprised a serpent-arch fibula with disc foot, the typical man's fibula, a lance head and a pair of tweezers. Bronze razors are often found with men's graves – the male citizen of ninth-century Gabii was evidently clean-shaven.

A woman's inhumation tomb, no. 144, had vases of a different character. They are normal size. Like the man, the lady had open bowls and cups, although more of them. But the containers are different and there is an unmistakably feminine article, the spindle whorl, recalling the constant activity of spinning wool which was the lot of peasant women of the Mediterranean down to our own day. The fibula (fastening the shroud or garment) was also the female or thickened-arch type.

The extent of excavation at Osteria dell'Osa has allowed for an analysis of the cemetery of the kind that Boni could not undertake. The northern and southern groups of the cluster under discussion are distinguished by mutually exclusive characteristics, as summarized by Bietti Sestieri:[8]

Specific features of the North group [central] cremations (graves 135, 137, 138, 139):

- the filling of the pit includes a large slab of yellowish travertine crust, usually just above the mouth of the *dolium*.
- in each grave, the bowl contains the same portion of meat, three or four caprovine ribs.
- all the fibulae (that are present in the three graves) belong to the *arco serpeggiante* type with disc-foot; the razors (in four graves) are

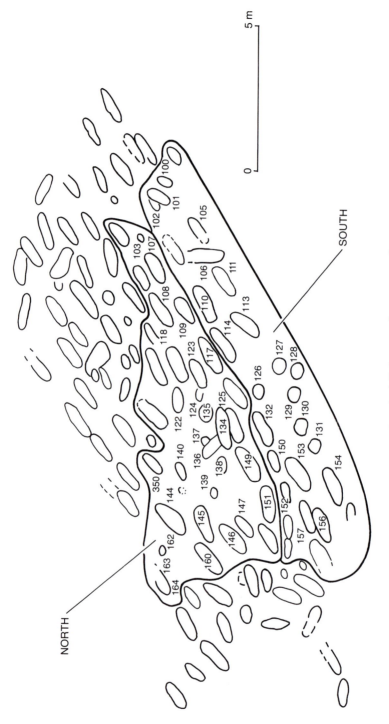

Figure 8.1 Osteria dell'Osa, northwest area of cemetery.

quadrangular; the spear-heads (in two graves) are of the socketed type with wooden stick.

- the pottery manufacture is extremely accurate and the majority of the vases are decorated; plastic motifs are quite frequent.
- the hut-urn appears in one case only (grave 137); in two graves (135, 139), the liquid container is a two-handled vase set on a high stand or *calefattoio*.

Specific features of the South group [central] cremations (graves 126–131):

- the filling of the pits includes two or more small white pebbles; in the majority of the graves, the upper layer of the filling is arranged in a ring of pebbles; the mouth of the *dolium* is covered by an *impasto* lid.
- the only preserved evidence of meat being included in the funerary offerings is a fragment of deer femur in the urn of grave 126.
- the fibulae are present in five graves out of six and belong to the so-called Sicilian type (*arco serpeggiante* with symmetrical foot); the razor (in one grave only) belongs to a lunate type; in another grave it is probably replaced by tweezers; the spears (in six graves) are all cast in one piece.
- the pottery manufacture generally is less accurate than in the North group; many of the pieces are not decorated; the existing decorations are incised, while plastic motifs are nearly absent.
- the hut-urn appears in all the graves; in five graves, the liquid container is a two-handled vase on a high conical foot.

The obvious inference is that the two groups are the graves of two different families, each with its own traditions. Granting this distinction is established, one can also appreciate the similar organization of the burial plots of the two groups. The center of each group of tombs is occupied by a group of men who were cremated (South 126–131, North 135, 137, 138, 139). Around these are grouped inhumations of adult women (South 113, 114, 132, 153, 154, North 123, 134, 145, 147, 149). In the North group they are joined by children (122, 124, 136, 140) and inhumed men (146, 151). The young women (12–20 years) are at the periphery (South 156, North 117, 163, 350). With them are other adult women, but possibly these are graves slightly later than the first burials of the group (South 106, 111, North 108, 118, 160). Here too are male inhumations, mostly of young men (South 102, 105, 110, North 107, 125) and children (South 100, 101, 150, 152, North 109, possibly 172 and 173). Infants were buried as part of the family. There are three male cremations at the edge of the group (North 103, 162, 164).[9]

The cremation graves in the center of the family groups, as interpreted by the excavator, represent men of authority, the *paterfamilias*. It is with these individuals that the symbolic miniature objects are buried, the house itself, either the complete house model or a jar covered with a hut roof to hold the ashes. The *paterfamilias* as warrior is emphasized by miniature weapons, as priest possibly by knives (Tombs 126, 127, 139) and the statuette with extended hand in an offering gesture (Tomb 126).

Miniaturization of grave goods, best known from the tombs of the Alban Hill communities, was on the wane in the ninth century and an important cremation grave in the North group (138) is already furnished with a set of full-size objects.[10]

Inhumations of men surrounding the central cremation tombs appear to be the graves of individuals still in the family and directly under their father's authority (*patria potestas*).

The women follow a congruent pattern of rank in the family. Concentrated around the *patres* in the central group are the well-supplied inhumations of adult women. One of them (South 153) also contained a knife, perhaps marking the grave of a priestess.

Young women on the periphery received particularly lavish burials containing objects of bronze and amber and glass paste ornaments. Such attention may well have been accorded nubile girls who died before marriage. Preadolescent girls were usually given a spindle whorl, often decorated, in addition to other grave goods, especially a biconical jug which seems to accompany the whorl in what Bietti Sestieri calls a "weaving set." A few women (Tombs 123, 147, 157) had poor burials, as preserved in the archaeological record – but may have been well equipped with perishable items in wood, leather, or cloth.

Such is the aspect of two small families of early Gabii as they appear equipped and arranged in death. The community to which they belonged would have been composed of several such families sharing a common culture but distinct in its expression such as one sees in the different details of the pottery of the two groups, in each case apparently made by a family member.

Change, however, was in the air. The beliefs expressed by the miniature funeral equipment were weakening around 800 and social organization was about to undergo a major transformation.

Another group of some sixty tombs located about 50 m (164 ft) from the first takes us into the eighth century and the Latian Period III (fig. 8.2). The graves were massed together. Intrusion of one into another is frequent. In some cases there was little left of the earlier grave or of its occupant. There was only one cremation, the grave of a woman in the center of the group (no. 259) paired with a man's inhumation (no. 262) and possibly representing the founders of this group. Placement of tombs with respect to rules of age, sex, and authority is no longer evident. Consistency of funeral gifts for men and women and age levels has been lost. Compared with the North group of the ninth century it seems that the identity of the individual has become lost in a crowd. But there was an apparent desire to place graves within a restricted area, which somehow identified them with others buried there. Let Dr Bietti Sestieri draw her conclusions from this striking change.[11]

The identification of the specific type of group affiliation documented by these graves is not beyond doubt: however, it is reasonably certain that we are dealing with a kinship structure; the subdivision of the graves by roughly separate clusters probably indicates the co-existence of different branches. The indicators of individual role and wealth are too scanty to allow the identification of consistent differences among these clusters; as regards the individual burials, it is not possible to decide whether the occurrence of graves with no funerary outfit relates to a structural difference in status among the members of the group (as seems probable) or is just another confirmation of the limited emphasis on individual attributions in the funerary ritual of this group.

However, it is at least possible to propose the hypothesis that these characteristics reflect the emergence and the earliest formation of a *gens* with its hierarchical structure, as we know it in the Latin society since the archaic period. In the wider context of the cemetery, the difference in ritual and funerary behaviour between the central group and the other contemporary graves probably indicated the beginning of a process of social stratification, based on the competition among the individual family groups which constituted the community since

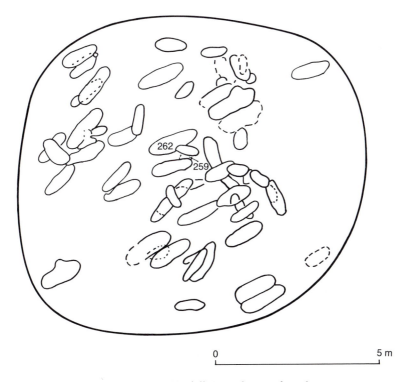

Figure 8.2 Osteria dell'Osa, cluster of tombs.

109

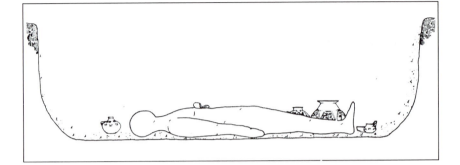

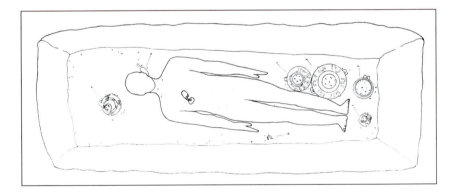

Figure 8.3 Osteria dell'Osa, Tomb 482–483, initial deposition.

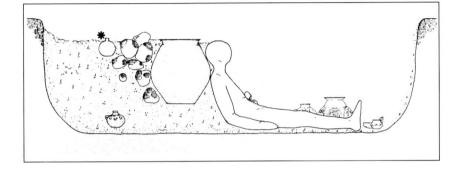

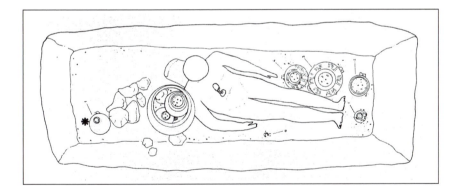

Figure 8.4 Osteria dell'Osa, Tomb 482–483, state after insertion of cremation burial. The star marks the vase with a graffito.

the 9th century and on the internal structuring and organization of some groups in contrast to others.[12]

In the cemetery of Osteria dell'Osa a pair of burials was made in a single *fossa*. The burials are contemporary, both belonging to the end of Period IIB about 770. From this tomb comes the earliest evidence of the use of the alphabet in Italy. The sequence of burials was this. First a man was inhumed in the *fossa* (fig. 8.3). The grave was left open and subsequently received the cremation of a woman, presumably his wife (fig. 8.4). The man's body and his funeral goods were rearranged for the purpose. All the woman's grave goods save two vases were contained, with the ash urn, in a *dolium*. One of the vessels placed outside the *dolium* was a globular-bodied vase with a low neck and a single handle. The graffito on its body is composed of five letters (fig. 8.5). Four (1, 2, 4, 5) are clearly E, Y, I, N. The third letter may be read as *lambda*, or, if the right arm of the *upsilon* did double duty as a side for the same letter, it could be a rectangular *omicron*. Since no composite letter is present, the place of the alphabet of the graffito within the various particular Greek alphabets is not certain, but the straight-line *iota* would agree with the Euboean practice. Despite the temptation to read the inscription εὔοιν[ος it is not certainly Greek. An Etruscan name perhaps, possibly a Latin name or one from another Italic dialect; these are the solutions preferred by A. La Regina in his presentation of the inscription, reading letter 3 as *lambda*.[13] The uncertainty of interpretation does not detract from the revolutionary importance of this document. In the first half of the eighth century a woman was buried in inland Latium with a vase bearing an alphabetic graffito which is at least a generation older than the earliest known inscription in Greece or in the Greek colonies of the west.[14]

Figure 8.5 Osteria dell'Osa, Tomb 482, graffito.

Objects from the Osteria dell'Osa cemetery point to the contacts of the community with the outside world. Amber, prized for its magical properties, came from the Baltic Sea. Four vases point to contact with Campania to the south or with the Villanovans closer at hand west of the Tiber. They are significant because they were made at Osa. Thus, like the graffito on the vase from Tomb 482, they show the presence of foreigners in the population of the town and their integration into this Latin community.

The first tomb discovered at Osteria dell'Osa, in 1889, provided a well preserved wooden coffin. It was a burial of the seventh century and included among the gifts was a silver jug of Cypro-Phoenician type.[15] A grave found more recently, but as a result of plowing outside the excavation area, belonged to a warrior whose equipment makes it appear that he was a Villanovan resident at Gabii. As Bietti Sestieri describes the tomb:[16]

> The grave-goods (or, at least, those which had been preserved) included a whole set of bronze-sheet vessels: the cinerary urn (a biconical or globular vase with two handles), a large helmet of Villanovan type, probably functioning as the urn's lid, three bowls, a four-wheeled stand, along with a sword and an iron spear-head. This burial belongs to a well-known category of warriors' graves, all dating from the last decades of the 8th century, which have been found in some of the main cemeteries of ancient Lazio (Latium) . . . and in southern Etruria.[17]

In Period II inhumation burial at Osteria dell'Osa was carried out in several stages. First the body was placed in the *fossa* in an extended position. The trench was left open until the muscles and ligaments gave way. The body was then rearranged. Finally the fossa was filled with earth and pebbles. Bietti Sestieri supposes that the rearrangement of the bones assisted in reassuring the living that the spirit did not have physical means to harm them.[18] There are also cases of unusually large and heavy tufa slabs placed directly above the body. This practice also hints directly at the desire to protect the living from the dead. In the eighth century men's urns were often surrounded by some small pieces of white travertine. In a single case a woman's grave was fitted in this way (no. 476). The occupant also wore a belt from which hung a piece of iron and a perforated bear's tooth. She was an uncommon person, whose powers crossed into the male sphere.[19]

9

CASTEL DI DECIMA; ACQUA ACETOSA, LAURENTINA; FICANA; AND CRUSTUMERIUM

CASTEL DI DECIMA

What Osteria dell'Osa has done for our knowledge of Latian society in the ninth and eighth centuries, two other recently discovered cemeteries, Castel di Decima and Acqua Acetosa, Laurentina, amplify for the seventh century. Of the two Castel di Decima has attracted more attention. The excavation was begun when the main road from Rome to Terracina, before the building of the Autostrada del Sole in the 1960s a major artery between Rome and Naples, was widened in 1971. It was a sobering thought for more than one Roman motorist and the archaeologists among them to realize that they had been driving over one of the richest cemeteries of the orientalizing age in Italy (the period of Near Eastern imports and influence). The "Casale" (big house) "at the tenth mile stone" was built beside the Roman road that cut a straight line through the countryside. The wide curve of the modern road passes along the rising ground to the west, skirting the edge of the woods of the formerly royal and now presidential hunting preserve of Castel Porziano. The excavation, which continued until 1975, was beset by all the difficulties of a rescue operation. The work was confined in a long band following the road's right of way; much of the cemetery is still to be explored. Worse still, the cemetery straddles the boundary between the Archaeological Superintendency of Rome and that of Ostia, each of which carried out part of the work. Publication of the results of the excavation is still in its initial stages. However, a wide selection of the material was presented at the exhibition Civiltà del Lazio Primitivo (Civilization of Early Latium) in 1976, for the first time illustrating the wealth of the seventh century at the very gates of Rome. An excellent interpretation of the results has also been made by Prof. Fausto Zevi, who was formerly Superintendent at Ostia.[1]

From Decima there are three hundred tombs, half of these belonging to the end of the eighth and seventh centuries, Latian IV (fig. 9.1). None is later than about 600. From the beginning of the cemetery to the end of its life the form of burial is the same: inhumation in *fossae* with a covering of stones or,

114

in the early sixth century, simply of earth. The nearby settlement had its origins at the beginning of the eighth century. The necropolis does not present a compact mass of tombs. Rather, it spreads out from the nucleus of the eighth century in small clusters of graves. The early graves were frequently invaded by tombs of the seventh century. There is a wide difference in funeral goods, the rich burials at one end of the scale and, in the majority, burials without grave goods or with only modest personal ornaments in bronze. To accommodate a growing number of grave goods, the richer tombs of Period III begin to have a niche hollowed out at the side of the *fossa* to the right of the corpse. The niche is no longer found in tombs at Castel di Decima after the end of the eighth century, although it lives on at other nearby cemeteries, Acqua Acetosa, Laurentina, and Riserva del Truglio. At the same time as it loses the niche, the *fossa* tends to be enlarged for the richer burials, which will be the subject of discussion from this point on.

The grave goods continue to be placed on the right side of the dead person. The tombs of men and women are clearly distinguished. The women were elaborately dressed, occasionally wearing gold jewelry such as fibulae which also occur in silver or ornamented with discs of amber. Fifteen women had objects of silver in their graves, but only two men. Two women had faience scarabs. Their robes were resplendent with amber and glass paste beads. Their hair was dressed in locks bound with silver wire coils (and in only one case bronze). The discovery of fibulae lying beside women's heads shows that they were wrapped in a mantle or shawl, while their main garment was held by two large fibulae, one at each shoulder. When present the silver fibulae are placed on the breast. Large ornamental bronze rings are of particular interest. The largest, made of thin bronze sheet, reach 42 cm (1.4 ft) in diameter. They were held in place by a fibula. Women were also buried with the instruments of domestic industry. Clay spindle whorls are numerous and there are four work baskets originally in wood, now decayed, but shown to have existed by the bronze strips with cutout designs that covered them. There were certainly others in simple wood or basketwork.

Men wore a garment fastened by a single fibula (generally of the "dragon" type descended from the serpent fibulae of Period II) usually on the right shoulder. They wore bronze bracelets suggesting a sleeveless garment. Arms are an almost universal part of the tomb groups. There is a lance in thirty-four of forty-four tombs; it was probably present in five others. Swords are less frequent. The lance was generally placed on the right side of the corpse point down (a position with the point laid upwards does occur). Sword and lance together appear in the very rich tombs, for example tombs with a chariot. Six light two-wheeled chariots are known from Decima, including one from a woman's tomb (no. 101). The sword was placed either at the head or at the feet.

As in Etruria of the orientalizing age, Latin tombs contained shields

Figure 9.1 Castel di Decima, Tomb 153.

covered in thin bronze sheet decorated in repoussé. Tomb 21 at Castel di Decima is typical of these. This was a warrior's tomb in which there was found a chariot, a lance (fitted both with a bronze head and with a pointed foot spike or *sauroter*), an iron sword with bronze-covered sheath, and a rectangular bronze breastplate. Directly over the body were laid three bronze-covered shields. Such objects, however, became more symbolic than functional. A woman's burial at Acqua Acetosa, Laurentina, as we shall see shortly, also contained three shields, placed along the wall of the tomb. Such shields in Etruria and Latium became wall hangings, and at the same time weapons were no longer buried with the dead. It is worth mentioning that the bronze spearhead was not a functional weapon at the time, when blades were all iron, but rather a symbolic reminder of a heroized past. Indeed, during the seventh century (Period IV) it is convivial display rather than the equipment of war that comes to dominate men's funeral goods. The size of the tomb is increased and the niche or *loculus* disappears. In the tombs one now finds large pottery stands made with perforated walls so that they imitate the lattice of folding bronze stands also known at Decima (figs 9.2, 9.3). These *holmoi* supported mixing bowls – known elsewhere with plastic griffin heads copying the imported bronzes such as are known from the Bernardini Tomb at Praeneste (see Chapter 12). The group of vases illustrated in fig. 9.3 was found with a *holmos* in a dump from the settlement at Ficana.[2] Similar are mixing bowls made together with their stand. These vessels, clearly intended for mixing and dispensing wine, when in the tomb seem to be the exclusive property of women, and from the same tombs come Punic amphorae showing a preference for what may be a Sardinian product among the imported vintages in Latium (fig. 9.4).[3] The popularity in the seventh century of a red surface for pottery may also be an imitation of the red-surfaced Punic wares. Greek pottery reached Decima in the last quarter of the eighth century (Thapsos cups, fig. 9.5) and there are Protocorinthian vases from the early seventh century. The tombs with the large wine-mixing bowls also have a wealth of cups and jugs and small amphorae (fig. 9.6), all now made by professional potters on the fast wheel. Family-made, hand-formed pottery is a thing of the past.

The Latian matron of the orientalizing age steps forth from the tombs of Castel di Decima in a role quite different from her later Republican counterpart but similar to her contemporaries in Etruria. She is mistress of the banquet and dispenser of wine. We may suppose that she drove her own chariot (and at times recklessly like Tullia of legend, the ambitious daughter of King Servius who drove on even when her father's dead body lay in her way). In her tomb the Latian matron could display shields like a man. The realization of the dynamic role of these ladies in early Latium, corresponding to tradition, has been one of the important results of the excavations at Decima and at Acqua Acetosa, Laurentina.

The excavations at Decima have also revealed evidence of funeral ritual.

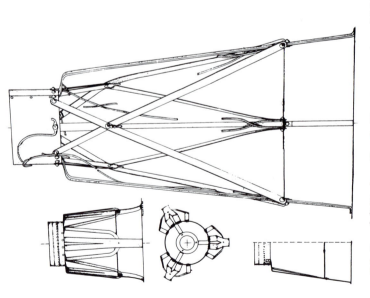

Figure 9.3 Ficana, group of vases belonging to a banquet service. The *holmos* in the center is derived from the oriental/ Greek griffin cauldron. The two-handled red *impasto* cup (d) has the form of a Greek *kotyle* embellished with the central Italian version of orientalizing decoration.

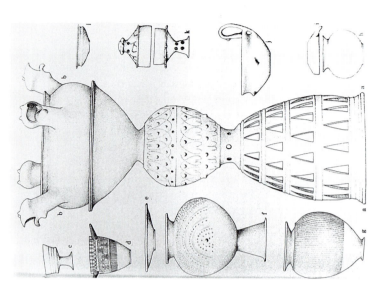

Figure 9.2 Castel di Decima, Tomb 15, reconstruction of fold-ing bronze tripod stand.

Figure 9.4 Castel di Decima, Punic amphora.

Figure 9.5 Castel di Decima, Corinthian "Thapsos Cup," Tomb 15.

Figure 9.6 Castel di Decima, Latian amphora with spiral decoration, Tomb 14.

During or at the end of the ceremony, various vessels were broken and the pieces thrown into the tomb. This happened after the corpse was placed in the *fossa* but before the grave goods were deposited. This practice of offering libations of wine to the dead is concentrated in the first half of the seventh century and has been noted in thirty tombs. The vessels employed are typically the small Latian amphorae decorated with incised spirals. Etruscan wares, although present among the grave goods, were never used for the ritual.

In the later orientalizing (Latian IVB) period, the tomb furniture becomes less numerous and less costly. Around 600 the life of the cemetery, as known at present, ends. It is important to note that the town at Castel di Decima continued to exist.[4] Its later tombs must be elsewhere.

ACQUA ACETOSA, LAURENTINA

If Castel di Decima seems close to Rome, Acqua Acetosa on the Via Laurentina near Tor dei Cenci, and within walking distance of Castel di Decima, is almost within sight of the ring road around the city.[5] Here 175 tombs have already been recovered, and others await excavation. The cemetery begins, like Castel di Decima's, in the early eighth century (Latian Period IIB). Unlike the cemetery of Castel di Decima, burials at Acqua Acetosa, Laurentina were still being made in the sixth century. The burials are inhumations. The same increase in expenditure for tomb furniture is found as at Castel di Decima. As was true at Decima, libations were poured during the funeral. There are, moreover, substantial traces of food given to the dead: lamb and goat, together with roasting spits for it.

More accentuated than at Castel di Decima is the development of the spatial distribution of the tombs. From the last quarter of the eighth century (Latian Period IV) a distance of up to 30 m (almost 100 ft) was left around conspicuous tombs for less important burials – for persons presumably related by blood or dependency to the occupant of the main tomb. The great tombs became underground houses, rectangular in plan and covered by a roof of wooden beams under a dirt fill. The corpse was placed on a couch-like pedestal of earth or on a wooden funeral bed (fig. 9.7). The grave goods were arranged to the right of the body. The richness of individual sets of offerings matches those of Castel di Decima and in the eighth century reference to wine and conviviality is strongly felt.

A woman's chariot from Tomb 70 is especially noteworthy (fig. 9.8). Unlike the small chariots documented elsewhere, this is a carriage with large wheels. Like the smaller chariots it was driven from a box and the forklike object found with the other parts of the chariot may be the top of an accessory to hold or separate the reins. The wheels of the chariot had six spokes. Their iron tires were secured by nails leaving the heads projecting for traction. The same detail is known from representations of Assyrian

Figure 9.7 Acqua Acetosa, Laurentina, Tomb 70.

chariots of the eighth century, which are also large wheeled vehicles. The axle was fixed to the wheels and turned (inside some kind of lubricated pad) through iron bands which were attached to the undercarriage.

The tombs of the sixth century, otherwise so difficult to locate in Latium, can be identified at Acqua Acetosa, Laurentina. They lack tomb goods – which must have been the general situation in tombs of this and the succeeding century – but at Acqua Acetosa, Laurentina the tradition of the underground chamber was kept up. The development of tomb architecture, however, sets these chambers apart from their seventh-century predecessors. The tombs are deeper and, instead of the couch-like pedestal, they have post holes in the floor for a funeral bed.

The results of these excavations are matched by the cemeteries of the eighth and seventh centuries at La Rustica (Tor Sapienza) and Ficana, as well as by scattered tombs elsewhere.[6] The same span of time is represented in the eighty-three tombs from Tivoli.[7] Grouped inside grave circles delimited by a low wall, after the fashion in the Sabine region to the east of the Tiber, these tombs still await publication. A special place in Latian archaeology is held by the necropolis of Praeneste, to which we shall return in a later chapter.[8]

Figure 9.8 Acqua Acetosa, Laurentina, reconstructed chariot from Tomb 70.

FICANA

Some 10 km (6.6 mi.) from the sea where the Tiber swings from its lower course temporarily toward the south, a low hill, Monte Cugno, rises close to its left bank. This site corresponds to the ancient Ficana, known to have been located 11 Roman miles from the city on the Via Ostiensis. This information comes directly from Marcus Antistius Labeo, the learned jurist of the age of Augustus, through Festus (298, 8 L) and it is worth quoting: "Fabius Pictor says that Puilia Saxa is located at a landing spot along the Tiber: Labeo believes this is the name of the spot where Ficana stood, at the eleventh milestone on the Via Ostiensis."[9] Fate has kindly preserved from nearby this very eleventh milestone of the Via Ostiensis, which was set up, to judge from the writing of the inscription, in the third century.[10] In the same neighborhood there has also been found a dedication to Mars Ficanus.[11]

The archaeology of Ficana is typical of the river towns along the Tiber. It is not a large site, occupying some 5 hectares (12.3 acres). Traces of occupation begin with Proto-Villanovan sherds. Cremation graves begin with *pozzo* burials of the Latian Period I. An *agger*, fronted by a *fossa*, ran across the western, more approachable, part of the site. The pottery from the fill of the *agger* places the date of this defensive work in the eighth century. To the Iron Age also belongs a single remarkable building. It is 21.5 m (70 ft) long and 3 m (10 ft) wide. It is not rectilinear but rather has the outline of a sausage-shaped balloon curving slightly to one side along its length. The floor was sunk below ground level. Further simple houses belong to the end of the eighth and the seventh century. One is oval (width 9 m, 29.5 ft) like the buildings at Lavinium and Satricum. Two show a rectangular plan, but with rounded corners. Four large posts placed in a square supported the roof. The walls and roof were wattle and daub construction. One of these buildings measures 6 × 12 m (19.6 × 39.2 ft), the other 6 × 7.5 m (19.6 × 24.6 ft). Beginning in the second half of the seventh century, such buildings were gradually replaced by houses built with stone socle walls and tile roofs. The construction of the walls varies from rectangular cut blocks to rubble construction. No complete plan is known but the buildings, of which two are well defined, belong to the courtyard/portico type and may be compared to the examples from Etruria and elsewhere in Latium (Satricum, Rome, Torrino).[12] One house is outside the line of the agger, and it is uncertain, though likely, that the early defense line was replaced in this period by stone walls.[13] Architectural decoration in terracotta is not lacking, but the remains are few and scattered. The most important is a female head antefix of the "Ionian" type comparable to the first series of Satricum. There are also fragments of a frieze with chariots.

The documentation of tombs outside the settlement area is restricted to *fossa* tombs of the seventh century. But within the settlement children's tombs are found in the sixth and fifth centuries as well. Indeed there is apparently no complete hiatus in the life of the community. The Roman king Ancus Marcius, according to ancient tradition, took Ficana and deported its population.[14] Whatever the worth of such traditions, the archaeology of the site does not support them, although an effort has been made to reconcile the disagreement by supposing exaggeration of the completeness of the sack.[15]

CRUSTUMERIUM

The Roman campagna has long been the object of archaeological reconnaissance. A century ago the excursions of Nibby, Ashby, and Comparetti were ventures into an underpopulated moorland that stretched to the Alban Hills on the south and the Sabine mountains on the east. The moors are fast disappearing as the modern metropolis of Rome swallows up ever more of its surroundings. The march of concrete and asphalt means that survey work carried out since the Second World War has been done just in the nick of time. An example of what surface archaeology could do was given by the south Etruria survey of the British School in Rome in the late 1940s and 1950s. In the following two decades the area along the left bank of the Tiber facing the territory of Veii across the river was investigated by two young archaeologists, Lorenzo Quilici and Stefania Quilici-Gigli. The Quilicis have published a series of volumes dealing with the river towns along this stretch of the Tiber (Antemnae, Fidenae, and Crustumerium) and one community situated deeper in the campagna (Ficulea) (fig. 0.2).[16]

Survey is the wide-angle lens of archaeology. By searching the surface it locates structures that are still above ground. And surface scatters of sherds, brick, and worked stone are a guide, if not a complete inventory, to what lies below the surface. Survey work emphasizes topography, roads, settlement density, and settlement pattern. It can never replace excavation, though this claim is sometimes heard; no site should be excavated without taking account of the wider setting surrounding it. The periphery illuminates the center. And the Quilicis' work in particular has shown how the Latin communities along the river, of which initially Rome was only one, developed.

The site of Crustumerium is not the upriver town closest to Rome. Much nearer was Antemnae, situated on the bluff where the Anio River, which descends from the Sabine Hills at Tivoli before crossing the Roman campagna, joins the Tiber. The site of Antemnae was seriously disturbed when the Italian army constructed a fort there in the 1880s, and it has now been surrounded by the advance of modern Rome. Upstream 5 km from Antemnae is Fidenae, another archaic Latin community, and after another 5 km Crustumerium. Like Antemnae, both occupied hills overlooking the river and could have controlled ferries crossing the Tiber. The development of these early communities can be studied from the Quilicis' investigations at any of these three sites, but Crustumerium offers what is probably the clearest picture.

At the time of its maximum development, just before the Gallic invasion reached the outskirts of Rome in 387 BC, the city of Crustumerium proper occupied a ridge about 1 km long. The town was defended by an *agger* and *fossa*. The *fossa* is still to be seen running for a length of 900 m (almost 3,000 ft) along the eastern side of the site where the gentler slope of the hill made it necessary to give the town additional protection. By that time a secondary settlement had been spawned on a hill just to the north and another had grown up beside the Via Salaria which skirts the bluff along the east bank of the Tiber's flood plain.

The Bronze Age has left its traces at Crustumerium, but the scatter of sherds becomes sufficiently dense to show the outlines of the town only in the Latian IIA–B period (ninth century BC) (fig. 9.9). There were two nuclei of settlement on the crest of the hill. By the late eighth century (Period III) these had both grown, and satellite occupation is found to the north and west, in the direction of the river. The occupation of the country becomes apparent in the seventh and early sixth centuries (Period IV), the time when the town proper reached the natural limits of the hill (fig. 9.10). The farmsteads and hamlets of the countryside multiplied in the sixth and fifth centuries (fig. 9.11). It was a time of prosperity reflected in chamber tombs and in one extravagant monument, the large tumulus, diameter 20 m (65.6 ft) at the base, located 1 km southeast along the road to Ficulea and Gabii.[17] This situation remained stable in the fifth century until the Gallic invasion. The Roman army met the Gauls at the River Allia, hardly a kilometer north of the city, and was routed by the invaders. After this disaster the area around Crustumerium seems to have recovered slowly, the population of the countryside not reaching the density of the pre-Gallic period until the second century AD. The town never recovered.

If Crustumerium is taken as a paradigm for Rome, one finds, not unexpectedly, an original Iron Age settlement of separate nuclei, some of which remain isolated even after the main site reached its natural limits. Similarly at Rome the Aventine was probably included within the perimeter of Roman defenses only at a late date (one might argue as late as the third century).[18] What is less apparent in the metropolis but is well documented at Crustumerium is the occupation of the countryside in the seventh and sixth centuries. Isolated villas of the archaic age are also known in the interior of the campagna and recent research has brought to light traces of the extensive network of roads which linked them.[19] The sudden appearance of wealthy tombs in Latium in the seventh century is thus only one aspect of the changing world of the period. Another is demography, growing population and a filling-up of the countryside. As survey work, such as that of the Quilicis, proceeds from sites along the river to the interior sites of Latium,

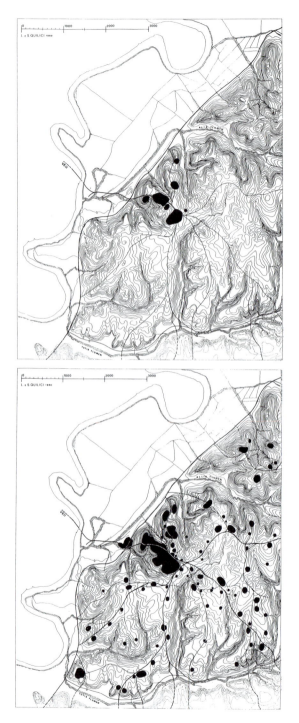

Figure 9.9
Crustumerium and sur-
rounding area in the
Latian II B period.

Figure 9.10
Crustumerium and sur-
rounding area in the
Latian IV B period.

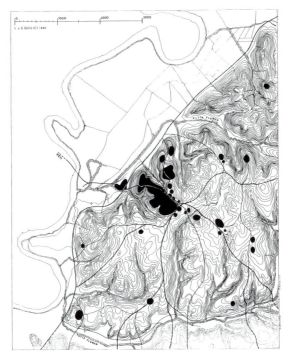

Figure 9.11 Crustumerium and surrounding area in the sixth century.

one will be in a position to judge the degree to which the development of places like Fidenae and Crustumerium was typical of Latium as a whole, or was more pronounced along the Tiber, and possibly along the Anio as well.

10

LAVINIUM

Following the sandy coast of Latium south from the mouth of the Tiber, one finds a taste of the primitive countryside in the hunting preserve of Castel Porziano. The primeval forest was long ago reduced to a Mediterranean macchia of stunted evergreens and thorny undergrowth. But the preserve, extending inland as far as the Via Laurentina, serves to punctuate the brief journey from Rome or Ostia to the cities of the Latian coast. The first of these, Lavinium, is the most important for the archaeology and history of Rome (fig. 0.2). Lavinium had the same situation as the Etruscan cities Caere and Tarquinia north of the Tiber. It was set on a low hill near the coast. It enjoyed the advantage of a harbor at the mouth of the Fossa di Pratica (ancient Numicus) which early maps show with a modest estuary. In the formative centuries of Rome the coast may have been marked by a barrier island and behind it a lagoon now filled in, thus providing a good harbor, possibly the best on this straight and sandy coast between Anzio and Civitavecchia.[1]

In the midst of the uncontrolled transformation of the coastal region into yet a further extension of the bedrooms and congestion of Rome, Lavinium has been in part rescued by the momentous archaeological discoveries made here since 1957, initially under the direction of Prof. Ferdinando Castagnoli and of his collaborator Prof. Paolo Sommella. In the early years of excavation, the undisturbed peace of Lavinium was still charged with the scent of history and hidden mystery. The hamlet of the Middle Ages and the Renaissance on the old arx, its houses facing inward in a protective circle to the church, seemed to have been asleep for centuries, first under the Massimi and then under its later masters, the Borghesi. There was a touch of magic in my first visit to Lavinium with Prof. Axel Boethius, whose readings of Virgil in this land of Aeneas made the shadows come alive with legend. We stopped beside the gate of the hamlet to eat a picnic lunch in the shade of the trees and creepers that cover the approach from the little valley below. As we were eating, a cart drawn by two snow-white bullocks appeared and made its way slowly up the ascent along the walls. I was quite prepared to find a priest, head covered in the Roman fashion, following behind. Nowhere would his presence have been more fitting. Upon entering office the chief magistrates of the Romans, consuls, praetors, and dictators, came to Lavinium to sacrifice to the Penates and to Vesta.[2] This was the city founded by Aeneas, where he was subsequently worshipped as Jupiter Indiges.[3] Although he was the great ancestor, the worship of Aeneas was not carried to Rome. With Lavinium, however, the Romans shared their most important cults: Vesta, Juturna, the Penates, Liber, Anna Perenna, and, as we now know from the excavations, Ceres and the Castores as well.[4]

The principal discoveries at Lavinium concern the areas outside the city itself on the sloping land to the south and across a small ravine to the east. The first area is that of the "Thirteen Altars" and of the hero shrine of Aeneas. The latter area has the sanctuary of Minerva (fig. 10.1).

The Thirteen Altars are placed in a row which curves only very slightly along its length (figs 10.2, 10.3).[5] They are typically Latian/central Italian, consisting of a base on which is set the offering table proper. The base itself has a strong bolster (torus molding) usually seated on a rectangular plinth. Both it and the plinth may be further defined by half-round moldings. The offering table is preserved on Altars 8, 11, 12, 13, and in part 1. The tables'

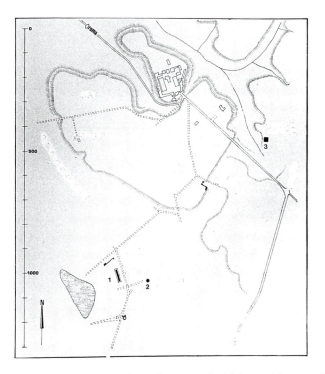

Figure 10.1 Lavinium, the archaeological area. 1, the Thirteen Altars; 2, *Heroon* of Aeneas; 3, sanctuary of Minerva.

moldings reverse those of the base. Between the molding and the base there may also be a transition in the form of a concave hawksbeak. In plan the altars are U-shaped, allowing for the ministrant to stand on one side of the altar in the opening between the wings. The altars were erected over two centuries. Although the moldings lost some of their protuberance over time, the altar form remained remarkably stable.

The Thirteen Altars were never in use together. The first (13) was built in the mid-sixth century and soon afterwards nos 8 and 9, in their first phases. By the mid-fifth century the earlier altars had been joined by four others (1–4), three of them (1–3) sharing a common foundation. Another altar (5) was situated between the two groups. The new altars show a slight change of orientation. In the first half of the fourth century Altars 6 and 7 were built. Their foundations appear to have been extended so as to include Altar 5 and its original underpinning, and to abut the foundations of Altar 4. It is not certain, however, that Altars 6 and 7 were not built before the pavement was laid. In this case one might envisage the extension of a widened foundation from Altar 5 in both directions. Finally, at the end of the fourth century another phase of reconstruction took place. Altar 13 was filled over. Altar 9 was rebuilt. In this case the new altar was moved beside Altar 8, and three new altars, 10, 11, 12, were added on a common foundation with it. Subsequently, before the sanctuary fell into disuse at the end of the third century, Altars 1, 2, and 8 were rebuilt.

The stratigraphy around Altar 8 is shown in fig. 10.4. Stratum D1 represents accumulation at the foot of the early altar of the sixth century. Stratum D2 is the stratum below the original ground level. When the second altar was built in the third century the ground level is represented by the boundary between Stratum C and Stratum B. Typical of the material from Stratum D is an Attic black figured *dinos* (wine-mixing bowl) decorated in two registers, the upper with a scene of merry satyrs and maenads (both companions of Bacchus and usually happy in each others' company) and below these the usual archaic bestiary (fig. 10.5). This piece was found in Stratum D2, much of it near Altar 8, but other fragments near Altars 6, 7, and 13. The material around Altar 8 was especially rich, including Etruscan *bucchero* vessels, fragments of another Attic *dinos*, an Attic cup, part of the latter found in the crannies in the base of Altar 8. These pieces represent some examples of the rich collection of imported pottery, Etruscan, Attic, and Peloponnesian (Laconian) from Stratum D. In this stratum there were also found numerous fragments of cooking pots – evidently used to prepare sacrificial meals – and their covers. Together with them there were fragments of storage vessels and basins.

It was in the area of Altar 8 on the trodden level connected with the final phase of the altar that one of the most striking discoveries at Lavinium was made, the inscription in honor of Castor and Pollux (fig. 10.6). The bronze plaque on which it was inscribed was 29.1 cm long (almost exactly 1 Roman

Figure 10.2 Lavinium, the Thirteen Altars.

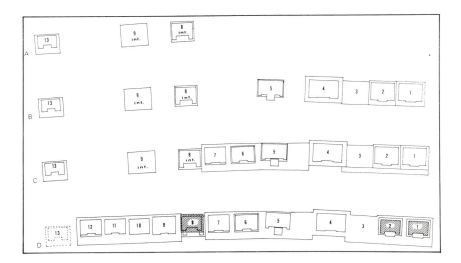

Figure 10.3 Lavinium, plan of the Thirteen Altars.

131

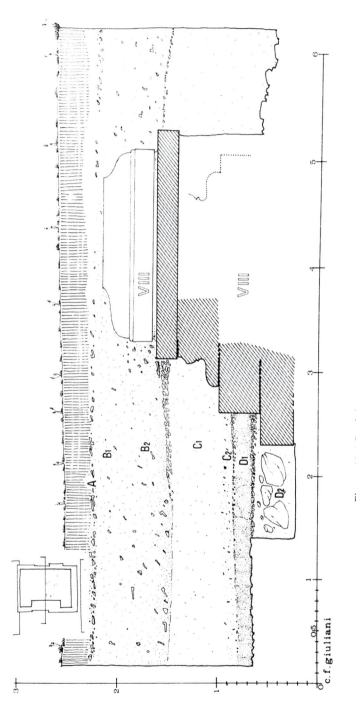

Figure 10.4 Lavinium, stratigraphy at Altar VIII.

Figure 10.5 Lavinium, Attic black figure *dinos*.

foot, 0.95 ft). Holes in the corners and middle show that the plaque was meant for attachment, certainly to the offering it accompanied. The dedication, written with characteristically archaic lack of concern for alignment of the text, reads, CASTOREI PODLOUQUEIQUE QUROIS (To the youths Kastor and Pollux). The text is somewhere between Latin and Greek. Castor, in the dative, was not a difficult name for the Latin speaker, who is shown to be a Latin speaker by the conjunction QUE joining the two divinities' names, as well as by the letter forms, which are normal for archaic Latin. But he stumbled over Pollux, which appears neither as Greek Polydeukes nor as Latin Pollux or Polluces. QUROIS is simply the Greek word "youths" in the dative.

The importance of the inscription can hardly be exaggerated. Not only does it emphasize the close and direct influence of the Greeks on Latium of the sixth century but once again it shows how close were the ties between Rome and Lavinium. The Roman Penates were identified with the Dioscuri.[6] And the path of these gods to Rome now unquestionably leads through Lavinium.[7]

The same may be said for Ceres. This goddess is also represented at Lavinium by a bronze dedication plate, which was found in a surface context. The letter forms belong to the third century.[8]

Stratum C represents material from the life of the sanctuary in the late sixth and fifth centuries. In this stratum simple buff-colored (*figulina*) pottery replaces *bucchero*. Miniature offering vessels in the form of wine-

Figure 10.6 Lavinium, inscription in honor of Castor and Pollux.

mixing bowls (Greek *krateriskoi*) become common. Imported pottery is noticeably absent. But there were imported works of art.

A beautiful bronze *kore*, height 22.5 cm (0.75 ft) with base illustrates relations with the Greek world and probably with Greek southern Italy (fig. 10.7). The *kore* stands on a rectangular base. She holds a flower and a mirror. She is wearing a crown and large disc earrings. Her features have much of the feline charm that is often associated with the art of Ionian Greece. She wears a simple sleeveless dress over a shift with sleeves. She was one of two such opulent votive objects from Stratum C, but of her companion only the base and one foot remain. More modest bronze figurines are divided between eleven male and seven female (fig. 10.8). These are local products similar to the examples from Rome.[9]

Terracotta votive sculpture and anatomical votives in terracotta are found only in the upper strata associated with the later life of the sanctuary.

Beside the sanctuary of the Thirteen Altars there stood an L-shaped building with a portico. Erected in the sixth century, it was enlarged but went out of use by the mid-fifth century. An interesting aspect of the building is its construction, wooden half-timbered work in rubble walling. Nearby there was a small kiln possibly used to produce votive terracottas.

Hardly 100 m (328 ft) distant from the Thirteen Altars are the remains of a small tumulus, which was investigated in 1968 by Prof. Paolo Sommella (figs 10.9, 10.10). The mound measures 18 m (59 ft) in diameter, and originally, in the seventh century, it covered a burial enclosed in a simply built rectangular tomb chest located in the center of the mound.[10] By the fourth century when the mound was restored and the tomb became the object of a cult, the whole must have been sadly dilapidated. At some time the tomb chest had been broken into and its contents rifled. Of the original occupant of the tomb nothing remained save a few fragments of bone. The tomb furniture was gone too. In its place, however, was a single amphora at least a century later than the original burial, probably a propitiatory offering to the *manes* (spirits) of the dead placed in the tomb by the intruders. At the moment of plundering one should envisage a clumsy pit dug by the robbers into the mound. It was in the bottom of this outside of the tomb proper that fragments of the metal objects originally buried with the dead man came to light. He was a person of standing and an augur, to judge from his *lituus*, the rounded augur's staff of which the spiral top in bronze is preserved, and a soldier; his spear and sword were with him. Iron fire dogs and spits were included in the grave goods. There was nothing left of precious objects such as those from the tombs of the same time at Praeneste and Castel di Decima, but there were some small objects in bronze, fibulae, and a bracelet that suggest the richness of the tomb. Beyond the area of intrusion, however, in a shallow pit beside the tomb chest, there was a deposit of pottery that accompanied the burial and gives us its date. It is mostly fine wares of central Italian manufacture of the early to middle seventh century.

Figure 10.7 Lavinium, bronze *kore*.

Figure 10.8 Lavinium, bronze *kouros*.

Figure 10.9 Lavinium, *Heroon* of Aeneas. The original tomb is the rectangular chest partially disturbed by the angle of the inner chamber of the later *heroon* chamber.

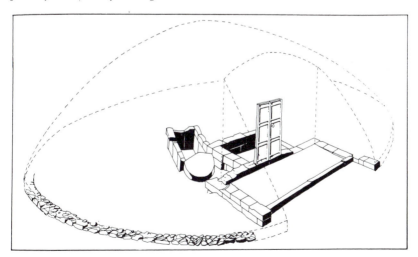

Figure 10.10 Lavinium, *Heroon* of Aeneas after restoration of the fourth century.

In the restoration work at the end of the fourth century the tumulus must have been reconstructed, filling in the robber pit and repairing the other ravages of time. But facing the pathway leading to the Thirteen Altars the new builders installed a porch, making a cut-out for it in the perimeter of the tumulus. The porch itself was fenced off from the outside and was intended to receive offerings (pottery was found in place). Behind a false door in stone, which was found broken but complete, there was an inner chamber with further offerings (pottery) which must have been connected with the dedication of the shrine. It is this pottery that dates the work in the years just before 300.

Various traditions surrounded the account of Aeneas' death. There was a strong belief (known to the Elder Cato) that Aeneas vanished and that no tomb of his was known.[11] This did not hinder his worship as Jupiter Indiges. But another tale had it that there was a tomb and we know how that tomb had been turned into a shrine. Dionysius of Halicarnassus writes concerning Lavinium:

> And for him the Latins made a hero shrine with this inscription "God the Earth Father who directs the stream of the river Numicus." There are those who say that this monument was built by Aeneas for Anchises [his father] in the year before this battle when the old man died. It is an earth affair, not large, and around it trees are set out in rows: well worth seeing.[12]
>
> (I, 64, 4–5)

This last detail makes it quite possible that Dionysius had visited Lavinium and had seen the shrine, which is almost certainly the tumulus restored in the late fourth century.[13]

In addition to the identification of this venerable monument, the archaeological evidence makes plain another aspect of Roman traditions: the shallowness of the historical past that lay behind them. About 300 a tumulus only 250 years old could be taken for the tomb of Aeneas. There can have been no memory at Lavinium of when the tomb was built or who the patrician was that originally lay within it. As in so many other cases, there is a caesura between early Rome and the time of Appius Claudius and his contemporaries in that first dynamic half century of Roman expansion after 338. It was in this age that the Greeks began making narratives of Roman history, and the hero shrine of Lavinium shows the reflection of this first chapter in Roman antiquarianism among the Romans themselves.

The area of the Thirteen Altars and the Hero Shrine of Aeneas are south of the town of Lavinium. The sanctuary of Minerva is to the east on a separate plateau (fig. 10.1). The area has been heavily disturbed. There is an enclosure (temenos) wall, but there is no trace of the temple's foundations, although architectural terracottas, including antefixes of satyr heads and of the Juno Sospita type (woman's head wearing a helmet with goat's horns), make it clear that the temple was built around or not long after 500 (compare fig. 11.10). The major discovery in this area was a pit below the level of modern disturbance, into which a mass of terracotta statues, certainly over one hundred of them, had been thrown. This was done at some time during the third century. The pottery in the deposit reaches down to that time. Characteristic material is various wares with stamped decoration which are now well documented and dated thanks to the work of J. P. Morel.[14] But there is also red figured pottery, both Italian and Attic, of the fifth century and local wares of the sixth century as well. The deposit seems to run the gamut from the building of the temple to the closing of the deposit some three hundred years later.

Among the material from the deposit there are small bronze *kouros* and *kore* figures and an Italic Mars. There is also a bronze hand holding a mirror reminiscent of the large bronze *kore* from the area of the Thirteen Altars. Among the terracotta figurines there are standing men and women and a Hellenistic Aphrodite. But the majority are seated women, often holding a baby.

Figure 10.11 Lavinium, terracotta statue of Minerva.

What is remarkable about the deposit, however, is the terracotta sculpture, from two-thirds life size to life size and above. The most startling is the giant Minerva (1.96 m, 6.4 ft high including the base), which must represent the divinity of the sanctuary, the Minerva of Lavinium (fig. 10.11). The iconography of the figure is romantically original. The goddess's helmet is the open-face or Thracian model.[15] Her shield is decorated with crescent moons and has snakes along its edge. The goddess's *aegis* (a short goatskin cape) has become a vest reaching below the waist in front, although only to the shoulder blades behind. Snakes abound, trimming the edges of the *aegis*, while one three-headed monster curls around the goddess's right arm. Her right hand held an attribute. It was not a lance, but it is broken away. The

139

Figure 10.12 Lavinium, terracotta statue of a woman.

aegis retains its traditional gorgon's head over the breast, and its scaly surface is indicated with incisions. The shield rests on a most unusual support, the figure of a small sea spirit, a triton. The triton is half man and half fish, the two sections joined together awkwardly atop the small stand on which the figure might (inaccurately) be said to kneel. In the words of Virgil, the Minerva of Lavinium was "Mightily armed, leader in war, the tritonian virgin."[16] Why Minerva (and the Greek Athena too) was called "tritonian" is an antiquarian matter which need not detain us, but the sea spirit's name made the verbal connection and was so used. The artistic source was the Parthenon (begun 448) where tritons like the Lavinium figure appear in the west pediment.[17] Our statue is, therefore, probably post-Parthenon in date. It might have been made at the end of the fifth century, or even later. In a terracotta like this the survival of an early fifth century look in the face is no surprise. The iconography of the tritonian Minerva is also known in one marble statue, the Athena Rospigliosi (Florence, Galleria degli Uffizi), a Roman copy of what may be a Greek original of the fourth century.

In the Lavinium deposit Minerva is represented by two other large pieces (though at one half the scale of the preceding), once with a goose, a most unusual iconography, and once with an *aegis* that has become an all-enveloping robe.

The other statues of the deposit represent youthful men and women. The group has yet to be definitively studied and published, but, even in the preliminary state in which it is known, it represents the most important such group of figures in existence. A woman's statue, for example, wears a *stola* over her tunic and holds a bird, an offering, in her right hand (fig. 10.12). On her head she wears a crown ending in feline heads; her ears have big plaque earrings. She has two necklaces, the lower one carrying a plaque and other matching pendents to either side. The men's statues are less opulent than the women's but the level of work, in a medium employing molds and thus tending toward the lifeless and ill-proportioned, is unusually expert, the most persistent problem being the difficulty of adjusting the scale of the bodies to that of the heads.

The statues of the Minerva sanctuary deposit play a central role in a far-reaching interpretive study by M. Torelli.[18] The author notes that in a hair style common among the female figures there are three clearly separated locks on either side of the face. This recalls the six locks mentioned by Festus as the hair dressing of a bride.[19] According to Festus this was an enormously old-fashioned style (*ornatus vetustissimus*), and Torelli points out that it must be the style for which spiral hair rings found in graves of the eighth and seventh centuries were intended. This observation is the starting point for a wide-ranging discussion of the ceremonies and beliefs connected with attaining adulthood in early Rome. According to Torelli, the terracotta sculptures represent maidens approaching marriage and youths about to assume the dress and responsibilities of men. The textual evidence from literary sources and the ancient calendars of Rome and Lavinium, and the problems of interpretation connected with them in relation to Torelli's thesis, are far beyond the scope of this treatment. One may note, however, that the "six locks" are not universal among the female terracotta heads, and one may safely characterize all of them as offerings without venturing further. Torelli's work adds a serious discussion and original ideas to the growing conviction that early Rome's connections with Lavinium were decisive to its development. The validity of that relationship will not be affected by the success or failure of Torelli's interpretation.

Further excavations at Lavinium have uncovered a portion of the city wall already existing in the seventh century and rebuilt during the sixth. Aside from the evidence of seventh-century dwellings, there has been revealed a part of the archaic town characterized by rectangular masonry structures.

11

SATRICUM

At the site of Satricum, 27.5 km (17 mi.) along the coast southeast of Lavinium, and about the same distance inland from the shoreline, there existed one of the most interesting cities of early Latium (fig. 0.2). Culturally Satricum was as close to Campania as to Latium, a fact reflected especially in the architecture of its archaic temple. The site has a low acropolis at its eastern end some 300 m (984 ft) across, while the entire distance across the site from the River Astura, which flows below the acropolis, to the *agger* which protected the town's western approach is on the order of 1 km (0.6 mi.). The identification is almost certain.

The settlement of Satricum in the seventh century and its houses have already been discussed. Above the seventh-century layer and immediately subsequent to it is the phase of archaic development of the acropolis dated by the excavators as beginning at the end of the seventh century (fig. 11.1).[1] There is already a recognizable temple (the *oikos*) facing the pond (*lacus*) in the center of the site, and behind the *oikos* another building aligned with it and referred to as the *sacellum*. As the site appeared in the middle of the sixth century the *oikos* and *sacellum* have been united and there was one building that has a fully rectangular plan centered on a courtyard 12 m (40 ft) across (fig. 11.2). There is a line of rooms bordering the courtyard on two sides. Across a 3 m (10 ft) street there is a similar building. Both have the look of the patrician courtyard house of the Acquarossa type, and the similarity is more than superficial (fig. 11.3). There are three sizes of rooms. Their proportions are the same as those of the Acquarossa houses, and, more than that, the basic unit of measurement, 4.8 m (probably equivalent to 16 ft, although a foot of 0.3 m rather than the Roman foot of 0.296 m) is the same. This evidence of common architectural design in southern Etruria and Latium takes its place beside the well-documented existence of traveling specialists in architectural decoration carrying their molds from one city to another in the same region.[2] At the same time small isolated rectangular buildings joined the larger courtyard establishments in the same area.

After 540–530, when there are traces of a general destruction, the two houses were replaced by porticoes, of which three are now known, as well as

142

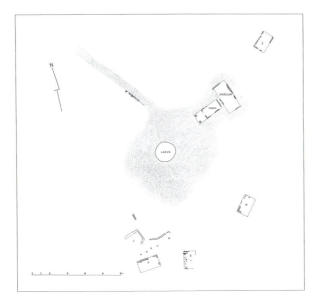

Figure 11.1 Satricum (Le Ferriere), late seventh and early sixth centuries.

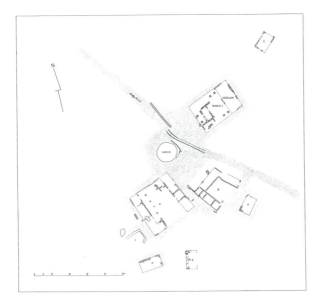

Figure 11.2 Satricum (Le Ferriere), mid-sixth century.

143

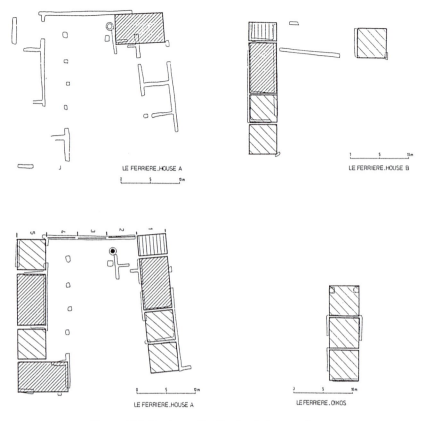

Figure 11.3 Satricum (Le Ferriere), house plans.

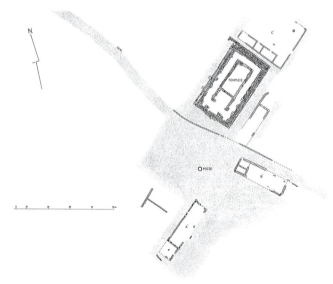

Figure 11.4 Satricum (Le Ferriere), about 500.

a fourth, which was built directly behind the temple with a courtyard enclosure not unlike the earlier buildings (fig. 11.4). These porticoes are unlikely to have been domestic buildings, and their appearance on the acropolis of Satricum, with its temple and spring, which seems to have been venerated from Iron Age times, raises the possibility that the "houses" of the sixth century were not domestic buildings. It has been shown that their large- and middle-sized rooms could be fitted comfortably with couches and thus could have been intended for communal banquets.[3] It is likely then that the houses, and then the porticoes, were intended for meetings of priest-hoods or other associations, like the "sodality" mentioned in the important inscription found reused in the temple foundations (see below). This possi-bility is reinforced by the fact that these buildings are not fragments of a widespread cityscape of the same character but seem to have stood in isolation, together with the temple, on the acropolis.

A second change in the rebuilding is that the temple and porticoes were positioned in a rectangular grid. Such rectangular relation between buildings had been notably absent in the earlier phase of the courtyard houses. This development at Satricum was undoubtedly influenced by the orthogonal planning practiced in the Greek cities of southern Italy and Sicily and entering Etruria at the same time.

The Satricum temple passed through three phases during the same period represented by the houses of the acropolis (fig. 11.5). The current exca-vations of the Dutch Institute at Rome have been faced with unusual difficulties in investigating the site, which was widely excavated between 1896 and 1898, but save for preliminary notices remained unpublished.[4] To judge from what seems to have been a dump of votive material recovered by the original excavators in the vicinity of the temple (one of three from the site), containing early Protocorinthian pottery (globular *aryballoi*) and other imported Greek pottery, there was cult activity on the spot by the late eighth century, in all likelihood connected with the pond (*lacus*) that remained a prominent feature of the acropolis throughout the history of the site.[5] The first rectangular structure would have been erected about 600 or shortly thereafter.[6] It was a simple *oikos* without porch measuring 6 × 12 m (19.5 × 39 ft: *oikos* is a basic Greek word for "house" often used with the connotation of a *hieros oikos* or shrine). To the *oikos* have been attributed roof terracottas of the type developed in Greek Asia Minor but for which the closest parallels are afforded by similar pieces from Caere in Etruria, making it not improbable that the building at Satricum was decorated by craftsmen from or related to a Caeretan workshop. Two major elements survive. First, there is a series of antefixes with female heads (figs 11.6, 11.7). These masked the joints of the tiles at the edge of the roof and overhung the roof edge. The tiles projected from the roof edge as well; their underside was decorated with palmettes. Second, we find a frieze of horsemen dressed for battle. This is topped by a strigilated crown below which is a meander

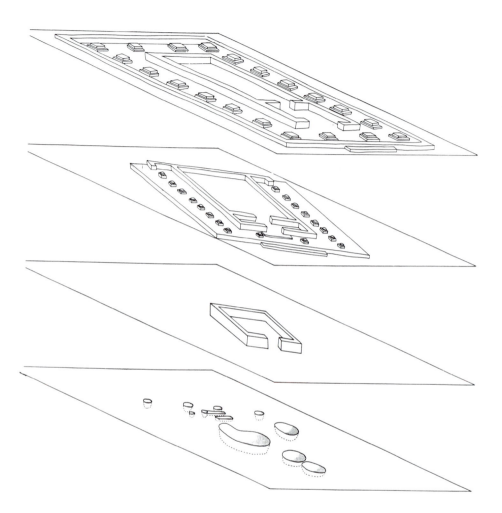

Figure 11.5 Satricum (Le Ferriere), development of the temple site.

punctuated by stars and water birds after the model also employed in the first phase of the Sant'Omobono temple at Rome. This frieze is restored immediately below the roof edge covering the ends of the rafters.

Temple I, as it is called, would have been built about 550 (and is so dated on the basis of the architectural terracottas attributed to it), but it was destroyed, together with the courtyard houses, between 540 and 530.[7] Its orientation was the same as the *oikos* it replaced. The plan had porticoes across the front and sides but none at the rear. There is a small *pronaos* (antechamber) before the *cella*. The architectural terracottas attributed to this building belong to the type known as Campanian, also found widely at this time among the Etruscan cities (fig. 11.8). Their ori-

Figure 11.6 Satricum (Le Ferriere), early antefix attributed to the *oikos*, Museo Nazionale di Villa Giulia.

gin, however, is in the Greek area at Naples, Poseidonia, and Himera. These terracottas are indicative of an opening-up of central Italy to architectural styles from the south, Greek innovations in the eyes of the Etruscans and Latins, if not in ours. This trend is further exemplified by the peripteral (surrounding colonnade) plan of the second phase of the temple at Satricum. The antefixes, now ending flush with the lower edge of the roof tiles, are female heads, palmettes, and *gorgoneia*. The flat tiles still project from the roof and their visible underside was decorated with circles. A frieze in the same position as the rider frieze of the *sacellum* may have had plastic lotus and palmettes topped by a painted guilloche and strigilations (ribbing) above (fig. 11.9).

The next phase, the peripteral temple, has been dated precisely to the 480s following the annalists' report of the capture of Satricum by Coriolanus in 488.[8] It had certainly ceased to exist by the mid-fifth century, although there are votive deposits that suggest continued if sporadic ceremonies on the spot.[9] There is an embarrassingly rich assortment of antefixes eligible for restoration on the peripteral temple. Some of them may well have decorated the porticoes surrounding the temple. There are satyr and maenad heads (fig. 11.10), the familiar head of Juno Sospita (fig. 11.11), but also antefixes in the form of full-figure sirens, satyr-tritons, and spirited groups of satyrs and maenads (fig. 11.12). The latter, shown in five different poses, have a charm that makes one forget their libidinous propensities and apotropaic function. The eaves-tiles of the building had plastic leading edges and behind this a gay

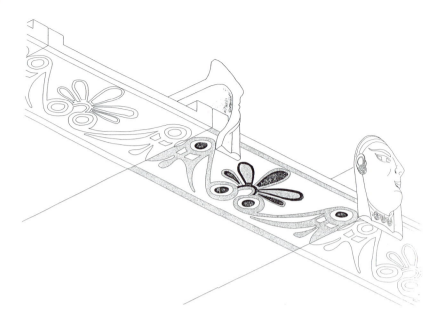

Figure 11.7 Satricum (Le Ferriere), eaves of the *oikos*.

Figure 11.8 Satricum (Le Ferriere), antefix of the Campanian type, temple first phase, Museo Nazionale di Villa Giulia.

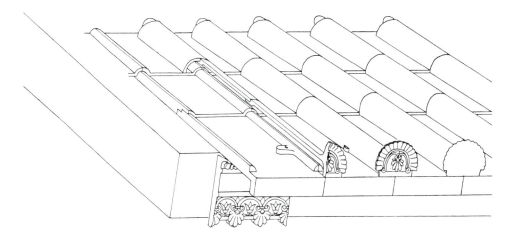

Figure 11.9 Satricum (Le Ferriere), reconstruction of the roof of the temple (first phase).

chevron pattern on their underside. Terracotta elements with strigilated tops covered the rafters. They have a central band with a meander and lotus and palmettes suspended below. The raking cornice was also strigilated, but above the strigilated band it carried an openwork of coils topped by palmettes. Below the strigilated band there is a bolster painted in a scale pattern and below that a meander (fig. 11.13).

The Dutch excavations discovered an inscription reused in the foundation of the second temple which seems to step directly out of early Roman history but does so in a way that raises new questions about the ancient tradition. The stones bearing the inscription, and other blocks set into the foundations of the temple beside them, originally belonged to the base of a monument (fig. 11.14). The inscription reads:[10]

... IEI STETERAI POPLIOSIO VALESIOSIO SUODALES MAMARTEI

in classical Latin

... STETERUNT PUBLI VALERI SODALES MARTIS

or

... STETERUNT PUBLI VALERI SODALES MARTI

149

Figure 11.10 Satricum (Le Ferriere), satyr head antefix from the period of the peripteral temple, Museo Nazionale di Villa Giulia.

Figure 11.11 Satricum (Le Ferriere), antefix of the Juno Sospita type from the period of the peripteral temple, Museo Nazionale di Villa Giulia.

Figure 11.12 Satricum (Le Ferriere), antefix of satyr and maenad from the period of the peripteral temple, Museo Nazionale di Villa Giulia.

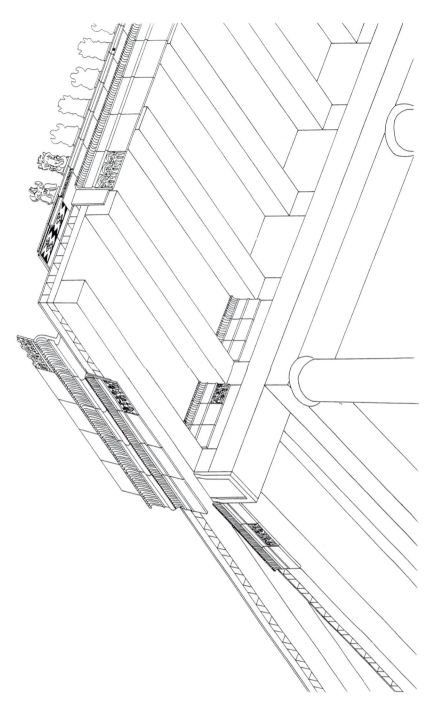

Figure 11.13 Satricum (Le Ferriere), reconstruction of the roof of the peripteral temple.

Using the second alternative one might translate: "The Companions of Publius Valerius erected to Mars." The word order, however, placing the genitive, *Publi Valeri*, before the nominative which governs it, *Sodales*, is awkward.

An alternative is offered by considering MAMARTEI a genitive rather than a dative. This produces "[lacking] of Publius Valerius erected, the Companions of Mars (erected)."

In the absence of the beginning of the inscription, the exact sense is in doubt.[11] But there is no doubt that a Publius Valerius is mentioned. Is he the Publius Valerius of Roman history, surnamed Publicola, and one of the heroes of the Roman Republic, consul of 509, 508, 507, and 504, who triumphed over the Tarquins and their allies of Veii, over the Sabines and again over the Veians, author of laws and the friend of the people? Although it is understandable as Latin, one cannot be completely sure that the language of the inscription is the Latin of Rome rather than the dialect of Satricum or of the Sabine region from which the Valerii are thought to have come. H. S. Versnel summarizes the possibilities: (1) Popliosios Valesiosios was a Sabine; (2) He was a notable resident of Satricum; (3) He was a member of the Roman *gens Valeria* but not necessarily the famous first consul or his son; (4) Popliosios Valesiosios was one of the only two men of this name known to us from the period.[12] The alternatives are open to debate.

Furthermore, the *sodales* of the inscription – are they members of a college of priests? Are they *gentiles* (clan members) of the Valerii? Or, as suggested by the reference to Mars, are they members of a war band? Remembering the Fabii who marched as a *gens* to fight against Veii,[13] one might think that the final two alternatives are not far apart. No doubt Popliosios Valesiosios in the course of his life was clan head, captain, and priest. What eludes us is which of the roles he may have played in the dedication at Satricum.

Recent work has led to the identification of another monument at Satricum.[14] This is a group of terracotta sculptures in which the most prominent element is the so-called Jupiter head from the old excavations (fig. 11.15). To that may be added a fragmentary statue of Minerva, a youthful god (Apollo?), Juno (?), and eight figures of giants, making twelve statues in all. In the opinion of P. S. Lulof this is not an architectural group but was intended to be set up as an independent monument.

During the recent excavations work has continued in the cemeteries of Satricum, bringing to light an extensive cemetery of inhumation graves in *fossae* of the fifth century. After the destruction of the temple n the fifth century, part of the acropolis was also the site of a cemetery (fig. 11.16), but religious gatherings appear to have continued around the site of the old temple.

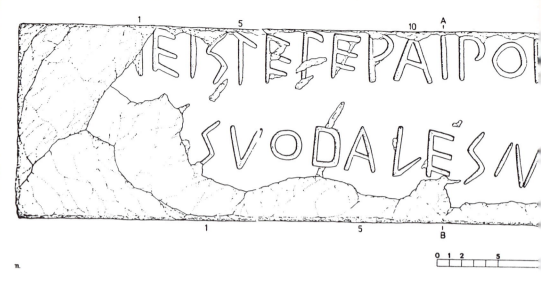

Figure 11.14 Satricum (Le Ferriere), inscription found reused in the foundations of the peripteral temple, the *lapis Satricanus*.

Figure 11.15 Satricum (Le Ferriere), head of terracotta statue, Museo Nazionale di Villa Giulia.

During the excavations of 1896, tumuli were identified outside the city, the oldest of them covering a grave of the ninth century. The material from the archaic graves excavated during the early campaigns is preserved in the Villa Giulia Museum in Rome.

154

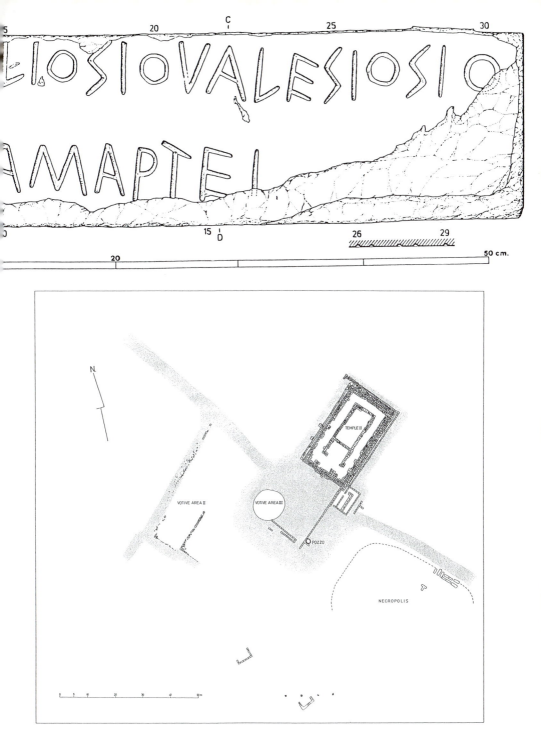

Figure 11.16 Satricum (Le Ferriere), plan of the mid-fifth century after the destruction of the temple showing the necropolis and votive deposits.

12

PRAENESTE

THE "PRINCELY TOMBS"

At Praeneste, the modern Palestrina, between 1855 and 1876, a group of tombs was discovered which for their sumptuous contents remain unsurpassed in Latium of the orientalizing period (fig. 0.2). The first discovery was that of the Barberini Tomb. No record was kept at the time of excavation, and it was only after some years that the contents were offered for sale and, following disappointing rejection by the museums of Berlin and New York, passed to the Italian state.[1] Despite the uncertainties which surround its discovery and history before coming to the Villa Giulia Museum, the tomb group is consistent and seems uncontaminated. As in the case of all the great tombs of Praeneste, however, the tomb group is not complete. In particular, the pottery found in the tombs was not considered worth saving, and its loss, with the exception of four fragmentary items from the Bernardini Tomb of 1876, robs the groups of their soundest chronological element.

In 1861–1862 two similarly rich orientalizing tombs were found at Praeneste. The tomb group from one of these passed into the hands of the collector Augusto Castellani.[2] Castellani's collection later passed to the Italian state. But only part of the contents of the tomb is now at the Villa Giulia Museum because other objects had already been given to the city of Rome (Capitoline Museum) and still others sold. One ivory from the tomb is in the British Museum. Of other similar tombs discovered at Praeneste down to 1900 there are only the vaguest reports and occasionally isolated objects such as the magnificent gold cup with decoration in gold granulation in the Victoria and Albert Museum.[3]

In 1876 the Bernardini Tomb, now the companion of the Barberini Tomb group in the Villa Giulia Museum, was unearthed at Praeneste.[4] On this occasion the tomb group passed immediately into public ownership and visitors to the excavation made notes at the site. The tomb was an inhumation in what has been described as a trench, 5.45 × 3.80/3.92 m (17.8 × 12.5/12.8 ft) and approximately 1.7 m (5.5 ft) deep (below the

156

Figure 12.1 Praeneste, Bernardini Tomb, gold fibula (only the casing above the actual pin is visible), Museo Nazionale di Villa Giulia.

Figure 12.2 Praeneste, Bernardini Tomb, gilded silver bowl, Museo Nazionale di Villa Giulia.

157

Figure 12.3 Praeneste, Bernardini Tomb,
ivory plaque with Egyptianizing motifs,
Museo Nazionale di Villa Giulia.

Figure 12.4 Praeneste, Bernardini Tomb,
bronze cauldron with attached griffin
heads on conical stand with orientalizing
motifs, Museo Nazionale di Villa Giulia.

modern surface). The walls of the trench were lined with tufa blocks. After
the burial the trench was filled with earth and sealed with further tufa slabs.
In the floor of the tomb there was a smaller trench in which a number of
grave goods were found, but the exact position of this feature, possibly
related to the loculi of earlier and contemporary tombs, is unclear.

Standing together in the Villa Giulia Museum, the objects from the
Barberini and Bernardini Tombs rival the great tomb treasures of the ancient
world from Ur to Sutton Hoo. The tomb groups, as we shall see in detail
below, are similar: gold clasps and fibulae of great size and complexity and
decorated in granulation technique by which tiny pellets of gold were
soldered onto the gold surface (fig. 12.1); silver bowls (one gilded, fig. 12.2)
with relief taken from the pseudo-Egyptian decoration of the Near East;
silver cups in the shape of Greek *skyphoi*; silver *oinochoai* of eastern
derivation; ivory in quantity, for the decoration of furniture and in the
Barberini Tomb handles possibly for fans, such as are documented in bronze
at Acqua Acetosa, Laurentina Tomb 70 (fig. 12.3). There are bronze tripods
from the Near East and cauldrons set on conical stands, the latter decorated

with orientalizing reliefs, the former decorated with griffin heads, as found in Greece and Cyprus, and winged genii also known in Greece but certainly native to central and eastern Turkey (fig. 12.4). The tombs contained bronze shields with miniature repoussé relief such as we have already met at Acqua Acetosa, Laurentina. Bronze vessels with repoussé siren heads and finally bronze offering bowls (*phialai*) complete the repertoire. Each of the tombs has its individually remarkable items. In the Bernardini Tomb there are silver discs with relief decoration and gold plaques with coiled "comb" ends, a cup of blue glass, a small gold cauldron adorned with Egyptianizing scenes – the rim surmounted by six snake heads, a silver dagger, its handle covered with amber and bound with gold wire (fig. 12.5). The Bernardini Tomb also contained two finials for staffs, or possibly chariot poles, their tubular elements meeting at right angles and each bearing a group of garishly amusing bronze figurines. The Barberini Tomb had numerous bronze vessels, an ivory cup and a chair covered with bronze sheeting and resembling a piece of Victorian wickerwork furniture.

The objects collected from these burials have the look of foreign origin or foreign models adapted in Italy.[5] The ivory pieces, so abundant in both tombs, were made from elephant tusks available only in Syria or North Africa. The scenes of the plaques from the Bernardini tomb are taken largely

Figure 12.5 Praeneste, Bernardini Tomb, silver dagger with amber-covered handle bound by gold wire, Museo Nazionale di Villa Giulia.

from the repertoire of pseudo-Egyptian art prevalent in Phoenicia and Cyprus. The Barberini ivories have a decidedly Syrian style. But they are not purely eastern. Among the figures of the handles in the shape of an arm there is a centaur in the early form of a full human figure attached by the back to a horse's mid-section and hindquarters. Only the ivory open-work fragments and monster's wings from the Bernardini Tomb are unquestionably imports.[6] The silver bowls can once again be characterized as Phoenician pseudo-Egyptian. Outside Italy, these objects are also known in Cyprus and the Near East, and at Praeneste one has a Phoenician inscription.[7] The silver *oinochoai* are similarly related to the Orient but not surely oriental.

It is entirely possible that many of these pieces were made by eastern craftsmen who had made their way to Italy. The plentiful ivories of Etruria show both the pseudo-Egyptian (Phoenician) and a Syrian style. And the Phoenician pseudo-Egyptian bowls are dispersed in Italy over an area from southern Etruria to Sybaris, in the instep of the Italian boot.

The gold cup from the Bernardini Tomb must be Etruscan, as shown by the four sphinxes done with granulation perched on its handles. The magnificent gold jewelry of the two tomb groups is surely Etruscan as well, both because of its typology and its granulated decoration. The workshop which produced the masterpieces of the two Praenestan tombs is known for examples of its work found both in Caere and Vulci and has been localized in the former city.[8]

It is only among the bronzes that there appear objects almost certainly manufactured outside Italy. These are the cauldrons, both those with griffin and with siren heads, as well as the stands with repoussé decoration thought to be incense burners adapted to a new use, and the less elegant vessels decorated with human and animal figures peering over the rims (fig. 12.6). The griffin cauldrons are a Greek invention. The other types have oriental sources.

The Bernardini and Barberini tombs have long been treated as examples of Etruscan culture extending southward into Latium, and with reason. The Regolini Galassi Tomb at Caere is a close cousin. There too one finds the elaborate granulated gold work, a Phoenician bowl, silver cups, and shields covered with bronze and repoussé designs. The parallels extend to tombs at Caere (the Cinque Sedie, Tomba della Nave II) and northward to Marsiliana d'Albegna, Vulci and Vetulonia and inland to Veii and Falerii Veteres (Civiltà Castellana). But tombs of the same era furnished with the same taste are now known in Latium at Decima, Acqua Acetosa, Laurentina, Torrino, and Rocca di Papa. There are such tombs at Cumae and near Salerno at Pontecagnano, while examples of such luxuries reached the Faliscans at Narce and Fabriano in the Picene region farther east. These tombs are a testimony of taste and style of burial common to those possessing sufficient wealth throughout a large area of Italy. It is a phenomenon to which we shall return in the context of the society that produced it (Chapter 13).

THE FIBULA PRAENESTINA

From the Janiculum Hill above the right bank of the Tiber the Villa Lante looks down on Rome. Built in the days of Raphael and Michelangelo, the villa has a simplicity and delicacy that set it apart from the "Casinos" of the Janiculum, the Casino Farnese, now the Villa Aurelia of the American Academy in Rome, and the Villa Doria Pamfili in its vast park or the Villa Sciarra with its charming gardens. In 1527, on the first morning of the sack of Rome, a German soldier in the army of the Emperor Charles V, awaiting orders to attack, cut his name and the date on one of the villa's tufa fireplaces. Today the Villa Lante houses the Finnish Institute in Rome, but for thirty years spanning the turn of the century it was the home of Wolfgang Helbig and of his wife, the Russian princess Nadejda Schakowsky.

With Helbig, who had come to Rome two years after his doctorate in 1863, we enter a world that seems far removed from archaeology of excavation and publication as we see it in the work of Boni and Pinza and their successors. This is the world of the salon, of the collector, of the rich and

Figure 12.6 Praeneste, Bernardini Tomb, bronze vessel and stand with figures, Museo Nazionale di Villa Giulia.

161

Figure 12.7 Gold fibula with engraved inscription, Museo Nazionale Preistorico ed Etnografico "L. Pigorini."

famous, of the dealer, of the masterpiece and the fraud. Helbig, a scholar of ability and success, to whom we owe the four-volume guide to the antiquities in the public collections of Rome (issued most recently in a revised edition between 1963 and 1972),[9] was Second Secretary of the German Archaeological Institute in Rome from 1865 until 1887. The Institute, which celebrated its fiftieth anniversary in 1879, had begun life as a spontaneous association of scholars, the Istituto di Correspondenza Archeologica. By the end of Helbig's time as Second Secretary it was the major branch of the Imperial German Archaeological Institute. The German Institute has remained the single greatest force in the archaeology of the Mediterranean and the Near East, and the Roman branch maintains a position of commensurate importance. Upon leaving the Institute Helbig did not seek another position but acquired the Villa Lante and remained in Rome, dedicating himself to archaeology but also to society and circles of influence in which he by inclination, and his wife by birth, felt a part. Even before moving to the Janiculum, "Helbig was swimming in the thick of society, well known to both the Roman and Piedmontese aristocracy, to the connoisseurs of art and to dealers": so wrote none other than Ulrich von Wilamowitz Moellendorf, the premier Hellenist of his day in Germany.[10]

The last item of Wilamowitz's list of his subject's acquaintances widens our picture of the man who on January 7, 1886 presented an unusual discovery at a public meeting of the German Archaeological Institute at its seat on the Capitoline. The object was a gold fibula with a long pin and the complicated type of bow that has given its name to the type "dragon fibula" (*fibula a drago*) (fig. 12.7). The type is characteristic of the seventh century. The singular element of the fibula was the inscription engraved on the catchplate:

MANIOS: MED: FHE: FHAKED: NUMASIOI

For many years after its presentation by Helbig and the epigraphist Ferdinand Dümmler, the "Fibula Praenestina," as it came to be called from its supposed find spot, stood revered as the earliest known Latin inscription.[11] Its meaning was not completely clear:

Manios made me for Numasios (Manios = a craftsman)
Manios had me made for Numasios (Manios = donor)

The Latin is archaic but consistent with the knowledge of the early stages of the language as it was already known in the late nineteenth century.

The fibula had no clear history. Helbig presented it as the property of a friend and as having been found at Praeneste. Soon afterward the friend was identified as Francesco Martinetti. It was Martinetti who donated the fibula to the newly founded Villa Giulia Museum in 1889 and almost simultaneously became a *cavaliere* (a courtesy title widely used by the Italian government; the title of *commendatore* – commander – was granted with greater circumspection). Martinetti is a shadowy but important figure in the surreptitious world of art and antiquities dealing in Rome at the end of the century. Even before 1860 under the Papal government regulations were in place to curb illegal traffic in art and following unification regulation was supported by a rising national consciousness regarding monuments of the Italian past. But when there is a customer there soon will be a merchant, and Martinetti plied his trade until his death in 1895. He became rich, though he remained a miser. (After his death various hidden treasures were reported to have been found in his house, one of which, a large group of ancient gems, was exhibited in 1990.)[12]

From his first days in Rome Helbig became Martinetti's confidant. The archaeologist also became the adviser to foreign collectors, notably Carl Jacobsen, the Danish brewer and founder of the Ny Carlsberg Glyptotek in Copenhagen. Helbig's activity as a counselor reached across the Atlantic when he participated in the sale of the so-called Boston Throne (a three-sided relief of Greek style of the fifth century) through the American dealer Percy Warren to the Boston Museum of Fine Arts. The Boston Throne has been repeatedly challenged as a fraud but has also been defended.

Already in 1905 doubts were expressed about the fibula by Giovanni Pinza, whom we have already encountered as a student of early Rome and who ranked as the leading expert of the day on archaeology of early Latium.[13] At the same time, however, the fibula acquired a more definite provenance: the Bernardini Tomb of 1876. Although this information contradicted Helbig's original statement that the piece was found in 1871, it was maintained on various occasions by Georg Karo, later director of the German Archaeological Institute in Athens, and tacitly accepted by Helbig for the second edition of his guide to the Roman museums (edited by Reisch).[14] The voices of criticism were not quieted. Dinsmore Curtis in publishing the Bernardini Tomb was dubious.[15] And Pinza held his ground, remarking to students that he even knew who had made the fibula.[16]

The value of Pinza's statements in the 1920s and early 1930s is clouded by the difficult circumstances of his life after returning from the trenches of the First World War, leading ultimately to seven years as a mental patient before his death in 1940.[17] More recently Margherita Guarducci, Italy's foremost Greek epigraphist, has launched a voluminous attack on the fibula and on Helbig's motives for presenting it in 1886. The fibula, she reasons, or if not the fibula, the inscription on it, is a forgery.[18] By means of this brilliant discovery Helbig hoped to secure the Directorship (First Secretaryship) of the German Institute (which he failed to do). Martinetti, for his part, became a *cavaliere* and curried favor with government officialdom. For Helbig, this episode is only one in a career of dubious dealing in antiquities and conspiring in the sale of fakes. Naturally, supporters of Helbig, the acknowledged scholar, have risen to his defense.[19]

Whatever the truth, we may take some comfort in Coleman's remark:

> Now it has to be admitted after all this that even if the inscription on the fibula could be proved conclusively to be an authentic representation of the seventh century or early sixth century Praenestine, it would not add a lot to what we would otherwise know or be able to reconstruct of the earliest period of Latin. Only "fefaked" was not predictable, though it is not surprising either.[20]

But no one can take comfort in an object deprived of its context, because even if it bears a written message like the Praeneste fibula, the message loses much of its meaning. And that is the archaeology of the salons, of the auction rooms, of museums of world art and, alas, of not a few scholars.

13

CONCLUSION

Rome was a river town. Like Cincinnati on the Ohio, like Memphis and St Louis on the Mississippi, like Cologne on the Rhine, Paris on the Seine, or London on the Thames, Rome's fortune lay in her location. The division of the river into two narrow channels below the Tiber Island and the shallows that formed there made bridging the river possible. The Pons Sublicius was supposed to have been built by Ancus Marcius.[1] And the curve of the river at the same point provided a good landing place. Salt came up the Tiber and was transshipped along the Via Salaria to the Sabine country and Umbria. Foreign goods and foreign merchants met Latins and Etruscans in Rome's emporium. Rome was not alone in having a good location on the Tiber and thus on the great river highway inland.[2] Immediately upstream Fidenae, Antemnae, and Crustumerium were all potential competitors. The greatest menace was Etruscan Veii, located within reach of the opposite bank of the Tiber. But destiny lay with Rome.

The thirty Latin communities, of which, in the beginning, Rome was only one, occupied the region from the Alban Hills to the Tiber. They spoke the same language and each year they gathered to celebrate the festival of Jupiter on the Alban Mountain. Three of the Latin towns, Ardea, Lavinium, and Antium, were on the sea.[3] But command of the river highway inland proved, as so often in history, more important than a harbor along the coast. So long as the Tiber carried nothing more than the wherries of the villages along the river, there would be little to alter the culture of Rome or any of her neighbors. As soon as the Tiber was penetrated by Greeks and Phoenicians, however, Rome and the Latins were propelled into a new world. Through the emporium on the Tiber, as much as through any port of Etruria or harbor of coastal Latium, new goods, new languages and new blood found their way to Rome. An image of this activity and its consequences, which found no part in annalistic history aside from the Tarquin Dynasty and is otherwise unknown save what can be gleaned from the history of foreign cults, notably Hercules and Apollo by the river bank, is the gift of archaeology to our knowledge of early Rome. At the same time, archaeology illustrates the inherent conservatism of the Romans through the remains of their cults away from the river bank.

In another direction, the study of Roman and Latian cemeteries shows how the family of the Early Iron Age ordered itself in death and conceived of the individual in relation to the tomb. It shows further how these conventions and the society they represented were replaced by new ways. It has been argued persuasively that this development includes the birth of a clan organization, the Latin and Roman *gens*, occurring at the same time as the first new influences from the Aegean and the Near East reached the region. In the seventh century archaeology illustrates the adjustment of the Latins and Romans to the material wealth of the new era. Archaeology also measures the expansion of population and settlement and at Rome gives the first indications of a true city with luxuries for its gods and mansions for its citizens in the sixth century.

Early in this work a complaint was entered against the use of archaeology as no more than a prop for the annalistic tradition. The temptation to write this kind of history is not peculiar to the study of early Rome. It arises wherever history seeks to objectify a legendary past through its material remains. For this reason, the problems of turning the archaeology of Bronze Age Greece into history are worth considering because they hold a mirror up to the history of early Rome. One critic of Aegean scholarship has written as follows:

> Basically, my point is simple. The prehistorian has four possible types of evidence: (1) archaeological artifacts, (2) language, (3) skeletal material, if he wants to use it, and (4) Greek myth and legend. It is now orthodox dogma that these types of evidence should be reconciled in any attempt to construct a legitimate historical picture. I want to show that this kind of reconciliation is the very crux of the difficulty, just because arguments and conclusions drawn from any one of the four categories are not necessarily applicable to any of the others. Failure to heed this caution results in complicated hypothetical constructs which are at best not logically necessary and which are at worst logically impossible.[4]

Substituting "Roman" for "Greek" in this quotation makes a fair characterization of a large segment of writing about early Rome in which history and archaeology mingle. There follows here one view of what can be learned from the archaeological evidence in isolation.

The first evidence that the Tiber has become a river of international trade comes from the Sant'Omobono sanctuary. In the fill between the archaic temple and its successors, there is a notable presence of sherds in the style of late Greek geometric pottery of the middle and later eighth century.[5] The following classes of Greek pottery have been identified: Euboean, second quarter to mid-eighth century (Middle Geometric), Cycladic, same period

(Middle Geometric), Corinthian, last quarter of eighth century (Late Geometric, Thapsos cups), Euboean, same period (Late Geometric), Cycladic, same period (Late Geometric), Ischian imitation of Corinthian, late eighth to early seventh century (early Protocorinthian), Cumean imitation of Corinthian, late eighth to early seventh century (early Protocorinthian).[6] Related to the finds at Sant'Omobono is the fragment of a *crater* from Boni's excavations at the Sepulcretum in the Forum and the appearance of wheelmade pottery fired to produce a fabric with a light background color after the Greek fashion in Period III.[7]

What was the river traffic on the Tiber in the eighth century? Two pieces of evidence make it clear that merchants from the new Greek outpost on Ischia came up the Tiber with their goods. First, Greek potters soon began to make versions of the Greek imports, at Rome or somewhere nearby.[8] They must have come up the river and most likely did so with their compatriots. The knowledge of writing also reached Latium and Etruria from the south. The date of the graffito of Tomb 483 at Osteria dell'Osa (Gabii) is so early, predating the foundation of any of the official Greek colonies in the west, that only Ischia, the offshore traders' haven, can have been the point of departure. Indeed, a strong case can be made for the adaptation of the Phoenician alphabet for Greek on Ischia where Greeks and easterners were living together in the eighth century.[9] The easiest way to Gabii from Campania is not overland but by sea and then up the Tiber and the Anio. And this is true whether we posit a series of literate individuals along the route of transmission or envisage a single literate woman coming to Gabii from the south.

Thus in the eighth century the traffic on the river changed, and so did Rome. Changes in the Latin communities at the same time, and even beginning earlier, can be seen in the necropolis of Osteria dell'Osa, where family burial customs change as a result of the families' acquisition of dependants and competition among these enlarged units.[10] Before the end of the seventh century it appears that Greeks were living in Rome, to judge from the graffito of one Ktektos on a Corinthian vase from the Esquiline cemetery.[11]

Phoenician presence on the Tiber cannot be shown before the seventh century, when characteristic Punic wine amphorae begin to appear as grave goods in Latin cemeteries. A summary of the distribution of these imports made in 1985 shows them to be present in the necropolis of Decima, Acqua Acetosa, Laurentina, Gabii, and at Ficana. The Punic amphorae at the first three of these sites almost certainly arrived through Rome.[12] They are characteristic of "rich" tombs at Decima and Acqua Acetosa, Laurentina. These are the burials including a chariot except for Decima, Tomb 93 (which had more than one hundred grave goods), and Acqua Acetosa, Laurentina, Tomb 123, which was only slightly below the "princely" level.[13]

The "rich" burials, at Castel di Decima, at Acqua Acetosa, Laurentina, and at Praeneste, like "rich" burials among the Etruscans, among the Macedonians and Thracians or among the Celts, almost automatically evoke another adjective, "princely." Fascination with royalty is still very much with us. In 1881 the Egyptian fellaheen lined the banks of the Nile to witness the passage of a barge carrying royal mummies of the New Kingdom from Thebes to Cairo, although more than thirty centuries separated them from their ancient kings. Heinrich Schliemann went to Mycenae to find the graves of Agamemnon and his followers. The quantity of gold in the tombs of the Grave Circle A satisfied him of his success. But this example of royal tomb hunting is instructive because the second grave circle at Mycenae, excavated in the 1950s, is, to a significant degree, contemporary with the first, which means that grave circles were not the exclusive property of monarchs; and it seems that Schliemann looked neither on the face of Agamemnon nor on that of one of his royal predecessors.[14]

Although the Barberini and Bernardini Tombs were assumed to belong to the rulers of Praeneste, the multiplication of similarly rich tombs at Castel di Decima and Acqua Acetosa, Laurentina, would suggest that such magnificent burials of the seventh century are a social rather than a political phenomenon.[15] The question at issue is to what degree the "rich" burials of the seventh century represent a change in the ideology of the Latins. Superficially, the earlier burials of the Iron Age seem not only "poor" in equipment but different because they begin with the widespread use of cremation and have no timber or rock-cut tomb chambers. By the sixth and fifth centuries burials have become suddenly "poor" again. So drastic is the economy of grave goods that formerly it was doubted that any burials of the time were known from Rome and only recently have some tombs without grave goods begun to be attributed to the period. Elsewhere, at Satricum for example, the grave goods tend to be scanty and cheap. This situation seems to be an intensified version of what happened in Etruria where tombs on the scale of the princely burials of the seventh century do not appear again but grave furniture remained important. In both areas chamber tombs became common. As far as is known, fresco decoration of the chamber tombs in Italy before the Hellenistic age was only practiced in Etruria and at Etruscan Capua.[16] What happened in Latium?

First of all it is essential to remember that the tomb and its furnishings are hardly the most important part of a funeral. We cannot go back to an archaic Roman funeral, but we do have eyewitness testimony to a patrician funeral of the second century BC. The source is the Greek Polybius, who was held as a hostage at Rome in honorable and comfortable conditions and lived to write the history of the wars between Rome and Carthage.[17] Polybius was deeply impressed by the majesty of the scene, the grand eulogies and the ghostly presence of the dead man's ancestors impersonated by living family members who wore the portrait masks and the official robes of the public offices attained by each. There is not a word about grave goods and had there been any they would have been insignificant compared to what was done and said on the occasion.

That rituals no less formalized and no less noble were practiced by the early Latins can be surmised from the tombs which reflect an intense conceptualization of the dead. Through miniature replicas they are provided with a house, table, cooking wares and knives, and arms. The figurines found in only a few men's tombs suggest a particular function of the deceased. And at Osteria dell'Osa the family remained gathered around the *paterfamilias* in death as it had been in life. Cremation was clearly a rite of honor, but the preference between cremation and inhumation was never absolute and in the later history of early Rome inhumation was more in fashion. In the age of the "princely" burials what is different, among the tombs of those who can afford to manifest the ideology of the burial in the most lavish material way, is the quantity and expenses of the furniture rather than the essential notion of the tomb. The tomb is still in some way a house. The deceased still has the needs of his or her social existence.

We have not yet answered the question why those with means to do so turned from Iron Age miniaturization and abstraction to conspicuous consumption. As traffic began to intensify along the Tyrrhenian coast and to move inland up the Tiber, the leaders of the emerging Roman and Latin *gentes* and their counterparts in the Etruscan cities to the north found themselves with an embarrassment of riches. Objects of gold, silver, and ivory had come their way by barter or by the gift giving that accompanies all manner of transactions. They could have ostrich eggs if they wished (known in nearby Etruria). Artisans working in precious materials and Greek pottery styles were setting up their workshops. But the essential economy of Latium was not ready for the infusion of such quantities of objects of high intrinsic value. In later centuries the Romans were fond of exaggerating the simplicity of early life in Latium.[18] But it is a fact that the Romans had no coin money until the third century and that down to the time of the First Punic War they were settling their accounts *per aes et libram* (by bronze and the scale, i.e. by weighing out raw metal, *aes rude*). The gold and silver and ivory and ostrich eggs that came into Italy, however proud their new owners might be of them, were outside the local system of value. They could be hoarded up for prestige but they were not easily turned into instruments of exchange. Some of this wealth might be consumed in gift exchange; some might go to sanctuaries; some could be kept from one generation to another; another part, with little remorse on the part of the heirs, could be handed over to the dead.[19]

This behavior may seem curious, but it is not unknown even today. In the later years of the existence of the communist state of Yugoslavia numerous families were faced with the dilemma of limited possibilities to employ their cash resources. They turned to the purchase of consumer goods to furnish ever more elaborate cottages at the family cemetery plots.[20] The dead, and their relatives visiting the tombs, were thus the recipients of languishing resources. A change in the economic situation, of course, would stop such practices.

Just such an abrupt change occurred in Latium at the end of the seventh century. Tomb furniture went from extravagant to frugal or non-existent. The Law of the Twelve Tables, assembled in the fifth century but certainly containing long-standing regulations, contained sumptuary laws controlling funerals. Excessive display, especially the practice of self-laceration by the women mourners, was forbidden. And gold tomb goods, except for crowns won through heroism or other public achievement, were prohibited.[21] But was the legal restriction on gold funeral goods the cause of the changes in burial or a manifestation of more fundamental economic conditions? Without falling prey to excessive trust in the annalistic tradition, it seems clear that around 600 Rome was drawn into the Etruscan orbit. According to tradition an Etruscan dynasty ruled the city. Whatever the truth of the stories believed in later centuries, Rome was now part of an urbanized region, and Etruscans were frequenting the Sant'Omobono sanctuary, as we know from the ivory lion of Araz Silqetena, and before long had given their name to the Vicus Tuscus. The luxury of Rome, as revealed by the imported materials and Greek pottery from the Sant'Omobono sanctuary, rivaled that of the great Etruscan cities. Domestic architecture vaulted ahead from simple thatched houses to *atrium* mansions built with cut stone walling and tile roofs. And the two such buildings standing side by side on the Sacra Via, like two Victorian city houses on a fashionable avenue, suggest that a growing population and congestion were now typical of Rome. Rome's population explosion can be inferred from the evidence at other towns along the river, Antemnae, Fidenae, and Crustumerium. Recent survey work, as we have seen, suggests that the seventh and sixth centuries were periods of vigorous growth not only of the town centers but in the surrounding countryside. It is clear that Rome is now a city in the true sense of the word.[22]

Archaic temple building in central Italy, shown in its first Roman example by the temple in the Sant'Omobono sanctuary, is no more precocious in Latium than in Etruria. But the inspiration for the decoration of the Sant'Omobono temple looks outside of central Italy to the heraldic felines who were placed in pediments of Greek temples of the period. The traffic along the Tiber, now just as much as two hundred years before when the first Greek pottery came to Rome, kept Rome in touch with distant places. The pace of the economy and thus the circulation of goods and materials representing a reserve of value accelerated, despite the cumbersome Roman methods of payment. The precious articles that formerly added prestige but not readily wealth to the Latin households were now more easily convertible. The dead could do without them. And they could do without the utilitarian equipment that had been added to the exotica of the "rich" tombs, some of them expensive and useful things like chariots. It cannot have been easy for the family to have put the high-wheeled chariot, surely in perfectly functioning condition, in the grave with the woman buried in Tomb 70 at Acqua Acetosa, Laurentina. But bury it they did, and there may well have been a general sense of relief as fashions changed. And rather than causing the change, one may suspect that the provisions passed down in the Law of the Twelve Tables simply put the public seal on what was already happening. What is important is that funeral customs give us no reason to think that the traditions and beliefs of the Latins did not continue essentially unchanged from the Iron Age down to the Republic. The phenomenon of the "rich" tombs of the seventh century is one of fashion, not of belief.[23]

The Tiber thus acted as a funnel of people, goods, and ideas. The two most important cities of the coast immediately north and south of the Tiber mouth, Etruscan Caere and Latin Lavinium, also played a conspicuous role in the process by which Rome assimilated foreign culture, Greek and Etruscan. Caere maintained a special relation with Rome. It was here that the Vestals and the *sacra* of the Roman state were sent for safety at the time of the Gallic sack.[24] And Caere was the university town where young Romans studied Etruscan lore and ritual.[25] To the south of the Tiber mouth was Lavinium. This Latin city was home to the Aeneas legend of Rome's distant past. It was here that the Romans looked for the origins of some of their most precious cults, Vesta and the Penates (later identified with the Greek divinities Castor and Pollux).

By the end of the sixth century Roman temples were being decorated with terracottas that belong to a central Italian *koine*, some of them produced from molds that were used in other cities, both Caere and Velletri. The itinerant craftsmen may have included Greeks. There was a story that the temple of Ceres on the slopes of the Aventine, erected in the fifth century, was decorated by Greeks, Damophilos and his associate Gorgasos.[26]

In fact there is one surviving piece of terracotta sculpture from Rome that is worthy of a Greek master. This is the torso of a wounded warrior from the Esquiline (fig. 13.1). There is no way of knowing how this superb piece of sculpture was displayed, but it must have come from a major shrine of the mid-fifth century.[27] The closest comparison for the piece is with the Amazon from the *metope* of Temple E at Greek Selinus in Sicily of about 460 BC.[28] The quality of the work has suggested a relation to the large-scale terracotta sculpture known at Greek Poseidonia.[29]

The Esquiline fragment is evidence for the prosperous and vigorous Rome of the fifth century. Although the quantity and quality of the Attic black figured vases, and pottery from other Greek cities, found in the Sant'Omobono sanctuary is striking, the finds of fragments of Greek figured pottery of the next century are by no means insignificant. It is wrong to say on the basis of pottery imports that Rome went into a depression in the fifth century.[30] Another index of the economic wellbeing of the time is provided by the sarcophagi made of imported Greek marble which come from the

Esquiline necropolis and which are now attributed to the fifth century.[31] Testimonia to statuary in Rome of an early date, especially portrait statues of the period of the kings and of the early Republic, are not lacking.[32] But only one example of major sculpture of the early age has survived, the Capitoline Wolf, preserved throughout the Middle Ages, first in the Lateran and from some time after AD 1438 on the Capitoline (fig. 13.2). The statue is housed today in the Capitoline Museum with the suckling twins added in the late fifteenth century, possibly by Antonio Pollaiuolo.[33] There has been speculation that this was the wolf which stood originally on the Capitoline and was struck by lightning in 65 BC. The statue, a wolf with the twins, was knocked off its pedestal. What happened thereafter is unsure, although it has been argued that the statue was buried and thus preserved. There were, of course, numerous wolf statues in Rome, in the Forum and in the Lupercal Cave especially.[34]

To the evidence pointing to the cultural continuity of Rome from the early Iron Age down to the Middle Republic one must add the character of the votive deposits from the city. In the "regal" period and during the fifth century they continue the tradition of miniaturization of figurines, vessels,

Figure 13.1 Torso of terracotta statue from the Esquiline, Antiquarium Comunale –
Musei Capitolini.

and clay models of loaves of bread. Together with the Latin language, Roman religion, for all its frequent adoption of foreign cults, as in the case of Ceres/Demeter with foreign priestesses and foreign rites, remained at bottom determinedly Roman.

The Romans during the three centuries and more between the arrival of the first Greek and Punic vessels in the Tiber in the eighth century and the suppression of the Latin League, earned their supremacy in Latium from their position on the river.[35] Because of the Tiber they gained a population, a diversity, resources, and sophistication that made Rome a city far different from the town of the simple farmers that it became in later tradition. The control of the Tiber, and of potential competitors, was an early objective. In later times the Romans wanted to believe that Romulus had already attacked the upstream towns Fidenae and Crustumerium and that Ancus Marcius had planted the flag at Ostia.[36] Eventually they did both, freed themselves from Etruscan rulers, pushed back their Etruscan neighbors by capturing Veii, and dominated the Latins. That they accomplished this, under the leadership of the senate, a priestly corporation that made itself into a council of state, is one of the feats of history.[37]

Figure 13.2 Bronze statue of a she-wolf, "Lupa Capitolina," Musei Capitolini, Palazzo dei Conservatori.

NOTES

1 INTRODUCTION

1 Reaching the year 390 Livy prefaced the chapter continuing his history with the remark that in the preceding period, "Events were much obscured by their excessive age just as if they were observed, but barely, far in the distance" ("res cum vetustate nimia obscuras velut quae magno ex intervallo loci vix cernuntur," VI, 1, 1–2).

2 B. W. Frier (1979) *Libri Annales Pontificum Maximorum*, Rome (*Papers and Monographs of the American Academy in Rome 27*).

3 There was also a fire in the Regia, which was occupied by the Pontifex Maximus, in 148, Julius Obsequens LXXVIII.

4 Of these inscriptions large fragments remain, *Fasti Capitolini: recensuit praefatus est indicibus instruxit Atilius Degrassi* (1947) Padua.

5 "His laudationibus historia rerum nostrarum est facta mendosior: multa enim scripta sunt in eis quae facta non sunt, falsi triumphi, plures consulatus, genera etiam falsa et ad plebem transitiones cum homines humiliores in alienum eiusdem nominis infunderentur genus."

6 M. Torelli (1975) *Elogia Tarquiniensia*, Florence. Note should be taken of the fragment of a mural with "historical" scenes from a tomb of the first half of the third century on the Esquiline celebrating the military exploits of a Quintus Fabius, *Roma Medio Repubblicana*, no. 283, E. La Rocca (1985), in *Ricerche di pittura ellenistica*, Rome: 169–191. For the scenes with figures from early Roman history in the François Tomb from Vulci see below, pp. 5–7.

7 Especially B. G. Niebuhr (1826ff.) *Römische Geschichte*, Bonn, translated quickly into English by J. C. Hare and C. Thirwall (1828–1842) Cambridge. Macaulay's *Lays of Ancient Rome* was an attempt to recreate the genre.

8 "Impudenter facta, negligenter praetermissa."

9 Diodorus, the Sicilian Greek writer, continued a Hellenic tradition in compiling a universal history recounted year by year. His account is fragmentary but is valuable for its independence from the traditions represented by Livy and Dionysius. Again moralizing in tone, there are the lives of Romulus, Numa, and Publicola in Greek by Plutarch (before AD 50 to after AD 120). Finally, of the early parts of the general history of Dio Cassius (*consul suffectus* before AD 210) only fragments remain.

10 Leading to the critical treatises of the seventeenth and early eighteenth century, J. Perizonius (1685) *Animadversiones historiae*, Amsterdam, L. Beaufort (1738) *Dissertation sur l'incertitude des cinq premières siècles de l'histoire romaine*, Utrecht. On the birth and growth of skepticism in Roman history, see

A. Momigliano (1980) "Perizonio, Niebuhr e il carattere della tradizione romana primitiva," *Rivista Storica Italiana* 92: 561–571, reprinted in (1984) *Settimo contributo alla storia degli studi classici e del mondo antico*, Rome: 155–170 and in (1989) *Roma arcaica*, Florence: 449–465, also R. T. Ridley (1989) "The Historical Observations of Jacob Perizonius," *Memorie dei Lincei* ser. 8, 32: 187–295.

11 Especially in (1913–1920) *Storia critica di Roma durante i primi cinque secoli*, 4 vols, Rome and in English (1905) *Ancient Legends of Roman History*, New York. For Niebuhr, see above, note 7.

12 (1854–1856) 3 vols, Berlin.

13 See below, pp. 20–36.

14 The initial discovery was made in 1907. For this and later excavation, see S. M. Puglisi (1951) *Gli abitatori primitivi del Palatino attraverso le testimonianze archeologiche e le nuove indagini stratigrafiche sul Germalo* (*MA* 41).

15 *CIL* I ed. 2 no. 1, *Inscriptiones Latinae Rei Publicae* no. 3, among discussions R. L. Palmer (1969) *The King and the Comitium*, Wiesbaden. The canonical story of Romulus' assumption among the gods might be at variance with the existence of the founder's tomb, but topographical tradition proved as strong as logic.

16 G. De Sanctis (1907–1923) *Storia dei Romani*, 5 vols, Rome; K. J. Beloch (1926) *Römische Geschichte*, Berlin and Leipzig.

17 I. S. Ryberg (1929) "Early Roman Traditions in the Light of Archaeology," *MAAR* 7: 1–118.

18 *Nuova Antologia* August 16, 1936: 405–416, reprinted (1936) *Pagine stravaganti di un filologo* 2, Florence, 3–21.

19 (1938) *BC* 66: 279–282.

20 (1953–1973) *ER*.

21 So R. M. Ogilvie (1976) *Early Rome and the Etruscans*, Hassocks, Sussex; L. Quilici (1979) *Roma primitiva e le origini della civiltà laziale*, Rome; A. Grandazzi (1991) *La Fondation de Rome*, Paris. Contra, H. Riemann (1969) "Beiträge zur römischen Topographie," *RM*: 103–121, A. Alföldi (1963) *Early Rome and the Latins*, Ann Arbor (Jerome Lectures, 7th Series) and (1976) *Römische Frühgeschichte, Kritik und Forschung seit 1964*, Heidelberg, J. Poucet (1985) *Les Origines de Rome*, Brussels.

22 Of the extensive bibliography see most recently S. Steingräber, ed. (1986) *Etruscan Painting*, New York, no. 178; F. Buranelli (1987) *La Tomba François di Vulci*, Rome; and A. Maggiani (1983) "Nuovi dati per la ricostruzione del ciclo pittorico della Tomba François," *DdA* 3, 1: 71–78 as well as the remarks of F. Coarelli, ibid.: 43–69. For historical questions in the frescoes, see R. Thomsen (1980) *King Servius Tullius*, Copenhagen: 96ff. and A. Momigliano (1984) *Settimo contributo alla storia degli studi classici e del mondo antico*, Rome: 147 and 183.

23 Arnobius *Ad Nat.* VI, 7, refers to an Aulus buried on the Capitoline. Aulus Vibenna is unquestionably an archaic Etruscan name; it is found on a graffito from Veii, *Testimonia Linguae Etruscae* II no. 35.

24 H. B. Walters (1899) *Catalogue of the Bronzes, Greek, Roman, and Etruscan in the Department of Greek and Roman Antiquities, British Museum*, London: no. 633; see J. P. Small (1982) *Cacus and Marsyas in Etrusco-Roman Legend*, Princeton: 13 and Appendix I.

25 Generally translated "king" but certainly with the sense of the Homeric *basileus*, i.e. "lord."

26 For the various members of the Tarquin family, see T. N. Gantz (1975) "The Tarquin Dynasty," *Historia* 24: 539–554.

27 (1973–1974) "La topografia romana e l'istoriografia della Roma arcaica," *AC*

25–26: 123–131.

28 The identification is certain. See Platner and Ashby ad verb., Richardson ad verb.

29 For the background of the cult at Lavinium see below, pp. 133–134.

30 I. Nielsen and J. Zahle (1985) "The Temple of Castor and Pollux in the Roman Forum. Preliminary Report I," *Acta Archaeologica* 56: 1–29, for the architectural terracottas, see also K. M. Phillips in E. M. Steinby, ed. (1989) *Lacus Iuturnae* I (*Lavori e Studi di Archeologia* 12), Rome: 277–302. *Grande Roma*: 4.1.5, 4.1.6, 3.4.1, 3.4.2.

31 *Grande Roma*: 3.2.

32 *Grande Roma*: 3.4.

33 G. Gronne (1987) "Ultime indagini nel tempio dei Castores," *AL* 8: 83–87.

34 On the historical circumstances surrounding the introduction of the Dioscuri at Rome, where they were equated with the Penates, see for example M. Sordi (1972) *La leggenda dei Dioscuri nella battaglia della Sagra e di Lago Regillo* (*Contributi dell'Istituto di storia antica, Università del Sacro Cuore* I): 47–70.

35 There are no remains of the superstructure. Dionysius of Halicarnassus (IV, 61) gives a precise description but modern restorations are completely hypothetical, as for example that of Gjerstad, *ER* III, which incorporates only three fragmentary terracottas from the Capitoline Hill (none of them clearly associated with the building) in an otherwise conjectural restoration, which draws largely on elements from the Sant'Omobono sanctuary. Any element of the building left after the fire of 83 was probably removed from the site, as happened after the later fire of AD 69 by order of the *haruspices*: Tacitus *Hist.* IV, 53.

36 F. Castagnoli (1974) "Topografia e urbanistica di Roma nel IV secolo a.C.," *Studi Romani* 22: 425–443, esp. 434.

37 *ER* III: 176–177; see also T. Hackens (1962) "A propos de la topographie du Capitole," *Bulletin de l'Institut Historique Belge de Rome* 34: 9–26.

38 So Tacitus *Hist.* III, 72 and Dion. Hal. IV, 61, 4.

39 Livy (VII, 3, 5–8) records that a nail was driven into the doorpost of the cella of Minerva of the Temple of Jupiter Optimus Maximus on the Ides of September. The rite would have been as old as the temple, and therefore should have given an exact count of the years elapsed since the dedication. However, the practice had been interrupted and revived ("Intermisso deinde more digna etiam per se visa res propter quam dictator crearetur"), thus robbing us of a promising chronological link between the Augustan Age and early Rome. Livy knew, apparently from Cincius Alimentius, whom he cites in this passage regarding similar rites in Etruria, of an ancient law ("lex vetusta est, priscis litteris verbisque scripta") that governed the rite and its execution by the praetor maximus. This official is otherwise unknown and his title has generally been taken as a synonym for consul, i.e. the chief magistrate of the state. There is more than a slight possibility, however, that this lex vetusta, like the inscriptions of the François Tomb, preserves a real element of early Rome, in this case perhaps the most important magistracy of its time, which had been forgotten in the annalistic tradition. In a similar fashion the term "comitatus maximus" used in the Law of the Twelve Tables (*XII Tabulae*, IX: 1–2), where one would expect the utmost verbal precision, may not be a synonym for one of the better known Roman assemblies but, like the praetor maximus, a genuine political artifact from the lost history of early Rome. On the praetor maximus see further A. Momigliano (1968) "Praetor Maximus e questioni affini," *Studi in onore di G. Grosso*, Turin: 161–175, reprinted in (1969) *Quarto contributo alla storia degli studi classici e del mondo antico*, Rome: 403–417 and (1989) *Roma arcaica*, Florence: 171–181.

40 This is the opinion of G. von Kaschnitz-Weinberg (1962) *Die Grundlage der republikanischen Baukunst*, Reinbeek: 58 and of H. Rieman (1969) "Beiträge zur

römischen Topographie II: Zum Kapitolinischen Tempel des Iupiter Optimus Maximus," *RM* 76: 110–121.

41 The supposition, frequently repeated, that the *quadriga* of 296 was a replacement for an early piece is without foundation.

42 The suspension of work on the building reminds one of the project of the Athenian tyrant Peisistratos (who ruled with interruptions from 561 to 527) for a giant temple to Olympian Zeus which was also interrupted. The continuation of the Athenian project was financed by Antiochos IV of Syria in the second century. It was from this building that Sulla took columns for the restoration of Jupiter Optimus Maximus after the fire of 83: Pliny *NH* XXXVI, 45.

43 "Ludos magnos ex senatu consulto vovit Veiis captis se facturum aedemque Matutae Matris refectam dedicaturam, iam ante ab rege Servio Tullio dedicatam."

44 "Romae foedum incendium per duae noctes ac diem unum tenuit. Solo aequata omnia inter Salinas ac portam Carmentalem cum Aequimaelio Iugarioque vico et templis Fortunae et Matris Matutae. Et extra portam est vagatus ignis sacra profanaque multa absumpsit." The limits of the devastation are defined north–south by reference to the Salinae at the foot of the Aventine and the Porta Carmentalis at the foot of the Capitoline. The Vicus Aequimaelius ran off the Vicus Jugarius between the Forum Boarium and the Forum Romanum and so serves to establish the limit that the fire reached along the Vicus Jugarius. If the topographical reference points of this passage are envisaged as functioning in this way, it would have been pointless for Livy to include the temple in the Sant'Omobono sanctuary, which must be located within a few meters of the Porta Carmentalis, wherever this elusive gate in the Servian Walls actually stood. The temples must have been mentioned as indications of the extent of the fire in another direction, perhaps toward the Palatine. The temples were rebuilt the year after the fire: Livy XXV, 7, 6.

45 "L. Stertinius . . . de manubiis duos fornices in foro boario ante Fortunae aedem et Matris Matutae unam in maximo circo fecit et his fornicibus signa aurata imposuit." Under the empire the passage between the two temples was partially occupied by a structure supported on six large pylons. F. Coarelli (1988) *Il Foro Boario*, Rome: 363–414, with appendix of G. Ioppolo: 443–450 and esp. fig. 112, p. 454, identifies this structure as an arch with cross passages (*janus quadrifrons*). It is only with the greatest difficulty that this structure can be interpreted as a successor of the arches of Stertinius, which stood in front of (*ante*) the temples of Fortuna and Mater Matuta, wherever they may have been located.

46 Castagnoli, cited note 27.

47 The evidence of the excavations, in so far as they have been carried out and published, suggests that the twin temples were not erected until the third century. Thus neither could be a restoration made by Marcus Furius Camillus in the early fourth century. See below, p. 80.

48 See below, pp. 91–101.

49 Recent excavations have revealed the early foundations of the Temple of Saturn in the Forum: G. Maetzke (1989) "Scavi nell'area occidentale del Foro Romano," *Archeo* 48: 66–73. Other *cappellaccio* (tufa) foundations on the northern end of the Capitoline (the arx), often considered parts of early fortifications or simple terraces, have been associated with the temple of Juno Moneta and the Auguraculum (space reserved for taking auspices) by G. Giannelli (1980–1981) "Il tempio di Giunone Moneta e la casa di Marco Manlio Capitolino," *BC* 87: 7–36.

50 For the general background, see A. P. Anzidei, A. M. Bietti Sestieri, and A. De Santis (1985) *Roma e il Lazio dall'età della pietra alla formazione della città*, Rome.

51 S. Omobono: *ER* III: 435–436; Capitoline: personal communication Dr Anna Sommella Mura.

52 See p. 44.

53 See R. R. Holloway (1991) *The Archaeology of Ancient Sicily*, London: ch. 1.

54 Summary R. R. Holloway (1992) "Italy and the Central Mediterranean in the Crisis Years," in W. Ward and M. Joukowsky, eds *The Crisis Years: The 12th Century BC*, Dubuque: 40–45.

55 The long-discounted interpretation of the Terremare as planned cities, championed especially by Luigi Pigorini, has recently found support in the results of the excavations at Poviglio (Reggio Emilia): see M. Bernabò Brea and M. Cremaschi (1989) *La Terramara di Poviglio, Le campagne di scavo 1985–1989*, Reggio Emilia.

56 In general see S. S. Lukesh (1984) "Italy and the Apennine Culture," in T. Hackens, N. D. Holloway, and R. R. Holloway, eds *Crossroads of the Mediterranean*, Providence and Louvain: 13–54 and A. M. Bietti Sestieri, "Central and Southern Italy in the Late Bronze Age," ibid.: 55–122. Specifically for Latium, see M. A. Fugazzola Delpino (1973) *Testimonianze di cultura appenninica nel Lazio*, Florence.

57 It is now known in Latium at Casale Nuovo near Satricum: M. Angle and A. Zarattini (1987) "L'insediamento protostorico di Casale Nuovo," *AL* 8: 250–252.

58 See the papers collected in (1979) *Il Bronzo finale in Italia* (Atti della XXI Riunione Scientifica dell'Istituto Italiano di Preistoria e Protostoria, 1977), Florence; G. Bartoloni (1989) *La cultura Villanoviana*, Rome: ch. 3; M. A. Fugazzola Delpino (1979) "The Proto-Villanovan: A Survey," in D. and F. R. Ridgway, eds *Italy before the Romans*, London and New York: 31–54.

59 For a summary of the Villanova culture, see G. Bartoloni, cited in note 58; H. Hencken (1968) *Tarquinia and Etruscan Origins*, New York and Washington.

60 See Anzidei, Bietti Sestieri, De Santis, cited in note 50: 137–139.

61 P. G. Gierow (1964–1966) *The Iron Age Culture of Latium*, 2 vols (*Skrifter* 24), A. M. Bietti Sestieri (1992) *The Iron Age Cemetery of Osteria dell'Osa (Rome) – A Study of socio-political development in central Tyrrhenian Italy*, Cambridge. For the relation between the earliest Roman tombs and the groups from the Alban Hills, see A. M. Bietti Sestieri and G. Bergonzi (1979) "La fase più antica della cultura laziale," *Il Bronzo finale in Italia* (Atti della XXI Riunione Scientifica dell'Istituto Italiano di Preistoria e Protostoria, 1977), Florence: 399–424.

62 G. Bartoloni, cited in note 58: 161, Bisenzio and Veii.

63 The Alban/Roman cemeteries are often compared to the Tolfa/Allumiere group north of the Tiber in the hills behind Caere, but this group is another, and independent, offshoot of the Proto-Villanovan.

64 See p. 125.

65 For Sicily, see Holloway cited in note 53. For southern Italy, see T. J. Dunbabin (1949) *The Western Greeks*, Oxford and more recently P. G. Guzzo (1982) *Le Città Scomparse della Magna Grecia*, Rome.

66 D. Ridgway (1984) *L'Alba della Magna Grecia*, Milan. English translation (1992) *The First Western Greeks*, Cambridge.

67 A. Rathje (1979) "Oriental Imports in Etruria in the Eighth and Seventh Centuries B.C.: Their Origins and Implications," in Ridgway and Ridgway, cited in note 58: 145–186.

68 F. M. Cross (1986) "Phoenicians in the West: the Early Epigraphic Evidence," in M. Balmuth, ed. *Studies in Sardinian Archaeology* II, Ann Arbor: 117–130.

69 See the discussion in A. M. Bietti Sestieri (1992) *The Iron Age Cemetery of Osteria dell'Osa (Rome) – A Study of socio-political development in central*

Tyrrhenian Italy, Cambridge.

70 Short description and color photographs in F. Coarelli (1974) *Guida archeologica di Roma*, Milan: 339–341; still basic, T. Frank (1924) *Roman Buildings of the Republic* (*Papers and Monographs of the American Academy in Rome* 3).

71 In Chapter 7 a possible use of the Anio stone in the third century will be suggested.

2 TOMBS OF THE FORUM AND ESQUILINE

1 Also shared by G. Pinza (1898) "Le civiltà primitive del Lazio," *BC* 26: 157.

2 Good general discussion by M. Taloni in *Roma Medio Repubblicana*: 188–196.

3 (1875) "Le antichissime sepolture esquiline," *BC* 3: 41–54.

4 (1885) "Necropoli arcaica romana e parte di essa scoperta presso S. Martino ai Monti," *BC* 13: 39–53.

5 *Monumenti primitivi di Roma e del Lazio primitivo* (*MA* 15), supplemented for the Esquiline by important topographical information in (1912) "Monumenti paleoetnologici raccolti nei musei comunali," *BC* 40: 15–102, esp. 15–24.

6 The cremation *pozzo* tombs of the Esquiline have not been preserved and are neglected in accounts of the cemetery; see below, p. 23 and note 15.

7 This material has been recovered in large part through the efforts of Dr Anna Sommella Mura: see (1988) "Il periodo orientalizzante a Roma: nuove acquisizioni," *Bollettino della Unione Storia ed Arte* 81: 17–21.

8 Ibid. On the inscription, see M. Guarducci (1967) "Un epigrafe greca arcaica a Roma," *RP* 49: 85–92. The name has also been read *Kleikles* or *Kleiklos*: G. Colonna (1987) "Etruria e Lazio nell'età dei Tarquini," *Etruria e Lazio Arcaico* (*Quaderni del Centro di Studi per l'Archeologia Etrusco-Italica* 15), Rome: 55–56, esp. 57.

9 Note the presence of the funeral couch in the tomb houses of wood of the seventh century at Acqua Acetosa, Laurentina, below, p. 120.

10 G. Colonna (1977) "Un aspetto oscuro del Lazio antico, le tombe del VI–V secolo," *Lazio arcaico e mondo greco*: 131–165, see also *Enea nel Lazio*: C68. Cremation continued in the same period: see the tomb described by G. Pinza (1912) *BC* 40: 78.

11 On the later material see especially I. Scott Ryberg (1940) *An Archaeological Record of Rome* (*Studies and Documents* 12: 1), London and Philadelphia.

12 G. Pinza (1905) *Monumenti primitivi di Roma e del Lazio primitivo* (*MA* 15): col. 206g and 562. Pinza knew of only one gold object said to come from the necropolis: ibid.: col. 552.

13 Ibid.: col. 246a; for others see Müller-Karpe (1959) *Von Anfang Roms* (*RM Ergh.* 6): pl. 16.

14 So charged by Pinza (1912) *BC* 40: 19.

15 De Rossi (1885) *BC* 13: 45 specifically mentions the discovery of a hut urn. This must be for a cremation grave, and De Rossi confirms the presence of such graves first by comparing the graves from Sant'Eusebio to the cremation burials of the Alban Hills and then by noting that as excavation continued, "Inhumation became frequent" ("L'inumazione divenne frequente"). A similar tomb is represented by Pinza, cited in note 12: CXII.

16 Reports (1902–1906, 1911) *NSc*.

17 Not the earliest; Lanciani published a balloon photo of the Forum in (1900) *BC* 28: pl. I.

18 Some corrections to the original identifications were made by C.-H. Hjortsjö and N.-G. Gejvall in *ER* II: Appendix II.

19 Some additions and corrections by H. Helback in *ER* II: 287–294.

20 Tombs A and B: (1902) *NSc.*: 96–111.

21 At this point in the excavation Boni identified a small mound of debris over the tomb the outline of which showed in the stratigraphic section of the excavation trench. This and several other mounds like it he took to be collapsed huts, but they are too small to be such and moreover contained fragments of roof tiles which did not come into use until the end of the seventh century. These features have never been explained satisfactorily.

22 (1903) *NSc.*: 146–159.

23 (1903) *NSc.*: 159–164.

24 A modern chemical substitute (polyethylene glycol) is now used because of the health and safety drawbacks of acetone and celluloid. It would be possible to carry out dendrochronological dating of the coffins from the Forum but this has not been done as yet.

25 (1903) *NSc.*: 381–393.

26 Four were infant burials without grave goods placed in jars whose mouths were closed by roof tiles. These come from upper strata and belong to an era when this part of the Forum was clearly occupied by rectangular buildings with stone foundations and tile roofs (after ca 625).

27 The relation of the early tombs of the Sepulcretum to other Iron Age burials of the time in Latium has been discussed in a penetrating article by A. M. Bietti Sestieri (1986) "Analisi di contesti funerari, i dati archeologici di fronte alla teoria," *DdA* n.s. 4: 249–263. The relationships are close, but the Roman tombs of the Forum are exceptional for the high incidence of cremation for women.

28 For two other unpublished tombs inside the podium of the Temple of Divine Julius, see E. Carnabuci (1991) "L'angolo sud-orientale del Foro Romano nel manoscritto inedito di Giacomo Boni," *Memorie dei Lincei* ser. 9, 1: 249–363, esp. 331, note 253.

29 *ER* I: 82–85. Gjerstad's retouched color photograph (fig. 59) of vases in situ with the caption "as found" was taken, of course, from the reconstruction in the Antiquarium of the Forum and Palatine.

30 (1932) *Giacomo Boni*, Milan II: 60.

31 Early Rome still makes news. I awoke one morning in 1968 to the report of the discovery of the *Heroon* of Aeneas at Lavinium on American radio. The "wall of Romulus" on the Palatine slope toward the Velia received similar coverage; see Chapter 7.

32 Varro *LL* V, 157.

33 Others at the time preferred to think that the vases were imitations of Iron Age pottery made in the time of Domitian! See *ER* I: 82–85.

34 There are occasional weapons in the Esquiline graves. But little weight can be placed on their absence in the Forum where there are sixteen adult inhumation graves with tomb goods to compare with ninety-four from the Esquiline.

35 G. Pinza, cited in note 12: 782–788.

36 Appeals to a long-standing tradition in the Forum, evidenced by the cremation burials and particularly by the close relation of the earliest of them to the cremation cemeteries of the Alban Hills (Latian par excellence) and the intrusive character on the Esquiline of the Sabines, whose grave goods were held to have more in common with a wider spectrum of Italic peoples of the peninsula (the so-called Fossa Grave Group), do not take into account the poorly documented but undeniable cremation graves in the Esquiline cemetery.

37 (1962) *Zur Stadtwerdung Roms (RM Ergh.* 8).

38 The presence or absence of cremation was not a distinguishing feature between Periods I and II in the Forum because two cremation graves (T and GG) belong to Period IIA.

39 (1960) "Per una nuova cronologia del sepolcreto arcaico del Foro," *Civiltà del Ferro*, Bologna: 464–499.
40 (1959) *Von Anfang Roms (RM Ergh. 6)*.
41 *ER* II.
42 "Preistoria e protostoria di Roma e del Lazio," *Popoli e Civiltà dell'Italia Antica* II, Rome: 275–346.
43 *ER* II: 282–286.
44 For further considerations concerning infant and child burials see the discussion of the evidence from the cemetery of Osteria dell'Osa in Chapter 8.

3 CHRONOLOGY

1 (1905) *Monumenti primitivi di Roma e del Lazio antico (MA 15)*.
2 (1980) *La formazione della città (DdA n.s. 2: 1–2)*.
3 H. Müller-Karpe (1962) *Zur Stadtwerdung Roms (RM Ergh. 8)*; R. Peroni (1960) "Per una nuova cronologia del sepolcreto arcaico del Foro," *Civiltà del Ferro*, Bologna: 464–499.
4 Discussed for early Rome by J. C. Meyer (1983) *PreRepublican Rome (Analecta Romana Instituti Danici* supp. 11): 39–40 who makes a smooth line right-side graph including the criteria of cremation/inhumation, *pozzo* or *fossa* grave, presence or absence of coffin, sex, age (adult/child).
5 (1979) "Preliminary Cluster Analysis of Iron Age Tombs from the Roman Forum," *Il Bronzo finale in Italia (Atti della XXI Riunione Scientifica dell'Istituto Italiano di Preistoria e Protostoria*, 1977), Florence: 461–475.
6 (1986) "Analisi di contesti funerari: i dati archeologici di fronte alla teoria," *DdA* n.s. 4: 249–263.
7 H. Müller-Karpe (1959) Beiträge zur Chronologie der Urnenfelderzeit nördlich und südlich der Alpen (*Römisch-Germanische Forschungen* 22), Berlin.
8 See the papers collected in (1979) *Il Bronzo finale in Italia (Atti della XXI Riunione Scientifica dell'Istituto Italiano di Preistoria e Protostoria*, 1977), Florence; M. A. Fugazzola Delpino (1979) "The Proto-Villanovan: A Survey," in D. and F. R. Ridgway, eds *Italy before the Romans*, London and New York: 31–54; A. P. Anzidei, A. M. Bietti Sestieri, and A. De Santis (1985) *Roma e il Lazio dall'età della pietra alla formazione della città*, Rome: 129–148.
9 P. G. Gierow (1964–1966) *The Iron Age Culture of Latium*, Lund (*Skrifter* 24).
10 R. Peroni (1979) "L'insediamento subappeninico della Valle del Foro e il problema della continuità di insediamento tra l'età del bronzo recente e quella finale nel Lazio," *AC* 31: 171–176. E. Carnabuci (1991) "L'angolo sud-orientale del Foro Romano nel manoscritto inedito di Giacomo Boni," *Memorie dei Lincei* ser. 9, 1: 249–363; M. Bettelli "Le evidenze protostoriche": 328–333 provides an appendix giving further evidence of the sub-Apennine character of lower strata of the central Forum.
11 E. Fabbricotti (1972) "Veio," *NSc.*: 246, fig. 36.
12 R. Kearsley (1989) "The Pendent Semi-Circle Skyphos," *University of London, Institute of Classical Studies, Bulletin* (supp. 44): esp. 126–128; cf. J.-P. Descoeudres and R. Kearsley (1983) "Greek Pottery at Veii, another Look," *BSA* 78: 9–53.
13 For other Greek eighth-century imports at Veii and elsewhere in Etruria and their local imitations see G. Bartoloni (1989) *La Cultura Villanoviana*, Rome: 98–102, 183–188.
14 R. R. Holloway (1991) *The Archaeology of Ancient Sicily*, London: 43–49. For supplementary evidence from the Near East, see J. N. Coldstream (1968) *Greek Geometric Pottery*, London: 302–327.

15 In the review of Müller-Karpe's *Von Anfang Roms*, in (1961) *Gnomon* 33: 378–382, also (1965) "Discussions concerning Early Rome 2," *Skrifter* 23 = *Opuscula Romana* 5: 1–74.

16 *ER* III: 276, fig. 170.

17 See Peroni, cited in note 10.

18 And possibly with a post-Hellenic rather than pre-Hellenic Cumae if the revisions in dating of the Greek cups reviewed above prove to be valid. In this summary I have not discussed Gjerstad's well-founded objection to Müller-Karpe's claim that horizontal stratigraphy of tombs could be found in the Forum sample; the space excavated is simply too small. Müller-Karpe's speculations on cultural relations between Latium and Minoan Crete are not central to his argument (although they influenced his early dating of Period I) and they were justly criticized by Gjerstad. See further P. G. Gierow (1983) "I colli albani nel quadro archeologico della civiltà laziale," *Skrifter* 29: 1 = *Opuscula Romana* 14: 1 = *Lectiones Boëthianae* 5: 7–18.

19 Cited in note 9.

20 Cited in note 6.

21 The disagreements between Gjerstad, his followers, and the holders of the *comunis opinio* as to the seventh century (Period IV) are less profound. They revolve around the dating of imported items from major Etruscan tombs. The focus of the dispute is a faience vase from a rich tomb at Tarquinia bearing the name of the Pharaoh Bocchoris (720–715): H. O. Hencken (1968) *Tarquinia Villanovans and Early Etruscans* (*American Schools of Prehistoric Research Bulletin* 23): 364. How long after it was made did the vessel come to Italy? How long before it was buried in the tomb? Traditionalists have favored earlier dates, the Swedish school later ones. The latter will now find support in the new studies of imported Greek pendent semicircle and chevron cups. As a result Latian Period IV (Etruscan III) may begin at the very end of the eighth century.

22 (1960) "Le origini di Roma," *AC* 12: 1–12 reprinted in (1979) *Saggi di Antichità* I, Rome: 214–247.

4 HUTS AND HOUSES

1 A. M. Bietti Sestieri, J. de Grossi Mazzorin, Anna De Santis (1990) "Fidenae: La struttura dell'età del ferro," *AL* 10: 115–120.

2 This is the analysis of M. Maaskant-Kleibrink (1991) "Early Latin Settlement-Plans at Borgo Le Ferriere (Satricum)," *BABESCH* 66: 51–114.

3 L. Crescenzi and E. Tortorici (1988) "Ardea, resti di capanne nell'area del tempio di Colle della Noce," *QL* 1: 29–32.

4 S. M. Puglisi (1951) *Gli abitatori primitivi del Palatino* (*MA* 41).

5 *ER* III: 63.

6 G. Carettoni (1954–1955) "Tomba arcaica a cremazione scoperta nel Palatino," *BPI* 64: 261–276.

7 *ER* III: 63.

8 M. Fenelli (1984) "Lavinium," *AL* 8: 325–344; M. Fenelli and M. Guaitoli (1990) "Nuovi dati degli scavi di Lavinium," *AL* 9: 182–194.

9 J. R. Brandt (1988) "Ficana: alcune osservazioni su capanne e fosse," *QL* 1: 12–28; L. Crescenzi and E. Tortorici (1988) "Ardea: resti di capanne nell'area del tempio di Colle della Noce," *AL* 9: 29–32. For similar buildings in Etruria etc., see Maaskant-Kleibrink, cited in note 2: 75, note 2.

10 (1903) *NSc.*: 126, 138ff.; *ER* I: 118.

11 Equus Domitiani, *ER* I: 45–46; Arch of Augustus, *ER* III: 268–269; Regia, F. E. Brown (1974–1975) "La protostoria della Regia," *RP* 47: 15–36.

12 I am grateful to Prof. T. Russell Scott, Prof. Brown's successor as director of this work, for kindly permitting me to anticipate the publication of his conclusions.

13 A second burial was discovered in a disturbed condition.

14 For the archaic material from the Temple of Vesta, see *ER* III: 310–320. For the archaic well nearby, see A. Bartoli (1959) "Pozzi dell'area sacra di Vesta," *MA* 45: 1–143, summary *ER* III: 359–374.

15 *ER* I: 139, fig. 130.

16 The section of street from just beyond the Sepulcretum up to the Arch of Titus would not have been the Sacra Via according to the hypothesis of F. Coarelli (1983) *Il Foro Romano* I, Rome: part 1.

17 G. Franciosi (1984) *Ricerche sull'organizzazione gentilizia romana*, Rome.

18 See below, pp. 109–112.

19 There is one exception, the tyrant's palace at Larisa on the Hermos; K. Schefold *et al.* (1940–1942), *Larisa am Hermos: die Ergebnisse der Ausgrabungen, 1902–1934* 1–2, Berlin.

20 The general publication appears in the various fascicles of *Skrifter* 38; cf. S. Stoponni, ed. (1985) *Case e palazzi d'Etruria*, Rome: 41–58.

21 D. A. Amyx (1988) *Corinthian Vase-Painting of the Archaic Period*, Berkeley and London: pl. 57: 1 (Louvre E 635); E. Simon and M. Hirmer (1981) *Die Griechische Vasen*: pl. XI.

22 K. M. Phillips (1989) "The Architectural Terracottas," in E. M. Steinby, ed. *Lacus Iuturnae* I (*LSA* 12), Rome: 277–301, esp. 277–279, pl. I.1.

23 *Grande Roma*: 1.9.

24 The following depends on F. E. Brown (1974–1975), "La protostoria della Regia," cited in note 11, and useful discussion with Prof. T. Russell Scott.

25 *Grande Roma*: 3.2.1–11.

26 Graffito, *Grande Roma*: 1.9.

27 For Satricum, see Maaskant-Kleibrink, cited in note 2; Lavinium in course of excavation; Torrino: A. Bedini (1984) "Scavi a Torrino," *AL* 6: 84–90. Prof. Maaskant is quite right to call into question the idea that these Italic buildings are somehow copies of Greek domestic architecture of the archaic age. What one witnesses in Italy is an organic development of a rectangular building with porch and courtyard on its interior. The only possibly imported element is the block of rooms built with cut stone foundations. But the importation was from the Greeks of south Italy and Sicily, who had the quarrying technique and whose eighth-century houses quickly developed from a single room to a rectangular block; G. Vallet, F. Villard, and P. Auberson (1976) *Mégara Hyblaea, le Quartier de l'Agora archaïque* (*MEFRA*, supp. 1), Rome.

28 I assume that the *atrium* was open rather than roofed in its original form. For the different types of *atrium* see Vitruvius VI, 3.

29 The *atrium* house is seen at its best at Marzabotto, the Etruscan city of the fifth century above Bologna. The development from open surroundings to courtyard houses in a congested cityscape happened earlier. In the central Mediterranean it is seen in the Bronze Age town of Ustica, I Faraglioni.

30 *ER* III: 78, with a group of archaic cisterns. For current excavations, including an archaic shrine, see P. Pensabene, in *Grande Roma*: 86–90 and P. Pensabene, P. Battistelli, L. Borrello, O. Colazingari, S. Falzone with appendix of M. Cristofani (1993) "Campagne di scavo 1988–1991 nell'area sud-ovest del Palatino," *AL* 11, 2: 19–38.

5 THE SANT'OMOBONO SANCTUARY

1 Full bibliography of the research in (1989) *Il viver quotidiano in Roma arcaica*, Rome. The general plan of the excavation has been published in only one place, by S. Panciera (1984) "Volusiana: Appunti epigrafici sui Volusii," *I Volusii Saturnini*, Bari: 83–96, fig. 4, p. 91. I am grateful to Prof. Panciera for this reference.

2 Livy V, 19, 6; Dion. Hal. XXVII, 7. Livy informs us that the Temple of Mater Matuta was restored by Camillus after the capture of Veii in 396.

3 *Roma Medio Repubblicana*: no. 89.

4 The name is also that of a figure of Italian mythology, the son of the river god Tiber: Virgil *Aen.* X: 198. There are a total of four Etruscan graffiti from Rome, two others from the Sant'Omobono sanctuary and a third found in the Forum at the foot of the Capitoline: G. Colonna (1987) "Etruria e Lazio nell'età dei Tarquinii," *Etruria e Lazio Arcaico* (*Quaderni del Centro di Studio per l'Archeologia Etrusco-Italica* 15): 55–66, esp. 58. The Etruscan presence in the neighborhood of Rome is marked by the town, on Monte Mario overlooking the Vatican on the right bank of the Tiber, known from its city wall, documentation exhibited in the Villa Giulia Museum, and its chamber tombs; C. Caprina (1954) "Roma, Via Trionfale," *NSc.*: 195–198.

5 (1977) "La decorazione architettonica del tempio arcaico," *Lazio arcaico e mondo greco*: 62–128, quotation from p. 64. "La ceramica e in particolare i numerosi frammenti di coppe laconiche, ioniche, attiche, rinvenute negli strati relativi alla distruzione e all'abbandono del tempio arcaico, offrono elementi utili per collocare nell'ambito del VI secolo le due fasi di vita del tempio stesso. Infatti, il termine cronologico più alto che possa essere posto in relazione al culto del santuario, è offerto dalla ceramica laconica trovata in strato, che pone la fase iniziale dell'edificio templare intorno al secondo decennio del VI secolo, mentre il termine cronologico più basso è offerto dalle più tarde 'coppe ad occhioni' databili non oltre gli inizi dell'ultimo decennio del VI secolo."

6 The Greek graffito from the Esquiline (see p. 22) adds the third unit to the linguistic make-up of early Rome.

7 The votive material described above excavated behind the temple has been attributed to the second rather than to the first phase of the temple with a consequent rise in date for the second phase to the first half of the sixth century: G. Pisani Sartorio and P. Virgili (1979) "Area sacra di S. Omobono," *AL 2*: 41–45; for considerations to the contrary, see F. Coarelli (1988) *Il Foro Boario*, Rome: 216–221.

8 A. Andren (1940) *Architectural Terracottas from Etrusco-Italian Temples* (*Skrifter* 6): 343, 409, pls 104, 126, 127, cf. (1971) "Osservazioni sulle terrecotte architettoniche," *Skrifter* 31 = *Opuscula Romana* 8: 1–16; A. Åkerstrom (1954) "Untersuchungen über die figurlichen terrakottenfriese aus Etruria und Latium," *Skrifter* 18 = *Opuscula Romana* 1: 191–231; T. N. Gantz (1974) "Terracotta Figured Friezes from the Workshop of Vulca," *Skrifter* 24 = *Opuscula Romana* 10: 1–22. From the Sant'Omobono sanctuary there are two other types of cornice plaques, both possibly intended for a lateral cornice, one with a similar scene of chariots but different crowning moldings, the other decorated below a strigilated (ribbed) hawksbeak with a relief meander punctuated by six-rayed stars and water birds. These revetments cannot be attributed to the second temple as long as the possibility remains open that there is another archaic temple waiting to be found in the sanctuary. The same circumstance weighs against considering definitive the restorations of the second temple made up to now.

9 As Coarelli, cited in note 7: 220.

10 For other hypotheses on the placement of the felines see (1989) *Il viver quotidiano in Roma arcaica*, Rome: pl. VII. M. Cristofani (1990) "Osservazioni sulle decorazioni fittili archaiche del santuario di Sant'Omobono," *AL* 10: 31–37 in *Grande Roma*: 133–137 offers a restoration combining these felines and sphinx *acroteria* in a single phase (late archaic) of the building and omitting the Hercules and Minerva group. This suggestion has been countered by G. Colonna (1992) "Le due fasi del tempio arcaico di S. Omobono," *Stips Votiva, Papers presented to C. M. Stibbe*, Amsterdam: 51–59.

11 Coarelli, cited in note 7: 301–328 making a learned connection between the eastern Aphrodite and Mater Matuta/Fortuna.

12 M. Cristofani (1981) "Riflessioni sulle terracotte decorative di prima fase," *Gli Etruschi e Roma*, Rome: 189–198.

13 G. Colonna (1987) "Il maestro dell'Ercole e della Minerva: Nuova luce sull'attività dell'officina veiente," *Skrifter* 44 = *Lectiones Boëthianae* 6: 7–41.

14 R. R. Holloway (1993) "Aedes Minervae in Foro Boario," in *Rivista do Museu de Arqueologia e Etnologia da Universidade de São Paulo*, forthcoming. The weaving implements, together with distinctive miniature fibulae ornamented with bone and amber and the alabastra, have already been noted as giving a distinctly feminine character to the cult: see *Il viver quotidiano in Roma arcaica*, cited in note 1, 555–556. F. Sbordone (1981) "Il gruppo di Eracle e Atene," *PP* 36: 28–31 identified the archaic temple with the cult of Hercules.

15 The estimate is that of G. Ioppolo (1972) "I reperti ossei nell'area di S. Omobono," *RP* 44: 3–39, esp. 17. The volume of the fill is staggering.

16 *ER* III: 392 (Stratum 11).

17 G. Lugli (1946)*Roma antica*, Rome: 543.

18 *Roma Medio Repubblicana*: no. 89.

19 P. Sommella (1968) "Area Sacra di S. Omobono, Contributo per una datazione della platea dei templi gemelli," *Studi di Topografia Romana*, Rome: 63–70.

20 If an explanation be sought for the abandonment of the cult of the archaic temple at the end of the "regal period," it may be found in the anti-Etruscan sentiments of the early Republic. When the Romans sought to sever their ties with Etruscans and things Etruscan, could it be that the cult of the Sant'Omobono sanctuary, where the Etruscan presence was so marked, was suppressed at this place for this reason? And was the suspension of work on the Temple of Jupiter Optimus Maximus perhaps a result of the same feelings?

6 THE *LAPIS NIGER* AND THE ARCHAIC FORUM

1 Beside the remains discussed in this chapter there is nothing of the Comitium proper that can be attributed to regal or early Republican Rome: see F. Coarelli (1983) *Il Foro Romano* 1, Rome: 119–138.

2 Festus 177, Dion. Hal. III, 1, 2.

3 Schol. Hor. Epod. XVI, 13, 14.

4 (1901) *NSc.*: 151–158, with the first discussion of the archaic *cippus* by G. F. Gamurrini, 159–169. This was to have been the first installment of the report, but nothing further was published by Boni.

5 So called from the bronze rams from warships captured at Antium in 338 which were displayed there.

6 It is not a base for the lion statues which were near the *lapis niger*, as reconstructed by Gjerstad (1941) "Il Comizio Romano dell'età repubblicana," *Skrifter* 5: 97–158.

7 A. Morandi (1982) *Epigrafia Italica*, Rome: 48, no. 6; A. E. Gordon (1983) *An Illustrated Introduction to Latin Epigraphy*, Berkeley and Los Angeles: no. 4;

Gordon terms the inscription, "Baffling and incomprehensible."

8 The stratigraphy can be followed best on the magnificent drawings prepared for Boni by the draftsman Ciacchi which have now been published in the monograph of P. Romanelli (1984) *Ricerche intorno ai monumenti del "Niger Lapis" al Foro Romano* (*MA* 52, Serie Miscellanea III: 1). A complete catalogue of the material that can now be identified was made by Gjerstad, *ER* III: 223–259. Thirteen graffiti on sherds from the deposit are known from a Boni photograph, ibid., fig. 146, 1–13, none sufficiently well preserved to give a useful reading.

9 See especially pl. III (Boni's field sketch) in Romanelli, above in note 8.

10 I find it difficult to believe that this kerbing could be the Graecostasis from which ambassadors addressed the Comitium, although other remains, such as those farther north beyond the column and *cippus* could be such. See fig. 6.1.

11 See the lengthy discussion by F. Coarelli (1983) *Il Foro Romano* I, 161–199. Fig. 47 on p. 175 shows Coarelli's reconstruction of the column topped by the statue of Horatius Cocles which stood in the Volcanal.

12 See pp. 47–49.

13 *ER* I: 75.

14 Gjerstad connected this paving with the pebble paving of the Comitium (see p. 83) some 50 m (164 ft) away. He proceeded to draw general conclusions as to the political development of Rome, the Forum paving making the division between the pre-urban and the unified city: *ER* VI: 89ff.

15 (1990) "On the Origins of the Forum Romanum," *AJA* 94: 627–646.

16 See p. 80. If estimates are correct the quantity of fill in the Forum Boarium would have exceeded that in the Forum.

17 On the Cloaca Maxima see E. Tortorici (1991) *Argiletum* (*BC*, supp. 1): 21–31; Richardson, ad verb.

18 Gellius II, 10. In general see G. Bartoloni (1989–1990) "I depositi votivi di Roma arcaica: alcune considerazioni," *Scienze dell'Antichità* 3–4: 747–759. The term *favissa* used generally to describe votive deposits is a misnomer. Basically it means a cistern or reservoir of water connected with a temple; it is only on the Capitoline that it acquires the significance in which it has entered archaeological literature, possibly because former cisterns were used for such deposits there: see T. Hackens (1963) "Favissae," *Etudes étrusco-italiques*, Louvain: 71–100.

19 Gjerstad, *ER* III: 190–201. Etruscan graffiti, Capitoline, *Grande Roma* 1.7, 1.8.

20 I. Sciortino and E. Segala (1990) "Rinvenimento di un deposito votivo presso il Clivo Capitolino," *AL* 10: 17–22.

21 Gjerstad, *ER* III: 145–160; M. De Rossi (1878) "Intorno ad un copioso deposito di stoviglie ed altri oggetti arcaici revenuto nel Viminale," *BC* 6: 64–85.

22 *Roma Arcaica*, depositi votivi, no. 9.

23 A. E. Gordon, cited in note 7: no. 3. The only clear phrase is "Duenos med feced," "Duenos made me" or possibly, if *duenos* is to be understood as *bonus*, "A good man made me."

24 Symbolic miniaturization continued in later times in figurines exchanged on the occasion of the Saturnalia in December: Varro *LL* V, 65; Macrobius *Saturnalia* I, 7, 32–24–29.

25 See pp. 69–75.

26 L. Cordischi (1990) "L'area sacra (il IV sacrario degli Argei sull'Oppio)," *BA* 1–2: 181–183 and (1993) "Nuove acquisizioni su un area di culto al Colle Oppio," *AL* XI, 2: 39–44.

7 WALLS

1 Livy XXVI, 9, 9.

2 (1969) "Beiträge zur römischen Topographie I: Zur frühesten Stadtummauerung Roms," *RM* 76: 103–109; for the discoveries made during the building of the railroad station in 1948 see S. Aurigemma (1961–1962) "Le mura 'serviane', l'aggere e il fossato all'esterno delle mura presso la nuova stazione ferroviaria di Termini in Roma," *BC* 78: 18–36.

3 G. Säflund (1932) "Le mura di Roma Repubblicana," *Skrifter* 1, hereafter Säflund.

4 Nor is cut stone masonry necessarily especially post-archaic. It is known in houses since the later seventh century and very likely masonry defenses in Etruria, such as those of Tarquinia and Vulci, could have been built at any time over the next two centuries.

5 Dion. Hal. IV, 13, 2–14, 1, recounting how Servius added the Viminal and Esquiline hills to the city and fortified the "seven hills."

6 (1924) *Roman Buildings of the Republic (Papers and Monographs of the American Academy in Rome* 3).

7 The tradition regarding King Servius Tullius had already been called into question by O. L. Richter (1901) *Topographie der Stadt Rom*, ed. 2, Munich: 43. Single blocks of *Grotta Oscura* stone, for example the block of the *cippus* below the *lapis niger*, must have arrived earlier.

8 "Murum a censoribus locatum saxo quadrato faciundum."

9 Säflund: 109–111.

10 G. Säflund (1937), "Unveroeffentliche Antike Steinmetzzeichen und Monograme aus Unteritalien und Sizilien," *Scritti in onore di Bartolomeo Nogara*, Città del Vaticano: 409–420; for Bolsena, see M. Pallottino, ed. (1986) *Rasenna*, Milan: fig. 378.

11 Säflund: 113–114.

12 Cited in note 6: 73.

13 E. Nash (1962) *A Pictorial Dictionary of Ancient Rome* I, London: ad verb.

14 (1912) *BC* 40: 78–80. "Entro il recinto a grossi blocchi presso la porta Fontinale, che era in fondo della rientranza delle mura ad imbuto – uno dei lati del quale si conserva tuttora nel giardinetto di via Magnanapoli e l'altro in parte conservato comprendeva l'usuale feritoia conservata nel palazzo Antonelli, destinata alle macchine di difesa e scambiata a torto per una porta – si rinvennero i resti di una necropoli del III periodo, cioè con corredi contenenti materiale ellenistico o etrusco campano. Sull'alto del colle restavano delle tombe individuali a fossa ed una 'a buco', come l'avrebbe detta gli scavatori toscani, con cinerario di antica fabbrica attica. Più verso la valle, nel pendio, si apriva l'àdito ad una delle solite tombe a camera incavate nella roccia. Questa tomba, bloccata dal muro tuttora esistente in parte nel giardinetto di piazza Magnanapoli, fu posta in luce negli sterri per la sistemazione della via, e allora si vide che era piena di terre, tra le quali si raccolsero vasi etrusco-campani. La incertezza della notizia lascia àdito a due ipotesi: si può supporre cioè che i vasi stessi appartenessero ai corredi funebri sepolti nella camera sepolcrale, ma non si può escludere che fossero frammisti a terre di scarico penetrate nel sepolcro. La prima ipotesi è la più probabile, anche perchè in armonia con la vicinanza delle altre tombe individuali, presumibilmente coeve, avvenuta, come ho detto, un po' più in alto, presso la chiesa di S. Caterina di Siena; ma questa tomba ebbe l'ingresso troncato, o almeno fu bloccata dalle mura a conci di tufo giallognolo, le quali perciò dovrebbero ritenersi posteriori al sepolcro e quindi non anteriori alla prima diffusione del vasellame etrusco-campano. Resta l'altra ipotesi, la quale però non muta le conclusioni prese intorno

alla cronologia delle mura in rapporto al sepolcro, poichè le terre da scarico contenenti i vasi campani poterono essere state introdotte in quella tomba forse prima, ma certo non dopo la costruzione delle mura, le quali, essendo state costruite a ridosso della porta della tomba e destinate a sorreggere gli scarichi per il terrazzamento del pendìo interno occupato dalla necropoli, dovettero impedire definitivamente ogni ulteriore manomissione della tomba. Quindi anche in questa seconda ipotesi, che è la meno favorevole alle precedenti conclusioni cronolo-giche, cioè supposto che le terre ed il frammisto materiale etrusco-campano fossero stati scaricati nella cella funebre duranti i lavori di terrazzamento compiuti a ridosso del muro, ne seguirebbe che gli sterri dai quali si traeva il materiale interessavano a loro volta depositi funebri o d'altro carattere, con materiale etrusco-campano, la cui prima diffusione risulterebbe pertanto ugualmente anter-iore alla costruzione dell'opera in tufo granulare giallognolo.

"Si può inoltre dimostrare che anche il tratto esquilino fu compiuto non prima che incominciasse il III periodo, giacchè entro al recinto è stata ritrovata la tomba LXI, la quale conteneva, secondo i rapporti dell'ispettore della Commissione, una 'tazza ordinaria etrusca con ornati in nero nella parte concava, priva del piedu-ccio.' Gli ornati in nero di una tazza 'etrusca', non ostante la imprecisione del linguaggio, presuppongono necessariamente una decorazione dipinta; d'altra parte la descrizione di quell'oggetto da parte del Marsuzi prova che fu acquisito al demanio comunale: non vi è dubbio, quindi, che debba rintracciarsi tra i cinque o sei piattelli di fabbriche dell'Italia meridionale, ornati a pittura nera su fondo giallo, tra i quali, escludendo prima quelli con testa muliebre dipinta nel mezzo, alla quale avrebbe certamente accennato il Rapporto, e gli esemplari ancora muniti del pieduccio, si giunge ad identificare con ogni sicurezza, per esclusione, il piattello del quale ragiono nell'esemplare qui riprodotto (fig. 24), sufficiente a dimostrare che l'intero corredo della tomba LXI, certamente individuale, spetta al III periodo." Challenges to this account, such as I. Scott Ryberg (1929) *Early Roman Traditions in the Light of Archaeology* (*MAAR* 7): ch. IV, do not convince me. More serious are the observations of G. Colonna (1977) "Un aspetto oscuro del Lazio antico, le Tombe del VI–V secolo a.C.," *Lazio arcaico e mondo greco*: 131–165, who claims the Quirinal sarcophagus tombs but not the chamber tomb for the fifth century.

15 *The Genucilia Group: A Class of Etruscan Red-figured Plates* (*University of California Publications in Classical Archaeology* III, 4), Berkeley and Los Angeles.
16 E. A. Arslan and E. M. Moretti (1980) *Gli Etruschi a Cerveteri*, Milan: Tombs 199 and 200.
17 G. Colonna reviewing Del Chiaro in (1959) *AC* 11: 134–136. In general also J.-P. Morel and M. Torelli in *Roma Medio Repubblicana*: 43–50.
18 F. E. Brown in *Roma Medio Repubblicana*: 115. For the question of Roman origin of some Genucilia plates, cf. Morel and Torelli, ibid.: 50.
19 Säflund: 83.
20 (1910) *NSc.*: 495–513.
21 *ER* III: 38.
22 (1910) *NSc.*: 511. Boni's words are, "Frammento di vaso attico del V sec. a. Cr. a figure nere" ("Fragment of an Attic vase of the fifth century BC in black-figure"). This suggests a late black-figured piece. Of course, if Boni was still employing the chronology for Attic pottery accepted until the turn of the century, it could mean black-figure of the best period. Gjerstad wished to substitute a red-figured sherd, *ER* III: 40 and 41, fig. 15:3, but I see no reason to attribute a careless error to Boni.
23 There is a further period of construction represented by a *cappellaccio* wall with a

cement core nearby in Via Carducci. Säflund: 77–80, Quirinal E. As Säflund suggests, this must be an amplification of the line of defenses represented by the remains at the Ministry of Agriculture in Via Salandra.

24 Säflund: 69, L III.

25 This is the length of Säflund, "Prima cinta" (first circuit).

26 Veii 194 hectares, Caere 148, Tarquinia 121, Naples 72: C. Ampolo (1988), in A. Momigliano and A. Schiavone, eds *Storia dei Romani* 1, Turin: 232.

27 Sybaris ca 500 hectares, Agrigentum 450, Syracuse 315 (built up), 814 (within the walls); figures from Ampolo, cited in note 26.

28 Säflund: general plan. This would have been the "murus terreus Carinarum" (earthen wall of the Carinae) mentioned by Varro *LL* V: 48.

29 For the various visible sections, see Nash, cited in note 13, II: 104–116. The most important addition to Säflund's material is the stretch of wall in Largo Santa Susanna, not far from Via Salandra and belonging to the same line of defenses, which was brought to light in 1938: 104, fig. 804; cf. *Grande Roma*: 43, fig. 10.

30 For a recent interpretation in relation to the Temple of Juno Moneta, see G. Giannelli (1982) "Il tempio di Giunone Moneta e la casa di Marco Manlio Capitolino," *BC* 87: 7–36.

31 Attributed to the period of the Marian–Sullan civil war: Säflund: 101, photos; *Grande Roma*: fig. 9.

32 Säflund: 8–9, C I–II. For the walls of the Capitoline and Palatine in general see R. Thomsen (1980) *King Servius Tullius*, Copenhagen: 222–235.

33 I. Ruggiero (1990) "La cinta muraria presso il Foro Boario in età arcaica e medio-repubblicana," *AL* 10: 23–30.

34 F. Coarelli (1988) *Il Foro Boario*, Rome: 36. Apropos, see Ruggiero, cited in note 33, who sees two separate and parallel walls and questions the hypothesis that these are remains of fortifications and continues (p. 31): "The heavy wall of 4 × 6 m and 4 m height identified in the most recent publication in Piazza Bocca della Verità in front of the western corner of S. Maria in Cosmedin and which constitutes the basis of the theory of defense walls parallel to the Tiber in reality never existed" ("il grande muro di m 4 × 6 e alto 4 m localizzato nelle ultime pubblicazioni in Piazza Bocca della Verità davanti l'angolo occidentale di S. Maria in Cosmedin e che costituisce il fondamento della teoria delle mura parallele al Tevere in realtà non è mai esistito"). For other walls of *Grotta Oscura* tufa completing the circuit of the Aventine, see *Roma Medio Repubblicana*: 26–31.

35 A. Carandini (1990) "Palatino, campagne di scavo delle pendici settentrionali," *BA* 1–2: 159–165. I am grateful to Prof. Carandini for the opportunity to discuss these discoveries with him and to visit the excavation in April 1992.

36 J. B. Ward Perkins (1961) "Veii: The Historical Topography of the Ancient City," *BSR* 29: 32–38 and (1959) "Excavations beside the North-west Gate," *BSR* 27: 66–67, 79.

37 I am grateful to Dr Stefano Musco for discussion of these discoveries.

38 One may also observe that only one quarry mark, back-to-back recumbent Vs, is visible at Veii: (1961) *BSR* 29: pl. XIII.

8 OSTERIA DELL'OSA

1 F. Piccarreta (1981) "Saggi di restituzione e interpretazione di fotografie aeree, II, Gabii," *Ricognizione archeologica e nuove ricerche nel Lazio* (*QITA* 9): 13–57; M. Guaitoli (1981) "Gabii, osservazioni sulle fasi di sviluppo dell'abitato," ibid.: 23–58; cf. M. Guaitoli (1981) "Gabii," *PP* 36: 152–173.

2 A. M. Bietti Sestieri (1984) "Castiglione (Roma): Abitato dell'età del bronzo e necropoli dell'età del ferro," *Preistoria e Protostoria nel Territorio di Roma* (*LSA*

III): 160–170.

3 A. M. Bietti Sestieri (1992) *The Iron Age Cemetery of Osteria dell'Osa (Rome) – A Study of socio-political development in central Tyrrhenian Italy*, Cambridge and (1992) *La Necropoli Laziale di Osteria dell'Osa*, 3 vols, Rome. The latter title is the definitive publication of the excavation.

4 Approached only by the excavation at Caracupa in southern Latium: L. Savignoni and R. Mengarelli (1903) "La necropoli arcaica di Caracupa tra Norba e Sermoneta," *NSc.*: 289–344; cf. (1904) *NSc.*: 407–423 and (1909) *NSc.*: 241–260. Also M. Angle and A. Gianni (1985) "An Application of Quantitative Methods for a Socioeconomic Analysis of an Iron Age Necropolis in Latium," in *Papers in Italian Archaeology IV: The Cambridge Conference* 3, eds C. Malone and S. Stoddart (*British Archaeological Reports*, International Series 245): 145–163.

5 (1878) New York.

6 The "New Archaeology" is rapidly becoming passé in a flurry of post-modernist deconstructionism, which is not relevant to our discussion. In Europe the same questions raised by the Anglo-Saxon "New Archaeologists" have been put in a structuralist framework, especially in France. This movement, not without influence in Italy, is also extraneous to our subject.

7 Despite the obvious difficulties in the case of cremation graves and not without problems in the case of inhumations because of the acidic nature of the soil, age and sex determinations have been made for most of the occupants of the tombs.

8 (1985) "The Iron Age Cemetery of Osteria dell'Osa, Rome; Evidence of Social Change in Lazio in the 8th Century B.C.," in *Papers in Italian Archaeology IV: The Cambridge Conference* 3, eds C. Malone and S. Stoddart (*British Archaeological Reports*, International Series 245): 111–144, quotation from 117–120.

9 To which group to attribute *fossa* graves 98, 155, and 158 is in doubt.

10 Two cremation graves of men with miniature offerings were found on the periphery (98, 158, also 155, damaged in Roman times). Bietti Sestieri explains these tombs as those of mature men who are not yet *patresfamiliarum*.

11 Cited in note 8: 138.

12 The *gens*, for which the best English translation is "clan," was composed of individuals bearing a common gentile (or "family") name. Blood ties between them were not necessary for them to enjoy membership in the *gens* and the fiction of common descent. See R. Rix (1972) "Zur Ursprung des römisch-mittelitalischen Gentilnamensystems," in H. Temporini, ed. *Aufsteig und Niedergang der Römischen Welt* 1, 2, Berlin and New York: 700–708 and J. Poucet (1985) *Les Origines de Rome*, Paris: 89 with references; and further G. Franciosi (1984) *Ricerche sull'organizzazione gentilizia romana*, Rome.

13 A. M. Bietti Sestieri, A. De Santis, A. La Regina (1989–1990) "Elementi di tipo culturale e doni di prestigio nella necropoli laziale di Osteria dell'Osa," *Scienze dell'Antichità* 3–4: 65–88, esp. 83–88.

14 The Osteria dell'Osa graffito raises the possibility that the Greeks adopted the alphabet in the west, very possibly at Ischia in the Bay of Naples where a multilingual community including Greeks and Phoenicians existed from the early eighth century: see R. R. Holloway and N. D. Holloway (1994) "Where Did the Greeks Learn to Write?," *Archaeological News*, forthcoming, also regarding dubious claims made for Greek graffiti before 750.

15 G. Pinza (1905) *Monumenti primitivi di Roma e del Lazio primitivo* (*MA* 15): cols 394–398, figs 1141–1144.

16 Cited in note 3 from manuscript.

17 Bietti Sestieri draws attention to Esquiline Tomb 94 (*ER* II: 232) and Castel di Decima, Tomb 21 (see below).

18 Cited in note 3 from manuscript.
19 After this chapter had been written, Dr Bietti Sestieri's complete presentation of the necropolis was published: (1992) *La necropoli laziale di Osteria dell'Osa*, 3 vols, Rome.

9 CASTEL DI DECIMA; ACQUA ACETOSA, LAURENTINA; FICANA; AND CRUSTUMERIUM

1 With G. Bartoloni and M. C. Dini (1982) "Aspetti dell'ideologia funeraria nella necropoli di Castel di Decima," in G. Gnoli and J.-P. Vernant, eds *La Mort, les morts dans les sociétés anciennes*, Cambridge and Paris: 257–273, with essential bibliography. What follows depends heavily on this article.
2 A. Rathje (1983) "A Banquet Service from the Latin City of Ficana," *Analecta Romana Instituti Danici* 12: 7–29.
3 Survey F. Zevi (1985) "La situazione nel Lazio," *Il commercio etrusco arcaico* (*Quaderni del Centro di Studio di Archeologia Etrusco-Italica* 9), Rome: 119–129; M. Botto (1990) "Considerazioni sul commercio fenicio nel tirreno nell'VIII e VII secolo a.C. – le anfore da trasporto nei contexti indigini del Latium Vetus," *AION* 12: 199–216. Aristocratic display at table in the ancient world has occasioned discussion for centuries: Baron de Montesquieu (1749) *De l'esprit des lois*, nouvelle édition, Geneva, chs 9–10. The role of the archaic hostess has been much discussed of late. L. Bonfante's study "Etruscan Couples," in H. P. Foley, ed. (1981) *Reflexions on Women in Antiquity*, New York, London, Paris, 1981: 323–342 is an excellent discussion. M. Gras has taken up the contradiction between the archaeological evidence and the prohibition on the use of wine by women reported in ancient sources: "Vin et société à Rome et dans le Latium à l'époque archaique," in G. Nenci, ed. (1983) *Modes de contact et processus de transformation dans les sociétés anciennes*, Paris and Pisa: 1067–1075. Although one may, with Gras, make a clever distinction between wine in a religious context and wine at social occasions, there is another explanation: the traditions in the sources (Plutarch *Quaest. Rom.* 6; Aulus Gellius X, 23; Pliny *NH* XIV, 90; Dion. Hal. II, 25, 6) are simply fanciful (could they derive ultimately from ancient comedy mistakenly taken for objective comment on social usage?).
For the wine service in a domestic context at Ficana, see A. Rathje, cited in note 2, and (1989) "The Adoption of the Homeric banquet in Central Italy in the Orientalizing Period," in O. Murray, ed. *Sympotica*, Oxford: 279–293. This group is illustrated in fig. 9.3. The connection between the imaginary world of the Greek epic and seventh-century Italy is more evocative than concrete. As the author states ("A Banquet Service," p. 23), "The Greeks which had connections with Tyrrhenian Italy are 'homeric' and we are justified in using Homer as a source in the description of the 'hellenisation' that happens in the 8th and 7th centuries BC". But this hellenisation often consists of no more than an imported vase or two and some local imitations of Greek articles. The services of Canton trade ware that graced American tables in the nineteenth century did not turn Americans into pseudo-Chinese nor did the Persian prayer rugs on their floors make them into Mohammedans. Prehistoric Italy had developed social usages long before the eighth century. These are best known in Sicily, where in the Bronze Age the interior of the house was dominated by a great mixing bowl, as has been documented most clearly near Licata at Madre Chiesa: G. Castellana (1990) *Un decennio di ricerche preistoriche e protostoriche nel territorio di Agrigento*, Agrigento: 39–45. The tomb architecture of Bronze Age Sicily was an imitation of the house, and tomb furniture was a table service also centered on a great mixing bowl: see L. Maniscalco (1985–1986) "Tipologie funerarie nella

Sicilia del tardo bronzo: Pantalica, Dessueri, Caltagirone," *Archivio Storico per la Sicilia Orientale* 81–82: 241–65. Our documentation of domestic and funeral contexts of the mainland in the Bronze Age does not lend itself as easily to the identification of the social traditions, but there is no reason to believe that they were less developed than in Sicily. And there is no reason to believe that these traditions did not persist in the eighth and seventh centuries, albeit with foreign trappings. For the question of "Homeric" taste and funeral goods in seventh-century Latium see pp. 167–170.

4 For the settlement, see M. Guaitoli, F. Piccarreta and P. Sommella (1974) "Contributi per una carta archeologica del territorio di Castel di Decima," *QITA* 6: 43–130.

5 A. Bedini (1990) "Abitato protostorico in località Acqua Acetosa Laurentina," in M. R. Di Mino and Marina Bertinetti, eds *Archeologia a Roma*, Rome: 48–64, Tombs 70 and 133, and (1992) "L'insediamento della Laurentina, Acqua Acetosa," *Roma, 1000 Anni di Civiltà*: 83–96, Tomb 70, complete documentation.

6 G. Carettoni and P. Zaccagni (1976) "La Rustica," *Civiltà del Lazio Primitivo*: 153–165; Ficana: see below.

7 D. Faccenna and M. A. Fugazzola Delpino (1976) "Tivoli," *Civiltà del Lazio Primitivo*: 188–212.

8 The site of Torrino, 3.5 km (2.17 mi.) from Acqua Acetosa, Laurentina, has much the same character: see A. Bedini (1981) *AL* 4: 57–68; (1984) *AL* 6: 84–90; (1985) *AL* 7: 44–64. Another important city of early Latium not treated separately here is Ardea: see E. Tortorici (1981) *AL* 4: 293–296; C. Morselli (1982) *Ardea* (Forma Italiae); (1983) *Ardea, immagine di una ricerca*, Roma; L. Crescenzi and E. Tortorici (1983) *AL* 5: 38–47; (1984) *AL* 6: 345–350. For Antium (Anzio), see G. Bergonzi (1976) *Civiltà del Lazio Primitivo*: 318–322.

9 "Puilia Saxa esse ad portum, qui sit secundum Tiberim, ait Fabius Pictor: quem locum putat Labeo dici, ubi fuerit Ficana, via Ostiensi ad lapidem undecimum."

10 *CIL* VI: no. 31585; M. Floriano Squarciapino (1955) *Il Museo della Via Ostiense*, Rome: 31.

11 Ibid.: 22.

12 Etruria: S. Stopponi, ed. (1985) *Case e palazzi d'Etruria*, Rome; Satricum: M. Maaskant-Kleibrink (1987) "Settlement Excavations at Borgo Le Ferriere," *Satricum* I, Groningen; (1991) "Early Latin Settlement Plans at Borgo Le Ferriere (Satricum)," *BABESCH* 66: 51–114; Rome: Gjerstad, *ER* 1, 130–152; Torrino: A. Bedini (1984) "Scavi a Torrino," *AL* 6: 84–85.

13 Traces have been found; see M. Cataldi (1984) "Ficana: Campagne 1982–1983," *AL* 6: 91–97.

14 Livy I, 33, 3; Dion. Hal. III, 38.

15 E. Jarva in (1980) *Ficana una pietra milliaria sulla strada per Roma*, Rome: 88–95.

16 (1978) *Antemnae* (*Latium Vetus* I); (1980) *Crustumerium* (*Latium Vetus* III); (1986) *Fidenae* (*Latium Vetus* V); (1993) *Ficulea* (*Latium Vetus* VI).

17 Quilici, *Crustumerium*: no. 88; for the chamber tombs, see F. di Gennaro (1988) "Primi risultati degli scavi nella necropoli di Crustumerium," *AL* 9: 113–123.

18 See pp. 92–99.

19 A. Bedini (1990) "Un compitum di origine protostorica a Tor dei Cenci," *AL* 10: 121–133.

10 LAVINIUM

1 F. Piccarreta (1981) "Saggi di restituzione di fotografie aeree," *QITA* 9: 7–22.
2 Macrob. III, 4, 11; Servius *Ad Aen.* II, 296.

3 Virgil *Aen*. I, 1–7, worship of Jupiter Indiges; Naevius ap. Macrobius VI, 2, 31; Livy I, 2, 6. Sanctuary at the mouth of the Numicus: *Aenea nel Lazio*: 167–168. In the sanctuary at Tor Tignosa, 7 km east northeast of Lavinium a fourth-century *cippus* has been discovered with a dedication, read by M. Guarducci (1956–1958) "Cippo latino arcaico con dedica ad Aenea," *BC* 76 (*Bullettino del Museo della Civiltà Romana* 19): 3–13 as to Lare Aineia (as well as others to Parca Maurtia and Neuna Fata); in general L. Quilici (1968) "Una domus culta della Campagna Romana: La Salforata," *Bollettino della Unione Storia ed Arte*, 61: 5ff. Doubts on the reading of the inscription have been expressed by H.-G. Kolbe (1970) "Lare Aineia," *RM* 77: 1–9, but see Guarducci's reply (1971) "Enea e Vesta," *RM* 78: 73–89.

4 References in F. Castagnoli (1972) *Lavinium* I, Rome: 71–75.

5 F. Castagnoli and P. Sommella (1974) *Lavinium* II, *Le Tredici Are*, Rome.

6 Servius *Ad Aen*. III, 12; cf. S. Weinstock (1960) "Two Archaic Inscriptions from Latium," *JRS* 50: 112–118.

7 The more dramatic debut of the Dioscuri was as allies of the Romans at the Battle of Lake Regillus against the united Latins in 496. The temple supposedly vowed by the Dictator Aulus Postumius Albinus was dedicated, according to tradition, in 485 (Livy II, 20, 12 and II, 42, 5). There was also a long-standing worship of the Dioscuri at Tusculum: Cicero *De Nat. Deo*. I, 98.

8 Cited in note 5: 443 L 2.

9 See Chapters 5 and 6.

10 P. Sommella (1971–1972) "Heroon di Enea a Lavinium," *RP* ser. 3, 44: 47–74.

11 Ap. Servius *Ad Aen*. IV, 620.

12 καὶ αὐτῷ κατασκευάζευσι οἱ Λατῖνοι ἡρῶον ἐπιγραφῇ τοιᾷδε κοσμούμενον. Πατρὸς θεοῦχθονίου, ὃς ποταμοῦ Νομικίου ῥεῦμα διέπει. εἰσὶ δ᾽ οἱ λέγουσιν ἐπ᾽ Ἀγχίσῃ κατασκευασθῆναι αὐτὸ ὑπ᾽ Αἰνείου, ἐνιαυτῷ πρόστερον τοῦ πολέμου τούτου τελευτήσαντι. ἔστι δὲ χωμάτιον οὐ μέγα καὶ περὶ αυτὸ δένδρα στοιχηδὸν πεφυκότα θέας ἄξια.

13 There are skeptics, among them E. S. Gruen (1992) *Culture and National Identity in Republican Rome*, Ithaca, New York: 25, with references to others of the same opinion.

14 For the Roman area: (1965) *Céramique à vernis noir du Forum et du Palatin*, Rome; (1965) "Etudes de céramique campanienne I, L'atelier des petits estampilles," *MR* 81: 56–117.

15 The modern name should not be taken to have any ancient significance.

16 *Aen*. XI, 483, "Armipotens, praeses belli, tritonia virgo."

17 J. Boardman (1985) *The Parthenon and its Sculptures*, Austin: 230.

18 (1984) *Lavinio e Roma*, Rome.

19 454 L.

11 SATRICUM

1 M. Maaskant-Kleibrink (1987) "Settlement Excavations at Borgo Le Ferriere," *Satricum* I, Groningen, and (1991) "Early Settlement-plans at Borgo Le Ferriere (Satricum)," *BABESCH* 66: 51–114.

2 As documented by A. Andren (1940) *Architectural Terracottas from Etrusco-Italian Temples* (*Skrifter* 6) and A. Åkerstrom (1954) "Untersuchungen über die figurlichen Terrakottenfriese aus Etruria und Latium," *Skrifter* 18 = *Opuscula Romana* 1: 191–231.

3 "Early Settlement-plans," cited in note 1: esp. 104.

4 The architectural Terracottas from the temple, the tomb groups, votive deposits and the seventh-century material from the habitation debris, with few exceptions

all from the excavations of 1896–1898, constitute one of the outstanding parts of the collections of the Villa Giulia Museum in Rome; for some of the earlier material see G. Colonna (1976) "Satricum," *Civiltà del Lazio Primitivo*: 324–346.

5 The development of the Acropolis of Veii was similarly conditioned by the presence of a *lacus*: Maaskant-Kleibrink, "Early Settlement-plans," cited in note 1: 64–66.

6 J. de Waele (1981) "I templi della Mater Matuta a Satricum," *MNIR* 43: 7–68, earlier date brought down to 590/580 by M. Maaskant-Kleibrink, cited in note 1: 85 and R. R. Knoop (1987) *Antefixa Satricana* (Satricum, *Reports of the Satricum Project* I), Leiden.

7 M. Maaskant-Kleibrink (1992) "Gli scavi più recenti svolti a Borgo Le Ferriere (Satricum)," *AL* 11, 1: 53–64.

8 Livy II, 39.

9 Maaskant-Kleibrink, "Early Settlement-plans," cited in note 1.

10 C. M. Stibbe, G. Colonna, C. De Simone, H. S. Versnel (1980) *Lapis Satricanus* (*Archeologiche Studien van het Nederlands Instituut te Rome, Scripta Minora* V), The Hague.

11 I am grateful to Prof. Silvio Panciera for discussion of the problems presented by the *lapis Satricanus*.

12 Cited in note 10: 129.

13 Livy II, 49–50.

14 P. S. Lulof (1991) "Un gruppo di statue fittili tardo-arcaiche da Satricum (Le Ferriere)," *MNIR* 50: 87–101.

12 PRAENESTE

1 C. Densmore Curtis (1925) *The Barberini Tomb* (*MAAR* 5).

2 F. Zevi (1976) "Praeneste," *Civiltà del Lazio Primitivo*: 213–217 and no. 76.

3 F.-W. von Hase (1974) "Die frühetruskische Goldschale aus Praeneste im Victoria und Albert Museum," *AA*: 85–104.

4 F. Canciani and F.-W. von Hase (1979) *La Tomba Bernardini di Palestrina* (*Latium Vetus* II), Rome, replacing C. Densmore Curtis (1919) *The Bernardini Tomb* (*MAAR* 3).

5 On the silver bowls in particular, see G. Markoe, (1985) *Phoenician Bronze and Silver Bowls from Cyprus and the Mediterranean* (*University of California Publications in Classical Studies* 26), Berkeley and Los Angeles.

6 Canciani and von Hase, cited in note 4: no. 118; Curtis, cited in note 4: no. 45. Compare the appliqués from the throne of Tomb 79 of Salamis in Cyprus: V. Karageorghis (1969) *Salamis in Cyprus*, London: pls IV–V.

7 The inscription does not specify whether it refers to the maker or owner, which gives the inscription an odd character: see M. G. Guzzo Amadasi (1967) *Le iscrizioni feniche e puniche delle colonie in occidente* (*Studi Semitici* 28), Rome: appendix 1.

8 M. Martelli in M. Cristofani-Martelli (1983) *L'oro degli Etruschi*: 35–47.

9 *Führer durch die öffentlichen Sammlungen Klassischer Altertümer in Rom*, ed. H. Speier, Tübingen.

10 "Helbig schwamm im vollen Strome des gesellschaftlichen Lebens bekannt mit dem stadrömischen Adel und den Piemontesen, mit Kunstfreunden und Kunsthändlern," (1928) *Erinnerungen 1848–1914*, Leipzig: 141. The reference to "Roman" and "Piedmontese" aristocracy reflects the situation after the unification of Italy under Piedmontese leadership in 1870 and the establishment of the national capital at Rome.

11 Until 1901 in the Museo di Villa Giulia, thereafter at the Museo Etnografico

"L. Pigorini." The bibliography is vast: see A. E. Gordon (1975) *The Inscribed Fibula Praenestina (University of California Publications in Classical Studies* 16), Berkeley and Los Angeles, and recently C. de Simone (1989–1990) "*Numasie/ *Numasio – le formazioni etrusche e latino-italiche in -sie/-sio," *Studi Etruschi* 56: 191–215 and R. Coleman (1990) "Dialectal Variations in Republican Latin," *Proceedings of the Cambridge Philosophical Society* 216: 1–25, a reference I owe to Dr Nicholas Horsfall.

12 (1990) *Il tesoro di Via Alessandria*, Milan.

13 (1905) *MA* 15: col. 561.

14 M. Guarducci (1980) "La così detta Fibula Prenestina, antiquari eruditi e falsari nella Roma dell'ottocento," *Memorie dei Lincei* ser. 8, 24: 415–539 (with physical analysis tending to support Guarducci's views by G. Devoto, 546–554); (1984) "La così detta Fibula Prenestina: elementi nuovi," *Memorie dei Lincei* ser. 8, 28: 131–174; (1987) "Una falsa ermetto di marmo rosso antico (appendice alla storia della 'Fibula Prenestina')," *Rendiconti dei Lincei* ser. 8, 42: 28–32; (1992) "Nuova appendice alla storia della 'Fibula Prenestina'," *Rendiconti dell'Accademia dei Lincei* ser. 9, 2: 139–146 (providing evidence that the inscription was cut with a modern engraver's tool), with full references. Karo later expressed doubts about his assertions. Guarducci believes he was acting as a prop for Helbig.

15 (1919) *MAAR* III: 13.

16 Guarducci (1984), cited in note 14.

17 See the moving necrology by B. Nogara (1940) in *RP* ser. 3, 16: 99–111 particularly in reference to Pinza's contribution to ordering the Etruscan collection of the Vatican Museum. His multi-volume work on Latium remained unfinished.

18 For reference see above, note 14.

19 H. Lehmann (1989) "Wolfgang Helbig: 1839–1915," *RM* 96: 7–86.

20 Cited in note 11: 19.

13 CONCLUSION

1 Livy I, 33, 6; Plutarch, *Numa* 9, 2–3. The Roman Pontiffs took their name from their priestly responsibilities with bridge building.

2 See (1986) *Il Tevere e le altre vie d'acqua del lazio antico = AL* 7, 2.

3 We should not count Circei as originally Latin, despite Dionysius of Halicarnassus' inclusion of the people of Circei among the members of the League in the early fifth century: V, 61, 3.

4 R. A. McNeal (1972) "The Greeks in History and Prehistory," *Antiquity* 46: 19–28, quotation from 19–20.

5 E. La Rocca (1977) "Note sulle importazioni greche in territorio laziale nell'VIII secolo a.C.," *Lazio arcaico e mondo greco*: 375–397; (1982) "Ceramica d'importazione greca dell'VIII secolo A.C. a Sant'Omobono: un aspetto delle origini di Roma," *La céramique grecque ou de tradition grecque au VIIIe siècle en Italie centrale et méridionale (Cahiers du Centre Jean Bérard* III), Naples: 45–54; also on the Esquiline, (1974–1975) "Due tombe dell'Esquilino: Alcune novità sul commercio euboico in Italia centrale nel VIII secolo a.c.," *DdA* 8: 86–103.

6 La Rocca (1982), cited in note 5: 47–48. The dates for Middle Geometric cited in the text take account of the down-dating of the end of the period from about 770 to about 750 argued by J.-P. Descoeudres and R. Kearsley (1983) "Greek Pottery at Veii, Another Look," *BSA* 78: 9–53.

7 G. Colonna (1977) "Un tripode geometrico del Foro Romano," *MEFRA* 89: 471–498.

8 The question of Rome as a center of production has been raised but preference is generally accorded to Veii: H. P. Isler (1983) "Ceramisti greci in Etruria in epoca

tardo-geometrico," *NAC* 12: 9–48; compare the discussion of G. Bartoloni (1987) "Le comunità dell'Italia centrale tirrenica e la colonizzazione greca in Campania," *Etruria e Lazio arcaico* (*Quaderni del Centro di Studio per l'Archeologia Etrusco-Italica* 15): 37–53.

9 See N. D. and R. R. Holloway (1994) "Where did the Greeks Learn to Write?," *Archaeological News*, forthcoming.

10 As we have already seen above (Chapter 8), this development has been interpreted by A. M. Bietti Sestieri as the birth of the Latin (and Roman) *gens*.

11 See p. 22.

12 F. Zevi (1985) "La situazione nel Lazio," *Il commercio etrusco arcaico* (*Quaderni del Centro di Studio per l'Archeologia Etrusco-Italica* 9), Rome: 119–129.

13 At Rome there are Greek transport amphorae, Corinthian (type A) from the Regia, Chiote from the Palatine and another Ionian occurrence noted on the Capitoline: F. Zevi (1985), cited in note 12.

14 E. Kilian-Dirlmeier (1986) "Beobachtungen zu den Schachtgräber von Mykenai und zu den Schmuckbeigaben Mykenischen Mässergraber," *Jahrbuch des Römisch-Germanischen Zentralmuseums, Mainz* 33: 159–220.

15 In reference to the Praeneste tombs one still finds the term "dynast" persisting, for example in M. Pallottino (1991) *A History of Earliest Italy*, Ann Arbor: 72, who then draws the further conclusion that tombs of such wealth suggest Etruscan rulers at Praeneste. One should also be skeptical of a corridor of Etruscan "communications" via "Etruscan" Praeneste to the Etruscan cities in Campania. The inland road through the Sacco–Liris Valley to Capua (the route of the modern Autostrada del Sole) passed along a route bordered by or blocked by the Hernici, the Volsci, the Aurunci, and the Sidicini. Surely the sea route along the coast, and then up the Volturnus River to Capua, was better.

16 With one notable example among the Greek cities, the Tomb of the Diver at Poseidonia.

17 VI, 53–54.

18 And in some respects possibly true in comparison with early Etruria. For example, graves with arms and chariots are far more frequent in Etruria than in Latium.

19 Much has been made of the "Homeric" character of seventh-century central Italy: the accumulation of valuable and exotic goods and lavish gift exchange. See for example G. Bartoloni, M. Cataldi Dini, C. Ampolo (1980) "Periodo IV A," *DdA* n.s. 2 (La Formazione della Città): 125–164, esp. 141–145 and A. Rathje (1984) "I Keimelia orientali," *Opus* 3, 341–347. Homer describes funeral games and prizes and understands providing the corpse on the pyre with suitable state (funeral of Patroclus, bk XXI) but he knows nothing of riches added to the burial after the cremation. The central Italian practices are "Homeric" only in the eyes of modern commentators. For a tomb in Greece comparable to the rich Latian, Italic, and Etruscan burials one must go back to Protogeometric Lefkandi: M. R. Popham, E. Touloupa, L. H. Sackett (1982) "The Hero of Lefkandi," *Antiquity* 56: 169–174. The Italian practice is like that shown in the shaft graves of Middle Helladic III to Late Helladic I times. One may suspect that economic conditions similar to those of central Italy in the seventh century encouraged the donation of riches to the dead in Greece in the Bronze Age at the moment of passage from village to palace society.

20 *New York Times*, February 19, 1991: 4. I wish to thank Dr Susan S. Lukesh for bringing this item to my attention.

21 *XII Tabulae*, X, 2–11.

22 I refrain from following the analysis of A. Guidi (1985) "An Application of Rank-size Rule to Protohistoric Settlements in the Middle Tyrrhenian Area,"

Papers in Italian Archaeology IV, pt iii (*British Archaeological Reports*, International Series 245): 217–242, because his claim for the primacy for Rome at this time and in the seventh and sixth centuries is based on a speculative estimate of the area occupied by the primitive community and archaic city.

23 Some have seen the reduction in funeral gifts in the late seventh century as a direct effect of the need to pay for the public and private building with quarried stone walls and elaborate terracotta decoration: so G. Colonna (1977) "Un aspetto oscuro del Lazio antico, le tombe del VI–V secolo a.C.," *Lazio arcaico e mondo greco*: 130–165. See also G. Bartoloni (1987) "Esibizione di ricchezza e corredi funerari," *Scienze di Antichità* 1: 143–160, and papers published in (1984) *Opus* 3: A. Bedini, "Struttura ed organizzazione delle tombe 'principesche' nel Lazio," 377–382; G. Bartoloni and C. Grottanelli, "I carri a due ruote nelle tombe femminili del Lazio e dell'Etruria," 383–394 and C. Ampolo, "Il lusso nelle società arcaiche," 469–476.

24 Livy V, 40 and 49.

25 Livy IX, 36, 3.

26 Pliny *NH* XXV, 154.

27 F. Zevi (1987) "I santuari di Roma agli inizi della repubblica," *Etruria e Lazio arcaico*, cited in note 8: 121–132, esp. 129, hypothesizes that it was hauled to the Esquiline as trash from elsewhere and might have been part of the decoration of the Temple of Ceres.

28 R. Holloway (1975) *Influences and Styles in the Late Archaic and Early Classical Greek Sculpture of Sicily and Magna Graecia*, Louvain: fig. 126; V. Tusa (1984) *La scultura in pietra di Selinunte*, Palermo: pl. 11.

29 Holloway, cited in note 28: pl. 19.

30 Most recently, J. C. Meyer (1980) "Roman History in the Light of the Import of Attic Vases to Rome and Etruria in the 6th and 5th Century B.C.," *Analecta Romana Instituti Danici* 9: 47–68, has sought to create formulae for weighing the relative significance of Attic imports from Etruria (almost exclusively tomb goods) and Attic imports from Rome (largely sherds from urban contexts). I fail to see how these two bodies of evidence can be compared to judge the relative prosperity or poverty of any location. E. Paribeni (1956–1958) "Ceramica d'importazione nel Foro Romano," *BC* 76: 3–21, illustrates high-quality Attic red figure that reached Rome during the fifth century: compare *ER* III: 129 for the Palatine and *ER* IV, 2: 547–551 for Rome generally. In Tyrrhenian central–northern Italy Greek pottery imports declined generally after 450.

31 Colonna, cited in note 23.

32 Pliny *NH* XXXIII, 9, 24; XXIV, 19–30; cf. G. Lahusen (1983) *Untersuchungen zur Ehrenstatue in Rom*, Rome.

33 *Grande Roma*: 144, no. 6.10; *Roma, 1000 Anni di Civiltà*: no. 1.

34 J. Carcopino (1926) *La Louve du Capitole*, Paris; see also C. Dulière (1979) *Lupa Romana* (*Etudes de philologie, d'archéologie et d'histoire anciennes publiées par l'Institut Historique Belge de Rome* 18), Brussels and Rome: 21–43. The case for considering the Capitoline Wolf to be an archaistic statue is argued by O.-W. von Vacano (1973) "Vulca, Rom und die Wölfin, III, die Lupa Capitolina," in H. Temporini, ed. *Aufstieg und Niedergang der römischen Welt* I, 4: 550–583, placing the terminus post quem for the statue at 387; however, comparison of the head with the boar's head socket of the Monteleone Chariot in the Metropolitan Museum, New York, is sufficient to establish the archaic character of the only element of the Capitoline Wolf that might seem out of keeping with an archaic date: see especially L. Bonfante and F. Roncalli, eds (1991) *Gens antiquissima Italiae, Antichità dall'Umbria a New York*, Perugia and New York: illustration on p. 118.

35 The imported goods appearing with frequency in the cemeteries of Veii came this way: bibliography in G. Bartoloni (1984) *La Cultura Villanoviana*: 139. The same traffic went further upstream to the Sabine region and Umbria: see most recently F. Roncalli and L. Bonfante (1991) *Antichità dell'Umbria a New York*, Perugia and New York; and P. Santoro (1986) "I Sabini e il Tevere," *Il Tevere*, cited in note 2: 111–123.
36 Livy I, 11 and 33.
37 On the Senate, see R. E. Mitchell (1990) *Patricians and Plebeians*, Ithaca.

INDEX